Essentials of Service Design

Developing high-value service businesses with PCN Analysis

Second Edition

by Dr. Scott E. Sampson
Passey Professor of Service Operations
and Business Management
Marriott School of Management
Brigham Young University
Provo, Utah, 84602, USA
ses3-pba@sm.byu.edu

December 29, 2012
©2012 SES

Summary Table of Contents

Detailed Table of Contents

Synopsis

Services represent the largest portion of economic activity in developed nations, and are likely an important part of your business. Unfortunately, services traditionally have lacked the rigorous design tools we see used in designing physical products. This book describes a simple yet powerful service design tool known as PCN Analysis. The PCN tool will allow you to document and analyze the provider-customer interactions that take place in your business, showing where increased value can be realized by strategic repositioning of process elements. This book shows how firms can optimally design service operations to achieve value objectives. Firms that use this tool will be able to deliver exceptional service at lower costs than competing firms.

Preface

In undertaking this work, I stand on the shoulders of giants. There have been many service researchers who have provided us with tremendous insights over the years. People like Richard Normann, Christopher Lovelock, and others. I cite many specific references to the work of others, but that does adequately represent my appreciation for their work.

The book is organized with foundational material from Chapter 1 through Chapter 5. Chapter 6 through Chapter 9 focuses on managerial issues. Chapter 10 through Chapter 12 discusses ways PCN Analysis can be used to provide strategic advantage. Illustrative case studies are provided in Chapter 15 through Chapter 19.

The last two chapters are admittedly a bit esoteric. In Chapter 20, I demonstrate how PCN Analysis relates to and draws upon some of the major frameworks of service management from recent years. It is, of course, not at all exhaustive, but meant to show how PCN Analysis subsumes many of the major features of other important models. Chapter 21 in an expansion of some material that a journal editor did not allow me to publish, but which I think is a cool way of thinking about PCN Analysis.

Some of the text came directly from some of my previously published articles. In some cases I directly quoted my prior articles, as allowed by the journal copyright policies. That quoted text is spread throughout the book, making it difficult to identify specific passages. However, I need to give due acknowledgement to two recent articles:

Sampson, Scott E. "Visualizing Service Operations." *Journal of Service Research* 15, no. 2 (May 2012): 182-98.
Sampson, Scott E, and Martin Spring. "Customer Roles in Service Supply Chains and Opportunities for Innovation." *Journal of Supply Chain Management* 40, no. 4 (October 2012).

Dedicated to my wonderful students and my wonderful Kristin.

Chapter 1 – Services Designed to Disappoint?

Have you ever had an off-the-chart service experience? Can you think of a recent experience with a service provider that either left you in awe or, conversely, left you cringing with disgust? Do you find that you have been disappointed so often that you have lowered your expectations for service delivery? Could it be possible that the customers of your firm are having similar experiences? Would you believe that even world-class firms often struggle with service delivery?

Do you get the sense that many services are poorly designed and shoddily delivered? Do you have the feeling that service providers hardly know what they are doing, and respond to even tepid customer requests with confrontational chagrin or apathy? Have you ever found yourself on the phone with a "customer service" employee whose job description seems to include giving customers the runaround?

And, are you slightly worried that this may somewhat be describing your company?

One last question for now: Do you mind if I share a handful of my own experiences? (If so, skip the next section.)

The good, the bad, and the ugly

I like Walmart—many products, great prices. But there was the time that I went to Walmart to have the battery replaced in my minivan. My old battery from Walmart was under warranty but had been discontinued. As a result, they could not figure out how much to charge for the replacement. After more than an hour of painful interactions with Walmart employees and managers, including my offer to pay any price to get out of there (with my four upset children under the age of 10), I left. I told the police officer who met me in the parking lot that I offered to pay but they would not take it. The manager finally cut me a deal to let me take my kids home.

Last year I was in Europe giving seminars and had my wife and four of our children with me. At the end of the six-week trip they were to fly home through Paris on a day that I had one last seminar in Cardiff, UK. Later that day I found out that Air France had cancelled their flight to Paris. After waiting in the Bristol airport from 4:00 am until noon, the Air France representative told them that they would have to try again the next day. After some threatening my wife got Air France to put them up in a hotel in Bristol. The next day I was flying on a completely different set of flights back to the U.S., and was only able to get help aligning our flights by calling up Delta Airlines and reminding them of my "Medallion" frequent flier status.

I like Target. Except for their pharmacy. There was the time that I took a prescription to the nearby Target pharmacy. The physician had made an error on the prescription, and the pharmacy manager threatened to report me to the police, insinuating that I had doctored the prescription. Aghast at the false accusation, I suggested they phone the physician and get clarification. A few days later I got my prescription, vowing never to return.

A few years ago I purchased an HP computer from a local retailer. When I got home I found that the computer inside of the box did not have the SD memory card reader that was pictured on the outside of the box. So, I called HP customer service. The HP rep told me that the box label was a printing error, but I still wanted the memory card reader I thought I had bought. The rep finally agreed to send me one, but only on the condition that it would not be covered under warranty, since I would be installing it myself.

Some time ago I was eating at a department business dinner with some colleagues at an Olive Garden restaurant in Tallahassee, Florida. My pasta, unfortunately, had a small round piece of cardboard in it. I discreetly pointed it out to the waiter, who profusely apologized and offered to bring me more cardboard, I mean pasta. The waiter also offered to take my meal off of the bill, which did not matter to me since it was charged to my department anyway, and it did not make up for the fact that my replacement food came after everyone else had eaten.

On another occasion the battery in my Toyota Camry had died and would not hold a charge. I jump-started the car and drove it to Walmart. Instead of checking in at the auto service desk I drove to the service bay and honked, declaring "I cannot stop the car or the battery will die." The employee motioned for me to come in to the edge of a bay so that they could replace the battery immediately. Happy day.

On other occasion I had given a presentation in Southern California and was scheduled to subsequently give some seminars in Australia. My son was going to accompany me to Australia and was to meet me at the Los Angeles LAX airport, but his Delta Airline flight was snowed in in Salt Lake City. My son told me that the customer service desk at the Salt Lake City airport was clogged with stranded passengers, so I asked someone at the Delta desk at LAX what could be done. They handily put my son on a later flight, rescheduled our United Airlines flights to Sydney for the following day, and put us up in a nearby hotel—no haggling involved.

Last year I was at a department business dinner with some colleagues at a local restaurant called La Jolla Groves. The nice tablecloths hid the fact that two adjacent tables were not the same height. A piece of stemware placed on the ridge fell and shattered. The employees cleared the table and replaced all nearby food before anyone could practically lift a fork. At the end of the dinner an exuberant toast also resulted in a broken glass, with similar response by the restaurant staff. This is not a pricy restaurant, but well run.

What is it that makes customer service be sometimes a taste of heaven and other times the pains of hell? Why is it that even world class firms seem to have a difficult time maintaining consistency in the delivery of service? Why do minor variations in customer requirement send some services into confusion? Do you ever have the feeling that any variation from normal operating conditions leads many service providers to flounder?

Enough of the questions—let's get to the answers. I am going to address those questions in this book, and show how you and your firm can systematically design and deliver services that shine under all types of conditions, build customer loyalty, reduce cost of delivery, and improve competitiveness. But first, I need to tell you about my son, Ryan.

Becoming a Design Engineer

My son, Ryan, has a penchant for designing new and interesting devices. Even though he is only in the fifth grade, he has already expressed interest in becoming a design engineer, perhaps a mechanical engineer. He has asked me what it will take to succeed as an engineer. Here is my response.

First, he will need to graduate from high school with good enough grades to be admitted to a reputable university. At the university he will apply for admission to an engineering program. Admission will require good grades in calculus and other math classes, since engineering draws on those skills.

In the engineering program he will take courses on various topics. He will learn about the characteristics of materials that are used to build products. He will learn how products operate under specific design conditions. He will learn about fluid mechanics, thermodynamics, and kinematics.

Ryan will learn to use powerful design tools such as Computer-Aided Design (CAD) systems. With CAD tools he will learn how to develop and prototype products digitally, allowing him to explore design alternatives before actually investing in physical prototypes. He will learn how to design products that can be actually delivered, the so-called Design for Manufacturability (DFM). And that is just the undergraduate program.

Hopefully, Ryan will desire to pursue a postgraduate degree in engineering. There, he will hone his product-design skills. He might take advanced courses on plasticity, structural vibrations, microelectromechanical systems, biomechanics, metallurgy, acoustics, and composite structures. An advanced CAD course might teach him about "parametric surface and solid modeling, associativity, numerically-controlled tool path generation, etc."[1]

When he graduates he will likely get a job working in the engineering department of a product manufacturing company. He will look for positions titled "engineer," which will subsequently be printed on his business card. On the job, he will be responsible for using his expertise to create designs and specifications for products that will rock the world!

However, I must point out that product manufacturing is only a small portion of the U.S. economy. As of 2010, manufacturing accounted for only 11.7% of GDP, down from 14.2% in 2000.[2] I am sorry to report that the U.S. manufacturing sector has been on a steady decline, with many jobs going overseas, including engineering jobs.

Conversely, from 2000 to 2010 the finance and insurance sector grew by 10%, the healthcare sector grew by 27.4%, and the education sector grew by 28.5%.[3] The future of the U.S. job market seems to be in services. Perhaps Ryan could pursue a career as a design engineer in the service sector.

Further, there seems to be great need for improvement in the delivery of services. The American Customer Satisfaction Index (ACSI) is an annual survey of customer satisfaction

---

[1] From the course description for the BYU graduate course ME EN 578: CAD/Cam Applications.

[2] From The 2012 Statistical Abstract, U.S. Census Bureau, Table 670 - Gross Domestic Product in Current and Chained (2005) Dollars by Industry.

[3] ibid.

developed at the University of Michigan. ASCI researchers conduct more than 70,000 customer interviews each year involving a wide variety of companies, industries, and economic sectors.

Figure 1 shows recent ASCI scores for economic sectors as of July 2012.[4] Note that customers seem quite satisfied with manufactured goods and e-commerce firms. Satisfaction with hospitality and healthcare services is a bit lower. Then there is a serious drop off to financial services and retail services, and an even bigger drop off to transportation services and information services (telephone, cable TV, etc.). Industries within these sectors showed some disparaging ASCI scores. For example, hospitals (in the healthcare sector) got score of 76 and airlines (in transportation sector) got an unimpressive 67. The government sector (not shown in Figure 1) also got a paltry score of 67.

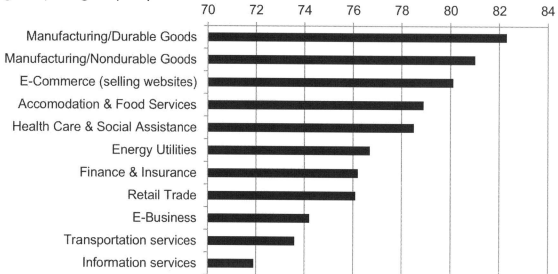

Figure 1: ASCI scores by economic sector (July 2012)

In other words, it appears that the manufacturing sectors are doing quite well right now, as least in terms of customer satisfaction. The bigger weaknesses of our economy seem to involve services. There seems to be a great need for improving the design and delivery of services if we are to see the same high standards of quality we see in manufactured products.

Perhaps Ryan could apply his analytical bent to help with this problem. Maybe he could become a Service Engineer and design exceptional and innovative services that could please customers and win increasing profits for his employer. But, what is the path to becoming a Service Engineer?

Becoming a Service Engineer?

I recently wrote a chapter for a book titled Introduction to Service Engineering (Sampson 2010b). However, I have actually never met a person with a degree in Service Engineering. Nor have I ever seen that title on anyone's business card.

---

[4] From The American Customer Satisfaction Index, http://www.theacsi.org/, retrieved August 9, 2012.

Surely, someone is responsible for designing innovative and well-crafted services, but who would that be? Service firms such as hotels and hospitals have "Engineering" departments, but they are primarily concerned with the operation of the building's air conditioning, electrical wiring, plumbing, etc., not the design of service offerings.

I have asked my professional seminar attendees the question, "who is responsible for service design at your firm?" The response I get is something like, "oh, marketing, since they are closest to the customer." But, are they trained in service design? What would happen if we let the marketing department design automobiles at GM or computers at IBM, instead of the trained engineers? The product engineers would revolt, since engineering is clearly difficult enough to require advanced degrees. Product engineering is not something you normally just pick up on the job.

Unfortunately, marketing degree programs and business schools have weakly addressed the issues of service design. Government statistics show that services represent 70 to 80 percent of GDP and employment in the U.S. and other developed nations. However, service businesses represent only cursory coverage in typical business school curriculum. The tradition of business management is in the so-called "industrial sector" that is preoccupied with manufacturing and selling physical products. Manufacturing management is a precise science with rigorous tools and techniques. Service management, on the other hand, is often considered to be unscientific and lacking strong methodologies.

What makes services so different—so lacking in formal mechanisms for design and innovation? The naïve have suggested that service design is "soft" and based on common sense, whereas product design is a hard science. I would beg to differ. Services can be very difficult to design and manage largely due to the onerous condition under which services are produced (discussed in Chapter 2).

Even if we did have formal programs to teach Service Engineering, what would we teach the students? What are the principles and tools that Service Engineers would use? Is there such a thing as a service CAD tool? I have seen computer simulations of service environments, but they are woefully imprecise and fail to account for the emotional response and personal variation that customers bring to service processes.

In Chapter 2 and elsewhere (Sampson and Spring 2012) I review tools like Service Blueprinting and process design techniques such as Business Process Modeling Notation (BPMN) and the Integration Definition for Function Modeling (IDEF0), but show how they are all inadequate for capturing the true nature and complexity of service processes.

The lack of rigorous service design tools was my primary motivation for developing a new analytical tool called *PCN Analysis*. I will define PCN in Chapter 3 and explain PCN Analysis throughout the book. For now I will simply say that PCN Analysis provides structure and methodology for approaching the difficult task of service design. It will show the complexities of service businesses and how they can be clearly conceptualized and systematically improved.

Services are indeed different

There have been various streams of thought that have hampered the science and study of services. For example, some have rejected the idea that services can be studied as a cohesive discipline. For example, a survey of service researchers conducted by Edvardsson et al. concludes, "On lower abstraction levels a general service definition does not exist. It has to be determined at a specific time, in a specific company, for a specific service, from a specific perspective" (Edvardsson, Gustafsson, and Roos 2005, p. 119). That idea suggests that services might be too diverse to study.

At the other extreme, some people have espoused a somewhat exaggerated concept that every business is a service business, and that everything is about service. Sometimes they couch this by saying that every business is in the business of satisfying customer needs, and they call that service. They do acknowledge that there are different models for satisfying customer needs, such as directly satisfying customer needs in interactive settings versus indirectly satisfying needs by providing customers with appropriate resources (that the customers can use to satisfy their needs). If every business offering were a "service" then generic business management should be sufficient—but it is not.

A related concept suggests that business is business, be it a service business, a manufacturing business, or whatever. However, it is easy to observe that traditional manufacturing management techniques function poorly when applied to services. For example, something as basic as identifying process bottlenecks on an assembly line becomes confounded when stations have arbitrary processing times due to the whims of customers at those stations, such as at a cafeteria line. Some may therefore conclude that services are a flawed form of manufacturing, which is like saying that a screwdriver is a flawed type of hammer. Flawed? Or different?

I strongly side with the camp that believes that services are operationally distinctive and managerially different. Some examples of the distinctiveness of service processes are shown in Table 1 (taken from Sampson 2012), which is similar to a table provided by Richard Chase (1978, p. 138). Non-service processes such as make-to-stock manufacturing have facilities that are organized to enhance process flow, focus employees on efficiency and consistency, and so forth. Conversely, service processes demand a customer-friendly layout, workers with interaction skills, and so forth.

Table 1: Managerial distinctions of services

Managerial issue	Non-service process	Service process
Facility layout	Organized to enhance process flow	Accommodate customer needs and expectations
Worker skills	Focus on efficiency and consistency; Rote training	Focus on interaction skills and responsiveness
Job design	Tightly defined with precise steps and cycle times	Broadly defined
Sales opportunity	Mass marketing	Personal selling

Managerial issue	Non-service process	Service process
Quality control	Based on formal specifications	Based on variable standards from customers
Asset utilization	Schedule assets for maximum utilization (ROI)	Balance asset utilization with customer responsiveness
Use of technology	Cost/productivity issues dominate	Customer acceptance issues dominate

My previous book, "Understanding Service Business: Applying Principles of the Unified Service Theory," outlined 50 major areas of service distinction relating to strategy, operations, quality management, human resource management, and marketing. This book will integrate an essential set of service management principles in a new and powerful tool.

We need a service design tool

The progress and development of services has been hampered by the unscientific and undisciplined ways in which they have been approached. This is evident as we have contrasted the systematic way that products are designed with the flippant way services are designed. Product design is rigorous. Service design is not—until now.

The need for better ways of designing and analyzing services has also been emphasized by leading researchers. Menor, et al, pointed out that the design of services is "among the least studied and understood topics in the service management literature" (2002). Bitner, et al, observed that "innovation in services is less disciplined and less creative than in the manufacturing and technology sectors" (2008, p. 66). Nie and Kellog asserted that services "must be studied in different ways, using different theories, skills, competencies, and language" than traditional manufacturing-oriented management research (1999, p. 352).

In other words, service design and innovation needs an analytical design tool that is more suited to the task. After years of research and development I am pleased to present a tool that addresses these concerns: PCN Analysis. This tool is uniquely suited to studying what is unique about services. To proceed, we need to clarify what makes services unique, which is the topic of Chapter 2.

Chapter 2 – Understanding Services

Before I introduce the powerful PCN Analysis tool, we need to discuss the fundamental nature of services. Few terms in business and economic parlance have been convoluted more than the term "service." We must begin by establishing an accurate understanding of what service businesses are.

Sometimes I get the feeling that defining services is like describing love—it may be hard to describe but we all think we know it when we see it. We define services as a set of industries—banking, hospitality, consulting, healthcare, garbage collection, etc.—which is what Judd called a "definition by listing" (Judd 1964, p. 58). Unfortunately, such an approach provides little intuition about what they have in common.

Or, defining services can be like describing salt. Try describing the taste of salt without using the word "salty." To be more precise in our understanding of services, we can consult a dictionary. The following are the first four definitions of "service" from the Merriam-Webster online dictionary:

1. "the occupation or function of serving"
2. "the work performed by one that serves"
3. "a form followed in worship or in a religious ceremony"
4. "the act of serving"

Except for number 3, this seems like describing salt as "salty."

Government economists have not provided us with any clearer depiction of services. They assert that services are part of the "service sector" as distinct from the manufacturing sector and the extractive sector (agriculture and mining). Then, they have referred to services as "non-manufacturing," implying that services can be defined by what they are not, with little indication of what they are (Morey 1976; Schmenner 1995).

That is like describing salt as being "not sugar," or describing night as being "not day," or describing men as being "not women." Judd astutely asserted that defining services by what they are not is inherently defective, in that "from the definition itself, nothing can be learned about what are the essential characteristics of a service" (Judd 1964, p. 59).

Two "services"

One source of confusion about services is that the term has been used ambiguously. The term "service" has been used in at least two distinct contexts in business parlance. The first and most common use considers "services" to be "intangible products." Numerous textbook authors and others have suggested that services are somehow intangible and fleeting, as opposed to "goods" that are tangible and durable. This is sometimes accompanied by an astute but confusing perception that "services are processes" whereas "goods are resources." True, but what is the point?

Some would suggest that the point is that firms that sell services sell processes, but firms that sell goods do not sell processes. That perspective is both naïve and myopic. Goods do not come out of nowhere, *ex nihilo*. So, where do goods come from? They come from processes! Processes are employed to produce goods. Customers buy goods. Processes are employed to use the goods and realize the benefits of the goods. Goods are enveloped in processes. Goods cannot exist without processes, and goods provide no value without processes including processes of use. When you buy goods you are buying an implied process of use.

Further, all services include goods and other tangible elements. Services cannot function without physical resources of some type. Psychiatry is considered a service, but it would not function very well without a comfortable couch for the patient and a pencil and notebook for the psychiatrist (or, perhaps an iPad running the "Psychiatrist helper" app). Banking would not function without computer equipment; the computer equipment may be located far from customer view, but is nonetheless essential for a positive customer experience. Where would hospitality services be without hotels and beds? Where would healthcare be without needles and MRI machines?

The naïve would argue that the distinction between "goods and services" is along the lines of ownership. With goods-producing industries the customer purchases and takes ownership of the goods, but it has been suggested that with services the customer does not take ownership of the goods (Judd 1964; Lovelock and Gummesson 2004). True, psychiatry customers do not get to keep the couch, bank customers do not get to keep the bank's computers, hotel customers do not get to keep the beds, and healthcare customers do not get to keep the MRI machines. Yet there are equally numerous examples of services where customers take ownership of tangible items: restaurant customers get to keep the food they order, retail customers get to keep the items they purchase, auto repair customers get to keep the replaced parts, knee replacement surgery customers get to keep the artificial knee, and so forth.

I call into question the traditional assumption that there is a dichotomy between goods and services (Greenfield 2002; Hill 1977; Zeithaml 1981). That assumption contributes to the service confusion (Sampson and Froehle 2006). A service is a type of process, and a good is a type of resource. All businesses involve both resources and processes that act on those resources, and, as mentioned above, it would be difficult to find a service process that does not involve goods. The bottom line is that defining services as "intangible goods" is inaccurate and a poor basis for analysis.

Service operations

The second way that the term "service" has been used in business parlance is to describe an operational process that involves a provider doing something productive in conjunction with resources that come from a customer. More precisely, services are business processes that act with or on customers, their belongings, or their information (Lovelock 1983; Sampson and Froehle 2006).

For example, the surgery process acts on customers' bodies, thus is a service. The auto repair process acts on customers' cars, thus is a service. The classroom process acts on customer's minds, thus is a service. The tax accounting process acts on customers' financial records, thus is a service. The business consulting process acts on customers' business problems, thus is a service.

What about the auto manufacturing process? What customer resource does the auto manufacturing process act with or on? Auto manufacturing is a fascinating process that typically involves procurement of parts and materials from suppliers, fabrication and assembly of components, inspection and control of quality, and delivery of finished goods. At no point do the customers, meaning the individual auto purchasers, need to be involved in the manufacturing process. In fact at this very moment an auto manufacturer could be producing a car that you might buy three months from now, and they are doing it without anything from you! They do not even have your permission!

Granted, you may have completed an auto manufacturer's customer feedback survey or attended one of their new product focus groups. However, the information you gave in those settings was not for your individual production; it was market segment data that would assist in understanding and meeting the needs of other future customers.

On the other hand, when you go to the dentist you will find that the dentist is waiting for you because the dentist cannot proceed with the dentistry process (cleaning teeth, filling cavities, etc.) without a key customer resource: the patient's teeth! Sure, the dentist can *prepare* for that productive dentistry process by procuring equipment, hiring staff, cleaning tools, and so forth. But the dentist cannot actually produce in the key value sense without those facial customer resources.

In other words, unlike the auto manufacturer, the dentistry process as defined (cleaning teeth, filling cavities, etc.) is dependent upon individual customer resources. This defining condition has various implications for the service provider that will be explained later. For example, the quality of dental work is extremely dependent on the processes and resources of customers, including eating and brushing habits. Conversely, auto manufacturers typically define production quality according to their own engineered design specifications, which are based on their expectation/hope that the specifications match future customer needs.

Unlike the "intangible goods" perspective on services, this second perspective on services is both universally valid and insightful. The name given to this enlightened perspective is the Unified Service Theory, but do not be dismayed by the reference to theory. As Kurt Lewin, the father of modern social psychology, reportedly declared, "There is nothing so practical as a good theory." The Unified Service Theory (or UST) is a very practical theory and simply states that the defining characteristic of all service businesses is process dependency upon customer resources—that the provider's processes are dependent upon resources that come from each individual customer. As we will see, this process dependency forms the basis for our ability to analyze and improve service businesses.

Service Supply Chains

The Unified Service Theory depicts services as a unique type of supply chain.[5] Supply chains are traditionally depicted as a series of firms that work together in a production of goods. Some firms provide and refine raw materials. Some firms fabricate components. Some firms assemble products. Some firms store and distribute goods. And so forth.

      An example of a traditional supply chain is shown in Figure 2, where we have a focal firm that receives resources from suppliers who in turn receive resources from still other suppliers (so-called "second-tier suppliers"). The focal firm has customers, who may themselves have customers. In this model the suppliers are considered to be "upstream" meaning that they ship goods down towards the focal firm. Customers are considered to be "downstream" meaning that the focal firm ships goods down to the customers. As such, the use of the terms "supplier" and "customer" in supply chain parlance is relative to whatever firm is considered the focal firm. However, that perspective does not hold true for Service Supply Chains, where customers are suppliers and suppliers can be customers! (I will provide alternate definitions for "customer" and "supplier" in Chapter 3.)

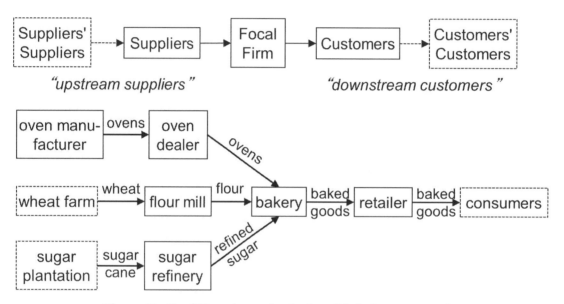

Figure 2: Traditional supply chain with bakery example

      Service Supply Chains are different from traditional supply chains in that each customer provides resources to the service provider for use in that customer's production. As mentioned above, those resources may be their selves (possibly including their effort), their belongings, or their information. Examples were given in the prior section. The customer resources are processed in conjunction with resources from other suppliers in order to meet customer needs. As such, customers are both upstream (meaning they provide input resources) and downstream (meaning they receive output resources). From the process perspective, they are two places at once, as depicted in Figure 3.

---

[5] Major portions of this section are from (Sampson and Spring 2012).

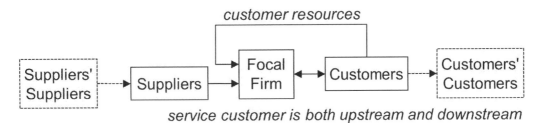

Figure 3: A Service Supply Chain

This Service Supply Chain relationship is bidirectional, meaning that resources move in both directions between the provider and the customers. The UST points out that services are, in fact, bidirectional supply chains. The bidirectional nature of Service Supply Chains has various implications, including the following: (Sampson 2000; Sampson and Spring 2012)

1. Service Supply Chains are generally shorter than product supply chains, meaning that customer resources pass between relatively few companies before getting back to the customer. For example, the product supply chain for a plastic door handle on a car begins with drilling for crude oil that is refined into plastic resin and shaped into pellets that are melted down and injection molded into a door handle that is assembled to a car that is shipped to a dealer—dozens of companies could be involved in producing and delivering that door handle. Compare that to the bidirectional supply chain of taking your car to the dealer to have the broken handle replaced.

2. Service providers typically do not pay for customer-provided resources. In the dentist example, the dentist does not have to pay the patient for providing his or her teeth. It is as though service providers receive customer resources on consignment, with the expectation that they will ultimately be returned to customer use.

3. Service providers inherently produce just-in-time (JIT), meaning producing according to demand, since the dependency on customer-resources precludes producing the service to inventory. (This will be explained in detail in Chapter 6.)

4. Services include implicit customer expectations for the value added by the service provider, since the customer sees both ends of the service process. In other words, service customers can compare what comes out of the service process to what they put into the process and thereby judge whether the provider is adding value.

Although Service Supply Chains are relatively short, they still can be quite complex. Figure 4 shows a dry cleaning Service Supply Chain. This is what has been a "two-level bidirectional supply chain" (Sampson 2000, p. 352). In that example, the dry cleaning firm receives a damaged garment from a customer, but outsources the repair of garments to a seamstress. The end customer only interacts directly with the dry cleaning firm. The repair offering is provided by using the seamstress as a service supplier, meaning that the seamstress processes customer inputs coming from the dry cleaning firm, only interacting with the end customer by way of the garment. (In Chapter 3 we will call this "surrogate interaction.")

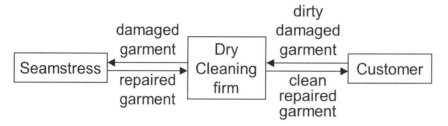

Figure 4: *A dry cleaning Service Supply Chain*

The auto insurance example shown in Figure 5 is the type of Service Supply Chain that later will be described as a Service Value Network. An insurance client (an individual or a firm) owns a car. The client provides the insurance company with risk that is based on the value of the car, the age and record of the driver, and so forth. The insurance company provides the client with assurance of mitigated risk. Insurance companies often employ reinsurance companies to take on some of the aggregate risk. Clients with questions about insurance coverage may call a company phone number that is routed to an outsourced call center. If the client has an auto accident, the client will likely go to an auto body shop that has contracted to do repairs on behalf of the insurance policy. Auto body shops do not usually do mechanical repairs, but outsource mechanical repairs to specialists like radiator shops.

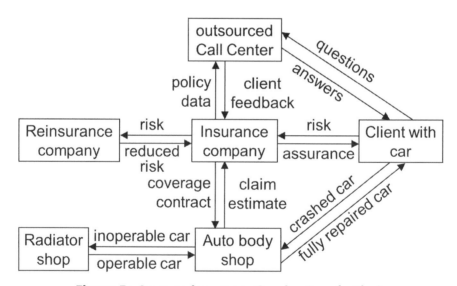

Figure 5: *An auto insurance Service Supply Chain*

An important issue we see from these examples is the complexity of relationships that can exist in Service Supply Chains. This points us to the fundamental underlying construct of PCN Analysis: interactions between entities. In one sense, PCN Analysis is a systematic way of studying and designing effective interactions.

Services are interactive processes

The term "service" has been used as an adjective to describe things of varying scope. We have already talked about how economists refer to the "service sector" which is comprised of "service industries." But again, they have been imprecise in telling us what constitutes a service industry, other than some vague idea that they "provide services." That classification is even more complicated by the variety of activities within the service sector. For example, education has been included in the service sector. Education includes firms that produce educational materials and firms that deliver education to students. Producing educational materials seems more like manufacturing, which contradicts calling services "non-manufacturing."

Even classifying *firms* as "services" is dubious, since firms also have a variety of operations of different types. For example, IBM used to focus on designing and producing computer hardware, and was considered a manufacturing firm. In 2002, IBM acquired the consulting arm of PricewaterhouseCoopers to bolster their information technology consulting business: IBM Global Services (IGS). According to recent financial reports, 60 percent of IBM's revenues come from their service operations. So, does that make IBM a service firm? Or just 60 percent of a service firm?

It makes much more sense to classify *individual processes* as being service processes or not service processes. The Unified Service Theory says that a service process of a firm is one in which the firm's customers, or beneficiaries of the process, each provide essential input resources to the process. A "non-service" process of a firm is one that the firm can perform *before* receiving resources from individual customers; after production is complete the customer may provide financial resources to the firm (e.g., pay for the goods), but those financial resources are used to meet the needs of *future* customers.

As suggested previously, dentistry operations include cleaning teeth, filling cavities, and so forth, which are service processes (dependent upon current patient inputs). Dentistry also includes procuring equipment, hiring staff, cleaning tools, and so forth, which are non-service processes (from the perspective of the patient). In fact, all firms have both service processes and non-service processes.

Granted, we *could* categorize businesses or industries according to the percentage of their processes that are dependent upon customer inputs, and maybe say that a firm with more than 50 percent of processes being service processes qualifies for being called a "service business." That may help the calculation of government economic statistics, but is a convoluted way to study services.

In this book we are going to treat service as a process, or more specifically an interactive portion of a process. We will see that all businesses have interactive service processes, as well as non-interactive processes that are not service processes. From this point forth, we will only use the term "services" to describe *customer-provider interactive processes*.

Visualizing interactive processes

If services are interactive processes then analyzing services means analyzing interactive processes. Processes are traditionally represented by flowcharts. Flowcharts, or "flow process charts," date back to at least 1921, when Frank Gilbreth gave a presentation titled "Process Charts—First Steps in Finding the One Best Way" at the annual meeting of the American Society of Mechanical Engineers (Graham 2004). Flowcharting and the various flowcharting tools have been useful in their own right, but they are limited in depicting distinguishing elements of interactive service processes.

Initially, flowcharts were primarily used in repetitive manufacturing processes, but they have since been adapted to other contexts, such as data processing and services. The original process charts included symbols for operation (i.e., processing step), transportation, inspection, delay, and storage. Process chart paper came pre-printed with all five symbols down the left side and room for writing process steps to the right, and symbols were connected with lines to represent process flow. Subsequently, instead of list form, the process charts were drawn on blank paper with annotated process symbols connected by arrows, which allowed for easier representation of non-linear processes. For example, the diamond represented decision steps with arrows pointing to different steps for different decision outcomes.

Figure 6 shows a simple flowchart for a pizza restaurant. In usual flowchart manner, the sequence of a process chain is indicated by arrows that connect one process step to another. The arrows generally represent a state dependency, meaning that one process step depends on some resource being in a state provided by another process step. For example the restaurant must first develop recipes before identifying ingredients, which is to say that "identify ingredients" is dependent upon the completed state of "develop recipes."

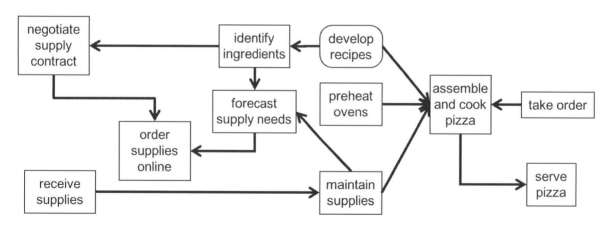

Figure 6: A simple restaurant flowchart

The arrows on flowcharts are different from the arrows on supply-chain diagrams such as was shown in Figure 2. Arrows in supply-chain diagrams often represent the flow of materials or information. Arrows on flowcharts represent state dependency, although movement of materials and information is an example of a state change. However, the arrows on flowcharts do not necessarily imply any flow of materials.[6]

Over the years, people have come up with new and more advanced forms of flowcharting, each being suited to analyzing particular types of processes. Unfortunately, prior flowcharting techniques have been inadequate at depicting interactive service processes and facilitating analysis. Chapter 3 will introduce the new PCN Analysis technique, which draws on key features of other flowcharting techniques.

For example, computer scientists use a tool called an Event-driven Process Chain (EPC), which is a flowcharting method used in business process modeling and is often used in enterprise resource planning (ERP) implementations. EPC flowcharts are valuable in representing not only processes but also events that precipitate process execution as well as entities responsible for specific processes (van der Aalst 1999). However, they are not particularly good at capturing processes that involve interaction between entities or the networks in which entities exist.

Another flowcharting tool used primarily in computer science is Business Process Modeling Notation (BPMN), which uses flowcharts that are similar to activity diagrams of the Unified Modeling Language (UML). BPMN organizes flowchart elements (process steps) into "swim lanes" that represent the entity that is performing the particular process step. A similar approach is used in "deployment flowcharts" of the Six Sigma tool set. For example, a sales process might be divided up into customer, salesperson, fulfillment, and billing swim lanes. However, by convention, each process step exists within one and only one swim lane, although it is conceivable that a step could span the border between adjacent swim lanes. Instead, interaction is depicted by dashed lines connecting corresponding steps in different swim lanes, which are referred to as cross-entity "messages" (White, Miers, and Fischer 2008).

A flowcharting technique that has been used for studying interactive service processes is Service Blueprinting, which will be discussed in Chapter 20. Service Blueprinting is helpful for studying interactions, but less helpful in showing how interactions fit within a broader picture of processes that are performed and shared by multiple entities.

PCN Diagrams build on the strengths of other flowcharting techniques, while emphasizing the unique conditions and design opportunities for interactive service processes. Chapter 3 will introduce PCN Diagrams through a simple example, and subsequent chapters will provide richer and more insightful examples.

---

[6] Flow of information is more complicated. It turns out all resources are information laden, meaning that all state changes imply a flow of information. However, that information may be embodied in some resource. For example, the "preheat ovens" step causes the oven to have implied information about its temperature.

Chapter 3 – Creating PCN Diagrams

The approach we will use for effective service design is PCN Analysis. The foundation of PCN Analysis is PCN Diagrams. PCN Diagrams will form the basis for analyzing service processes, networks, strategies, innovations, and other managerial issues. To proceed with this we need to first review the appropriate grammar and structure of PCN Diagrams, which will allow us to be precise in our subsequent discussions. This chapter may seem a bit mechanical, but is essential to unlocking the power of PCN Analysis.

The basics

A **process** is a sequence of steps. The base grammatical identifier of a process step is a verb. Process steps involve entities acting on resources, often multiple resources from multiple sources. Resources and entities are identified by nouns. In the PCN framework we use the term "resource" in a general sense, including physical items, knowledge, energy, and so forth. Even entities such as people or machines can be resources.

For example, the following are process steps from the pizza restaurant example of Figure 6:

- "develop recipes"
- "negotiate supply contract"
- "order equipment and supplies"
- "preheat ovens"
- "cook a pizza"

Notice that these process steps each have a verb followed by one or more nouns. You may notice that these process steps do not have a subject noun to identify who is performing the step, which will be explained below.

A PCN Diagram is a flowchart that exists within an analytical structure. PCN stands for Process Chain Network. A **process chain** is simply a sequence of process steps with an identifiable purpose. Chapter 2 described supply chains as sequences of companies that participate in the development of a product. For example, Figure 2 (on page 12) shows a simplified supply chain for a bakery.

Process chains, like supply chains, span and tie together multiple entities, although a service process chain may or may not result in the production of a physical good. However, all process chains have an identifiable purpose. In general, the purpose of process chains is ultimately to improve the well-being of some entity or set of entities, which is the concept of **value** (see, e.g., Grönroos 2008, p. 303). This concept of value will be expounded in Chapter 4.

Figure 7 shows a process chain with the purpose of serving pizza. Note that it has the same flowchart steps as Figure 6 (page 16), but it is structured within the framework of a PCN Diagram.

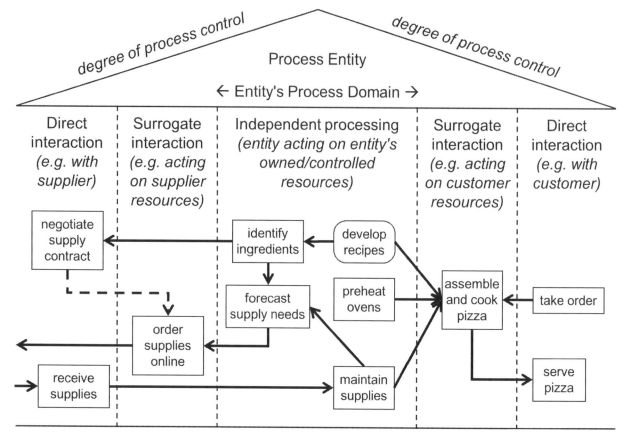

Figure 7: A simple restaurant PCN Diagram

As with a traditional flowchart (e.g., Figure 6), PCN Diagrams use arrows to indicate process step dependency. PCN Diagrams sometimes use dashed lines to represent a loose temporal dependency (i.e., one step may happen quite a while after the prior step). For example, the dashed line between "negotiate supply contract" and "order supplies online" implies that the supply contract could have been negotiated a long time before an instance of ordering supplies.

As mentioned above, process steps involve entities acting on resources. We define a **process entity** as any entity that participates in a process. Examples of process entities include firms, departments within firms, customers, agents of customers, and so forth. The key feature of a process entity is the ability to make decisions about the initiation or progress of some portion of the process. Process entities can perform process steps through the use of machines or automation, but the process entity still has cognitive control over the performance of the process steps.

The process entity in Figure 7 is a pizza restaurant, meaning the manager and employees of the restaurant. Alternatively, it could be depicted with two process entities, one for managers and one for employees, or the waiters could be considered one process entity and the cooks could be considered another. However, the decision making throughout the restaurant is probably unified, meaning that the pizza restaurant could be depicted as a single process entity.

Nevertheless, a PCN Diagram with only one process entity (like Figure 7) is illustrative but neither interesting nor realistic. Subsequent examples will be more useful by describing how process chains span multiple process entities with different decision perspectives. As will be discussed below, the "N" in PCN stands for Network, reminding us that process chains tie together a network of entities (to accomplish an identifiable purpose).

There are some useful ways of characterizing process entities. Some process entities *control* certain process steps—functioning as "operant resources" that act on other resources (Constantin and Lusch 1994), such as a surgeon, who acts on a patient. Other process entities function as "operand resources," meaning they are acted upon, such as the surgery patient. It is common for an entity to be an operant resource during some parts of a process chain and an operand resource in other parts of the same process chain.

All entities participating in a process chain—producers and consumers—are beneficiaries of the process chain, meaning that they participate with the expectation of value (see Sampson 2001, p. 330). We do not advocate eliminating the distinction between consumers and producers as some others have done (Vargo and Lusch 2008a, p. 257; Vargo and Lusch 2010, p. 146), but instead recognize that entities engage in interaction with two distinct types of value (i.e., benefit) motivations. Process chains tend to be configured to accomplish one or more specialized purposes. Entities that stand to benefit from a specific purpose of the process chain are **specific beneficiaries** of the process chain, and are generally called *customers* or *consumers*.

Other process entities participate in a given process chain in order to be able to subsequently meet well-being-improvement needs by other process chains. Usually, these process entities benefit from the given process chain by receiving a generic resource—money— that can be subsequently deployed to meet specific needs from other process chains. Firms such as "manufacturers" and "service providers" often fall into this category. They participate in a process chain not so much for specialized benefits of the process, but for the generic resource that can be used in other process chains, and as such are considered to be **generic beneficiaries** of the process.

For example, some employees of a deck and fencing company have been in my backyard installing a deck. I hired the deck company because of their apparent competencies in deck construction. These employees associate with the deck company not because they need decks, but because they need money for use in process chains that are outside of the deck company's process domain, covering things such as food, housing, entertainment, etc. These employees are generic beneficiaries of our relationship, since I provide money. I, however, am associated with the deck company because I specifically need a deck (which meets some relaxation or social need), so I am a specific beneficiary.

Of course, hybrid entities exist—being both a specific beneficiary and a generic beneficiary. For example, consultants are paid to engage in consulting projects (thus being generic beneficiaries), but also may desire to gain expertise in the business of a given client (thus also a specific beneficiary), and may therefore be willing to reduce the consulting fee charged that client. Another example is the teenage friend of one of my kids who was at our house recently. She mentioned she works as a lifeguard at the public swimming pool. When I asked why she works there she said it was because she likes swimming (thus a specific beneficiary), but I am pretty sure lifeguards also get paid (a generic beneficiary).

As shown in Figure 7, each process entity has a **process domain**, which is the set of process steps that are initiated, led, performed, and, to some degree, controlled by the process entity. In other words, an entity is an operant resource for process steps that fall within its process domain. A driving construct of a process domain is control, as symbolically noted by the triangle at the top of Figure 7. Entities can and do influence process steps outside of their process domains, but do not lead or directly control those process steps.

Three Regions of a Process Domain

In a study of various ways for classifying service processes, Urban Wemmerlöv observed that "contacts between a service system and a customer/client can be of three basic kinds": direct contact, indirect contact, and no contact (1990, p. 28). He gave an example that "a restaurant faces direct contact with its patrons in the dining area, has only indirect contact with them during the food preparation processes in the kitchen, and has no direct contact with them during its purchasing and maintenance activities" (1990, p. 29). These three types of processes are depicted in Figure 7.

At the extreme edges of the process domain in Figure 7 are process steps that involve **direct interaction** with other entities, such as suppliers and customers. This direct interaction means that people are interacting with people in some way, negotiating contracts, taking orders, and so forth. An example of a direct-interaction step in manufacturing is a salesperson negotiating the sale of a manufactured resource. An example from a hospital is drawing blood from a patient or consulting with the patient about the need to draw blood.

Adjacent to the direct interaction regions are areas of **surrogate interaction**, meaning that an entity is performing process steps that involve a non-human resource of another entity (see Chase 1978, p. 139). Examples are ordering supplies via a supplier website and assembling a pizza according to a customer order. The website is not the supplier and the order is not the customer, but are surrogates of those other entities. A manufacturing example is make-to-order production, where the order is a surrogate representation of the customer preferences (Sampson 2001, p. 142-144). A hospital example is analyzing a patient's blood in a laboratory.

At the center of an entity's process domain is the region of **independent processing**, which means processing that does not involve either direct or surrogate interaction with other entities. Make-to-stock manufacturing is a common example of independent processing. An independent processing example from a hospital is cleaning the facility, assuming that the person cleaning the facility is part of the hospital process entity. However, if the hospital cleaning has been outsourced to a separate entity, such as a janitorial firm, the cleaning function would be surrogate interaction in the janitorial firm's process domain. This idea will make more sense as we proceed to other PCN Diagram examples.

In Figure 7 it just so happens that the supplier-facing processes are shown on the left and the customer-facing processes are on the right, but it does not have to be that way. PCN Diagrams differentiate suppliers from customers according to beneficial relationships, not by relative positioning in and between process domains. In barter arrangements (see Normann 2001, p. 36), for example, both entities may be suppliers and/or customers, and either can be on either side of the diagram.

As suggested previously, the triangle at the top of the entity's process domain symbolically represents the degree of process control, with less control occurring with more direct interaction (Morris and Johnston 1987). Gary Thompson (1998) explained this concept by distinguishing between "uncontrollable work" such as "when customers and employees interact," and "controllable work", which "does not require the presence of customers" and therefore "management has some degree of temporal control" (p. 23). He described how service processes (i.e., process chains with interactive elements) contain both types of work, and managers can leverage the characteristics of each in order to improve labor utilization while meeting customer needs.

Multiple entities

A single-entity PCN Diagram like Figure 7 is not much more than an entity's process flowchart with categories. As mentioned above, it is much more interesting to study process chains that involve multiple entities, as shown in Figure 8 and subsequent figures. The essence of PCN Diagrams is documenting the interactive steps between the process domains of multiple entities in a service system, which will lead us to PCN Analysis.

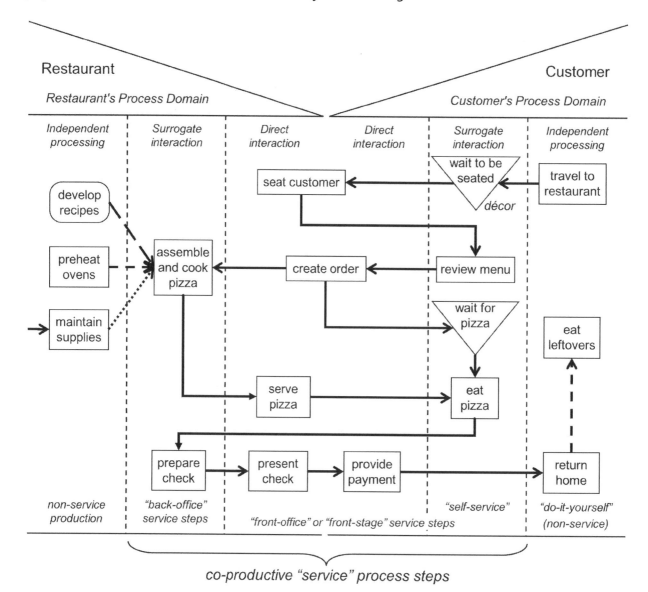

Figure 8: A PCN Diagram with two entities

Notice in Figure 8 how some steps occur between the direct-interaction regions of the entities. Seating customers involves direct interaction, but the step is executed primarily by the restaurant employee, and is therefore more within the restaurant's process domain. In this example, creating the order is led jointly by the employee and the customer. Serving the pizza and presenting the check are led by the employee, and the customer leads the step of providing payment. Each of these direct interaction steps are, by our definition, "service" steps. Further, all surrogate interaction steps are considered "service" steps. Note that both entities in Figure 8 are also engaged in some independent processing steps, which are "non-service" steps in this analysis. Were one to ask, "Is a restaurant a service?" the answer would be, "No, a restaurant is an organization that is engaged in both service (i.e., interactive) and non-service (i.e., independent) processes."[7] This emphasizes that the focus of analysis is the process segment[8], not the firm and certainly not the industry (see Chapter 2 and Sampson and Froehle 2006, p. 333-334). Firms are aggregations of resources and processes, including some service (i.e., interactive) process segments and some segments that are independent processing.

It is important to understand the use of grammatical constructs in a PCN Diagram. The subject, or predicated noun, of any step is always assumed to be the entity or a representative of the entity whose process domain the step falls under. In Figure 8, "develop recipes" is under the restaurant's process domain, implying that "restaurant employees develop recipes." If the recipes are developed by customers, then the box should be under the customer's process domain. If an outside entity like a cookbook publisher develops the recipes, then the process step should be under the publisher's process domain.

Since the subject of each process step is implied by the position on the diagram, the process steps can and should always start with verbs, reminding us that we are studying chains of process steps. The action verbs are followed by one or more object nouns, which are the resources being acted upon. Note that, by definition, object nouns under independent processing are normally resources owned and controlled by the given process entity.

However, for simplicity we allow steps that are outside the scope of the current analysis to be considered "independent processing," even if they are interactive. For example, Figure 8 shows "travel to restaurant" in the customer's independent processing, even though the travel may have involved a bus or a taxi. In that example, the interaction between the bus or taxi provider is outside of the scope of the pizza restaurant interaction being studied. At the end of this chapter we will review steps to create a PCN Diagram, including (1) identify the process to be analyzed and (2) identify the entities participating in the process. Those steps define the scope of analysis.

PCN – The N is for Network

A key feature of PCN Diagrams is that they can easily include multiple process entities in a network. Traditional service analysis techniques, such as Service Blueprinting, are useful for studying processes that involve two entities – a producer and a consumer – but limited in the ability to depict a full network.

For example, Figure 9 depicts a simplified PCN Diagram for a medical diagnosis process involving a patient who feels weak and needs a prescription based on a blood test. This example illustrates a process chain network involving four process entities: (1) a health clinic, (2) a patient, (3) an insurance company, and (4) a pharmacy. Standard flowchart connector symbols are used to show process dependencies that might span different pages or parts of the PCN Diagram. (Each connector has a letter followed by a number representing either the page, or in this example the entity number, where the step continues.) These and other flowcharting techniques can be used to depict PCN Diagrams of various levels of complexity.

---

[7] Elsewhere, I have advocated only using the term "service" as an adjective to qualify a specific noun, such as a service process, a service business, etc. Use of "service" as a noun is ambiguous, since it could refer to a service process, a service product, a service business, or a church meeting.

[8] A process segment is simply a part of a process. See (Sampson 2001, p. 38) .

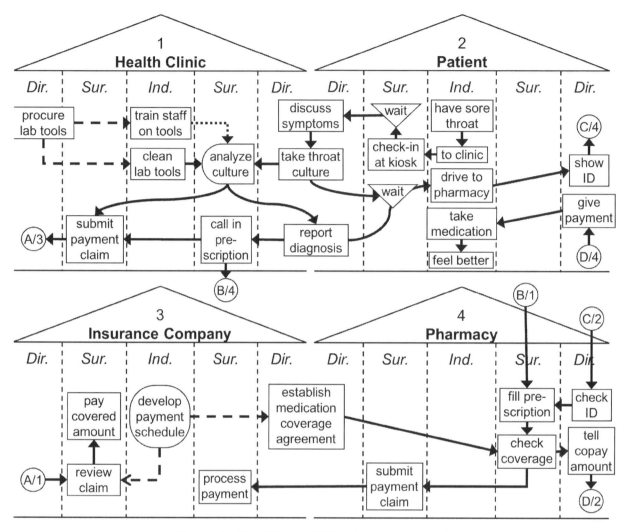

Figure 9: Healthcare PCN Diagram example

Again, PCN Diagrams can be used to visualize and analyze processes of varying levels of complexity and involving a wide variety of process entities. Chapter 13 will discuss the configuration of multi-entity process chain networks in greater detail.

Identifying the appropriate region

Summarizing, the three process regions of a process domain are:

- **Independent processing** steps are performed by a process entity acting on resources owned and controlled by that same entity.
- **Surrogate interaction** steps involve a process entity acting on the belongings or information of another process entity, but not with the person of the other entity.
- **Direct interaction** steps involve a process entity working in conjunction with one or more other process entities—people to people.

It turns out almost all process steps fit into one of these three process regions[9]. The initiator (operator) of the process step is the entity whose process domain the step falls within, or, in the case of direct interaction, jointly falls within. In the process step, the process entity is acting on, or integrating, resources. If the entity is acting on or with the person of another process entity, then the step falls in the domain of direct interaction. If the process entity is acting on the resources (belongings or information) of another process entity without direct interaction, it is surrogate interaction. If we have neither direct nor surrogate interaction, then the process step is independent processing—acting only on resources owned/controlled by the process entity.

Some processes may include composite steps that occur simultaneously in different process regions or domains. For example, an instructor may be giving a lecture as students are listening. Both are part of direct interaction, but the "give lecture to students" step is in the instructor's process domain and the "listen to instructor's lecture" step is in the students' process domain, with the latter being dependent upon the former. Or, an airline may be transporting passengers and their baggage at the same time: the "transport baggage" step is surrogate interaction and the "transport passengers" step is direct interaction, both in the airline's process domain, while "ride airplane" step is in the passenger's surrogate interaction region. It is helpful if the level of detail of analysis is fine enough to delineate the categorization of each step.

It is easy to recognize that every interactive process step, direct and surrogate, involves acting on customer-provided information. This is because people and belongings are always information laden. For that matter, every resource is information laden (Normann 2001, p. 29), meaning that every process step is, at some level, an information processing step. Information availability is the universal resource that ties process steps together in dependent relationships.

For example, an auto repair shop may receive some information about needed car repairs from a customer, but also receives information about the needed repairs from the customers' car by studying the car and performing diagnosis tests. The information coming from the car may actually be more accurate and informative than the information reported by the customer. The job of the auto mechanic is to use information coming from the customer and the customer's car to develop an appropriate plan of repair. Again, every customer-interactive process step involves acting on some information received from either a customer or from a customer-provided resource.

The functional and managerial distinction of these three elemental process step regions will be discussed in the subsequent chapters. In a nutshell, there are major differences in operating characteristics of the three regions, and, therefore, major differences in knowledge and skill requirements, even for process steps that exist within the same process chain.

---

[9] Machine-to-machine interaction can sometimes be represented in the surrogate interaction process region, even though it may not currently involve humans. (Of course, humans had to set up the machines and make decisions about how they would operate.)

PCN Analysis summary

This chapter introduced the concept of Process Chain Networks (PCN), which are networks of entities that are tied together by a process that accomplishes an identifiable purpose. The chapter also introduced foundational concepts of PCN Analysis, including:

- process chain – a sequence of steps with an identifiable purpose.
- process entity – an entity that participates in and makes decisions about steps of a process chain.
- value – the satisfaction of process entity needs (more on this in Chapter 4).
- specific beneficiary – an entity that participates in a process chain to have needs met by the specific competencies in the process chain.
- generic beneficiary – an entity that participates in a process chain to acquire generic resources (money) to meet needs from other process chains.
- process domain – portion of process chain that falls under an entity's control and responsibility.
- process regions – areas of a process domain for steps of a particular type...
- direct interaction – steps involving person-to-person interaction between entities.
- surrogate interaction – steps involving interaction with non-human resources of another entity (e.g., technology or information).
- independent processing – steps that are performed independent from other entities in the process chain network.

The foundation of PCN Analysis is a PCN Diagram that describes a process chain according to process entities, process domains, and process regions. The following is a summary of basic steps for creating a PCN Diagram:

1. Identify a process to analyze. As explained in Chapter 2, the appropriate unit of analysis is a process or process segment, not a firm. PCN Analysis takes place at the process level.
2. Identify the process entities that participate in the given process segment. This usually includes a focal firm and an immediate customer or customer segment. In many cases, especially B2B processes, the PCN Diagram should include the immediate customer's customer, so as to visualize how the focal firm facilitates the immediate customer accomplishing its customer-serving business objectives. The diagram might also include suppliers, partners, and others involved in the value network.
3. Record the steps that mark the start and end of the chosen process segment. Process segments often start with an identified customer need and end with the fulfillment of that need.
4. Fill in intermediate steps, showing which process domain and region each step occurs in, as discussed in the prior section. This may include steps in the process domains of the focal firm, customers of the focal firm, suppliers of the focal firm, and other entities in the process-chain network. As mentioned, the arrows between process steps indicate state dependencies (which may or may not involve product flows).

Creating a PCN Diagram is the just the beginning of PCN Analysis. The real power comes from understanding what goes on in various regions of process domains and how process chains can be configured and managed to provide superior value to customers and providers. The remainder of this book will show how to use PCN Diagrams to analyze interactive service processes and identify strategic opportunities for process improvement—in other words provide increased value to customers and providers. Chapter 4 will expound the concept of value and show how value is depicted in PCN Diagrams.

Chapter 4 – Identifying the Value Proposition

PCN Analysis proceeds by identifying the value proposition and elements contributing to that value proposition. A **value proposition** is a formal or implied proposal about why any particular entity should participate in a particular process chain. The basis of a value proposition is an expectation of benefits.

We briefly introduced the concept of value and benefits in Chapter 3. That chapter also described interactive entities of two types: generic beneficiaries and specific beneficiaries. The following is a brief review.

Generic beneficiaries (providers) participate in process chains with the intent of obtaining a generic resource, typically money, which can be subsequently used to acquire specific resources from other entities and other process chains. Specific beneficiaries (customers) participate in process chains to receive benefit coming from the specialized competencies of that process chain.

For example, a plumber repairs the pipes in a doctor's home. The doctor needs to take a shower, wash the dishes, etc. The doctor is a specific beneficiary (customer) of the plumbing interaction, receiving plumbing repair that meets his or her needs. On the other hand, the plumber goes to the doctor's home to fix plumbing, not to receive medical treatment or any other specific benefit. Instead, the plumber receives a generic resource, money, which he or she can subsequently use to buy food, go on vacation, buy a yacht, or whatever. As such, the plumber is a generic beneficiary of that plumbing interaction. Of course, some plumbers may plumb for the joy of plumbing, in which case they are also specific beneficiaries.

Despite the fact that generic beneficiaries and specific beneficiaries have different reasons for participating in a process chain, at the core they all have the same ultimate goal, which pertains to value.

The common goal

I often begin my professional seminars by asking participants to write down their answers to the following four questions:

1. What department do you work for in your organization?
2. Who are your primary customers?
3. What do your primary customers want from you?
4. What do you want from your primary customers?

Sometimes I pick a random volunteer to share his or her answers. The answer to the first two questions depends on the audience and individual. However, the answers to questions 3 and 4 always end up the same, regardless of the organization, the department, or the customer. How can that be? The answer is in the whys.

Here is a typical dialog, where the hypothetical participant is a manager at an auto dealership:

Me	Participant
What department do you work for in your organization?	the sales department – I am the sales manager
Who are your primary customers?	individuals looking for a new car
What do your primary customers want from you?	a car
Why do they need a car?	to get to work
Why do they need to go to work?	to get paid
Why do they need to get paid?	to pay their mortgage, etc.
Why do they need to pay their mortgage?	so they have a place to live
Why do they need a place to live?	so they are comfortable
Why do they need to be comfortable?	they're happier when they are comfortable
Why do they need to be happy?	I don't know. They just do.

It does not matter what organization/department/customer/whatever – it *always* ends the same. The ultimate reason customers participate in any business interactions is because they want to be happy. Happiness and related concepts of "well-being" or "quality of life" is the fundamental goal of all human existence. It is correspondingly the fundamental basis for participating in any and all business interactions.

This may sound like a rhetorical exercise, but it has major implications for why we make any business decision pertaining to customers. Ultimately, the success of a business is defined in terms of its ability to contribute to the happiness of customers – and others. I hear some of you saying "no, the success of a business is in its ability to provide an adequate return to stockholders, adequate wages to employees, etc. Success of a business is about sustained profitability." But you simply need to consider question 4: What do you want from your primary customers?

As suggested above, the answer to question 4 always turns out exactly the same as the answer to question 3. Here is the continuation of the above example:

Me	Participant
What do you want from your primary customers?	their business buying cars
Why do you need their business?	so that we can pay our employees and stock holders
Why do you need to pay you employees?	so that they will keep coming to work
Why do you need them to come to work?	so that our company will continue to make money
Why does your company need money?	so that I can be paid (among other things)
Why do you need money?	so that I can go on vacation
Why do you need to go on vacation?	so that I can relax
Why do you need to relax?	relaxing makes me happy
Why do you need to be happy?	I don't know. I just do.

If at this point you doubt that this is true, just try it. I have challenged my students and seminar participants on this for years, and have never, ever, come across a counter example. (Although I have had some people try to find one.) You can even try it in monopolistic situations – the result will be the same. Try some of these:

- Why do you pay taxes to the Internal Revenue Service?
- Why do people work for the Internal Revenue Service?
- Why do people run for political office?
- Why do bank robbers rob banks?
- Why do authorities put bank robbers in jail?
- Why do people eat hot dogs? (That one stumps me.)
- Why do terrorist terrorize?
- Why does anyone do anything?

If you follow the question with enough "whys" the answer will always end up being "because [I believe] it leads to happiness [or well-being or quality of life]." (Actually, it does not matter if the action is a business interaction, an interpersonal interaction, an individual action, or whatever. Since this book is about business interactions we will keep our focus there.)

We see a couple of tremendous principles come out of this exercise. As mentioned, we see that the fundamental basis of all business activity and interaction is to lead to the happiness of individuals. In addition, we see that the quest for happiness is universal, and must be sufficiently *mutual* in order for the business to function. In other words, there is a great symmetry in business interactions. Businesses exist to promote the happiness of customers, stockholders, employees, and others. The ultimate goal of all business activity is to promote the happiness of entities in the Process Chain Network.

This oversimplification is tempered somewhat by considering the complexity of happiness:

1. Happiness is a multidimensional construct. Individuals can be happy in different ways at different times. For example, after running a marathon a runner can be happy about the accomplishment and unhappy about the exhaustion at the same time.

2. Happiness is contextual. A person's frame of mind has major implications for their propensity for happiness. Sometimes happiness is easily achieved. In other cases, such as medical depression, the potential for happiness is limited even if all environmental conditions would favor happiness.

3. Happiness exists on a continuous scale. We sometimes treat happiness as a dichotomous state – something we either have or do not have. However, it is quite clear that happiness exists in degrees.

4. Happiness is relative to some baseline, and thus can occur in the negative region. There is probably not an absolute scale for happiness, but it is more practical to consider a degree of happiness relative to some alternative. This is important in PCN Analysis where we cannot measure happiness but we can estimate the impact a process change has on happiness.

5. Happiness is an emotion. Happiness is therefore latent, meaning that it is unobservable and not directly measurable. At this writing we can only estimate the existence of happiness by self-reported measures.[10]

The fact that happiness is difficult to conceptualize does not detract from its centrality in the occurrence of all human action. The popularity of attributing business success to financial profitability can largely be explained by the easy quantification of financial measures. However, we must not forget that money itself is only a surrogate measure of happiness potential. Overreliance on monetary measures of business success can lead to missing opportunities for providing happiness to various stakeholders, i.e., missing opportunities for value.

Happiness based value

The term "value" has been used and abused in academic discussions. Financial experts are concerned with the "valuation" of assets and organizations – such as used in determining whether to invest in a company's stock. Conversely, marketers may desire to provide value to customers in the form of benefits. Or, human resource professionals may desire to promote the culture of an organization by communicating company values.

I would argue that "financial value" and "customer value" and "organizational values" are all manifestations of the same core concept – individual happiness. Money only has value when it has the potential to satisfy needs and therefore promote happiness. We just discussed how customer value is ultimately rooted in providing happiness to customers. The values of an organization, as perhaps expressed in a mission statement, are simply a statement of things that the organization believes will lead to happiness.

Value, ultimately, is derived by an ability to provide happiness. Happiness comes from the satisfaction of needs, wherein I define needs as "conditions for happiness." This leads us to consider an important temporal element of happiness – present happiness versus future happiness.

Co-production and the timing of value

Reiterating, value pertains to satisfying needs, which are conditions for happiness (or well-being or quality of life). Value exists in two ways. A **value potential** is an ability to satisfy needs in the *future*. Value potential can be embodied in knowledge or other resources. An automobile has value potential because it has the ability to satisfy the transportation needs of a driver, which ultimately lead to increased happiness.

Value realization is the actual satisfaction of needs in the *present*, meaning that some knowledge or other resource is used to benefit some entity and increase their happiness. When an automobile owner actually drives the automobile to a destination, and is happier as a result, that value potential of the automobile is seen to enable a value realization to the owner.

---

[10] Of course, psychologists have attempted to measure emotional states by measuring electromagnetic brain waves. However, that is simply a surrogate measure of the emotional state.

Ultimately, value realization is or should be the goal of all organizations and individuals, but that can only be achieved by appropriately providing value potential. Usually, value realization occurs outside of providers' process domains. A goal of providers should be to provide value potential in a way that allows customers to have value realization in their own process domain. *This emphasizes the need for understanding what goes on in the customers' process domains.*

Some important concepts from the service literature are co-production and value creation (for example, see, Vargo and Lusch 2010, p. 143). The PCN framework considers "production" in a traditional value-adding sense: preparing resources so that they can subsequently be used to meet needs, which means the prepared resources have value potential (Grönroos 2008, p. 299). The prefix "co-" means "one that is associated in an action with another" (Merriam-Webster 2011). Therefore, **co-production** means two (or more) entities producing value potential together.

In common use, co-production is where customers participate in the development of the core offering of the provider firm, presumably in conjunction with the firm (Vargo and Lusch 2008b, p. 8). Co-production generally means that the customer and the provider both assume some responsibility for the execution of the production process, which may be working together (direct interaction) or may be one of them acting on the other's resources (surrogate interaction).

Subsequent process steps in the customer's region of independent processing are not co-production in the strictest sense, but may involve **value creation**, a phrase that has been used broadly to describe a realization of value by customers (Grönroos 2008). Although co-production always takes place in regions of direct or surrogate interaction, the realization of value can occur in interactive (service) process steps or independently (such as when a customer uses a product that was purchased from a firm to meet his or her own needs).

The phrase "co-creation of value" is often used in a confusing manner because it conflates both value potential and value realization. In a precise interpretation, "co-creation of value" would mean that multiple entities are simultaneously realizing benefit. However, what really happens is that the formation of value potential is done independently by providers and jointly between providers and customers. The realization of value on the part of providers and customers rarely happens simultaneously, therefore implying that "co-creation of value" is often a misnomer. "Co-creation of value" only makes sense if one ignores the temporal distances between value potential and value realization.

These manifestations of value are depicted in Figure 10. The operations of the auto manufacturer create value potential. The operations of the auto dealer provide both value potential and some value realization—by providing information that helps the customer make a selection decision. However, the primary value realization for the customer comes from the customer driving the car and thus satisfying his or her transportation need.

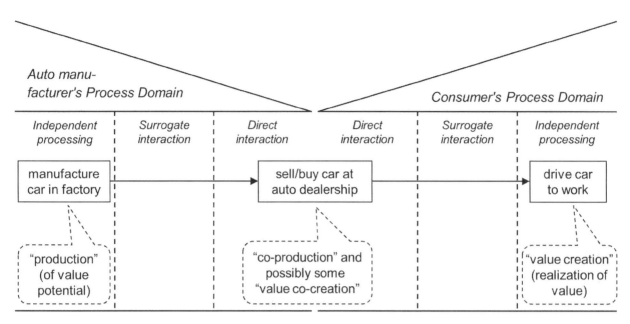

Figure 10: Value manifestations in automobile production and use

Value speculation and loyalty

There is a certain amount of speculation in creating or acquiring value potential. The owner may buy a car with the expectation of driving it, but may not for some reason. Still, the driver may realize value simply by owning the automobile, especially if it is a collector's edition.

Entities will enter into a process chain relationship only if they perceive that the relationship will ultimately lead to value realization. Therefore, the entities must speculate about the benefit potential of the other party or parties. For generic beneficiaries (providers) this speculation is a relatively straightforward, and includes assessing whether the other entity will provide the required generic resource (money) in a timely manner, which risk can be mitigated by enforceable sales contracts. It also includes guessing that the customer will not consume more provider resources than would be economically practical, which can be mitigated by pay-as-you-go requirements.

Interestingly, a local buffet restaurant had a problem at the height of the Atkins Diet craze. The restaurant charged a fixed fee to eat, even though some food items were more costly than others. Apparently a couple of Atkins Diet followers ate at the restaurant and consumed eighteen servings of roast beef and were told they could not have any more.[11] The company had to explain the difference between "buffet-style" and "all you can eat."

For specific beneficiaries (customers) the task of assessing a value offering is more difficult. Information about the value offering that comes from the provider may be biased. Information from other sources varies in reliability. Chapter 6 describes the ultimate source of information about a value offering: the customer's past experience. Still, customers take on a significant amount of risk by entering into a process chain relationship with a provider.

---

[11] Lisa Riley Roche, Chuck-A-Rama offers apology, Deseret News, April 30, 2004.

Therefore, we see a certain degree of risk asymmetry between providers and customers. Since customers bear the lions' portion of risk, they tend to be the decision makers in effectuating a process chain relationship. Providers will typically take generic resources (money) from any customer, but customers will not take specific resources from just any provider.

The key to sustainable process chain relationships is **trust**—the belief that the other entity will meet needs (i.e., provide value) in a way that is superior to alternatives (Sampson 2001, p. 303-304). This type of trust leads to **loyalty**, which is the propensity for one entity to make decisions that are in alignment with the other entity. Customer loyalty is an emotional response to available information about the provider, including about the provider's propensity and ability to act in the best interest of the customer. I like to think of loyalty as the selection emotion—the motivation of an entity, particularly a specific beneficiary, to choose to continue participation in a process chain relationship.

The reason loyalty is important is that, in my opinion, it is the most reliable indicator of a sustainable process chain relationship. Reichheld and Sasser (1990) showed how loyal customers are more profitable over time. Later, Reichheld (2003, p. 48) asserted that "the only path to profitable growth may lie in a company's ability to get its loyal customers to become, in effect, its marketing department."

Value is segment-based

Since value is the satisfaction of individual needs it stands to reason that value is customer specific, or more reasonably customer-segment specific. Customers can be grouped, or segmented, based on various factors: age, income level, gender, etc. Ultimately, the most relevant way to segment customers for service design purposes is according to their **value function**, which represents their needs and responses to a particular service offering. Segmenting customers according to their needs is very difficult, so we typically segment customers according to more observable factors that correlate with their needs.

For example, a restaurant may provide an offering that includes a large amount of food for a relatively low price, with little attention to other factors such as nutrition, facility décor, customer comfort, and so forth. The offering may be targeted at a custom segment with minimal financial resources and a voracious appetite. An identifiable segment that exhibits that value function might be students. Different customers segments might find the offering ill-suited to their needs.

It is important to remember that any estimation of customer value implies the value function of a given customer segment (i.e., a group of customers with similar conditions for happiness). Before we are able to estimate or identify customer response to a service design configuration we need to consider what customer segment we are addressing.

The B2B myth

This discussion of value is intuitive for business-to-consumer (B2C) services, where the customers are individuals that make decisions based on their emotional response. Some may assume that business-to-businesses (B2B) services may be different since the customers are firms and not emotionally-driven individuals. While it is true that business customers are bound by company policies and procedures for making purchases, it is incorrect to assume that B2B purchases are devoid of emotional effect. At the end of the day, B2B purchase decisions are made by individuals or group of individuals who are driven by emotional value functions.

One distinction of B2B services is that individual making the purchase decision may not be engaging the service provider on their own behalf, but instead on behalf of some other individual or group. As such, the need satisfaction of the purchasing decision maker is largely indirect, depending upon how well the service provider meets the needs of the intended recipient. However, it may also be direct in the way the process engages and facilitates necessary interactions with tat decision maker.

An illustration of this point is the old adage "no one was ever fired for buying IBM equipment." This adage referred to B2B purchasers selecting IBM equipment instead of equipment from less-known providers that may provide better equipment at a lower price. The adage recognizes that B2B equipment purchasers may tend to be risk-averse, with the risk of getting fired over a bad purchase having more emotional weight than the possible accolades and rewards for saving the company money.

The point is that even for B2B offerings we still must consider the emotional response of the purchasing decision makers. Value in B2B settings is, ultimately, the satisfaction of stakeholder needs that improves their happiness and wellbeing (or decreases the unhappiness of getting fired).

PCN depiction of value

Value propositions for generic beneficiaries can be represented on PCN Diagrams by placing -$ symbols by steps in which the generic beneficiary incurs monetary costs and +$ symbols by steps where generic beneficiaries receive monetary compensation. The magnitude of the costs and compensation can be depicted by the number of $$$ signs by each step, or omitted if the costs are trivial.

We recognize that compensation means receiving funds that represent value potential. Costs, on the other hand, represent giving up value potential. Financial profitability is the idea that the organization has a net increase in value potential, at least as far as measurable monetary instruments goes. Some nonprofit organizations may seem to have a net decrease in value potential, however if one takes into account the nonmonetary benefits, even nonprofits need to have a net increase in value (potential and realization).

The value to specific beneficiaries is usually emotional or attitudinal, since the satisfaction of needs leads to a positive emotional effect: increased happiness (or decreased unhappiness). This is true if the specific beneficiary is an individual or even if the specific beneficiary is a firm (as in B2B interactions). As discussed above, every individual or individual within a firm makes interaction decisions based on expectations for an emotional benefit.

In PCN Analysis we identify steps where specific beneficiaries (customers) receive specific benefits (i.e., need-filling value that provides motivation to compensate a provider) with ☺ symbols. We identify where the customers incur non-monetary costs (such as inconvenience) with ☹ symbols.

The ☺ and ☹ symbols can represent value realization, or can represent value potential that is directly perceived by the beneficiary. In the auto example from Figure 10 the customer may find happiness not only in driving the car, but also in buying a car that he or she believes will lead to future happiness. The ☺ and ☹ symbols depict the specific beneficiaries' (i.e., the customers') perspective on value.

This combination of tags therefore represents the value proposition to the various beneficiaries involved in a given interactive process. For example, Figure 11 shows the value proposition for a furniture retailer. In this situation, the furniture retailer designs, procures, and ships the furniture independently from customers. The customers recognize the need for furniture independently from the retailer. The customer browses the retailer's showroom and may ask a salesperson for purchase advice. (We sometimes place steps requiring judgment in rounded boxes, as discussed in Chapter 8 below.) The customer makes a selection, and the salesperson determines if the item is in stock. If the item is not in stock it is backordered. Eventually, the purchased item will be delivered to the customer, who can use the item.

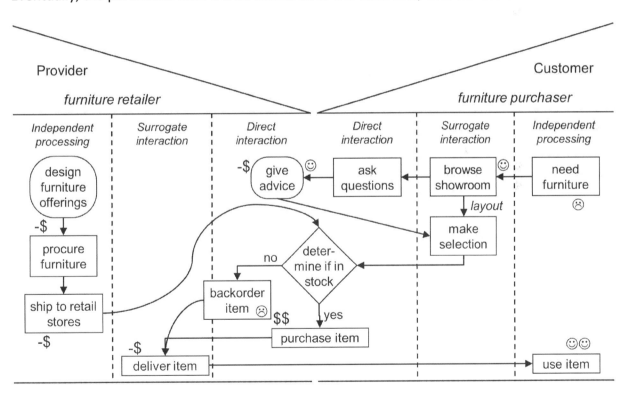

Figure 11: Value proposition of furniture retail

The furniture retailer receives value potential when the customer purchases an item. This value is a generic resource – money – that the retailer can use to meet various needs such as paying for labor, inventory, facilities, cleaning of facilities, and so forth. The retailer incurs costs in procuring inventory, shipping inventory, and delivering advice through qualified labor.

Although labor is also involved in backordering items and handling purchases, those steps are not nearly as labor-intensive as giving advice. (Whether or not to flag costs of a given step is up to the judgment of the person conducting the PCN Analysis.)

Figure 11 depicts two steps of non-trivial customer cost: needing furniture and the need for an out-of-stock item to be backordered. The need for furniture is a happiness deficiency due to lack of furniture. If that need is not filled, the customer may be disappointed in having to wait for the item to be backordered. Customer psychological costs are factors of reduced happiness, which means decreased value.

The customer realizes value at three steps of this process. First, this customer finds value in browsing the showroom, exploring alternatives and considering personal preferences. For this particular customer segment the "browse showroom" step is a pleasurable experience. This emphasizes that when we specify a "customer" entity we are really specifying a customer segment, which is a group of customers with a certain set of needs (conditions for happiness) and thus an assumed emotional response to the offering. If you do not like browsing showrooms you may not be in the customer segment being considered in Figure 11.

Second, the customer (from that customer segment) finds value in the advice coming from the salesperson. The knowledge imparted by the salesperson will help the customer feel more confident in making a selection decision. Third, the customer finds value in using the item. If it is a comfortable chair or couch, the customer realizes value each time he or she sits on the item.

What about all of the other steps that do not have ☺ benefit indicators? Are those other steps necessary? They may not produce a value realization (actually satisfying a customer need), but may provide important value potential. Value potential means that the steps enable subsequent value realization. The salesperson cannot give the best advice without some input from the customer, which takes place in the ask question step. The customer cannot use the item unless it has been purchased and delivered.

If any step of a process does not contribute to either value potential or a value realization, it should probably be eliminated. Some processes have steps that are followed due to habit or tradition or some other unjustified reason. Some steps might be performed in ways that are not very productive or efficient. Streamlining service processes be expounded with examples in Chapter 10 – Improvement through Lean Services. Configuring or reconfiguring a process in order to improve the value proposition is the topic of Chapter 5.

PCN Analysis summary

This chapter discussed the foundational purpose of all process chains and process chain networks, which can be stated various ways such as:

- the provision of value
- the satisfaction of needs of process entities
- delivering benefits
- providing for increased happiness (or decreased unhappiness)
- improving the well-being of process entities

These ideas are all embodied in the concept of value, as the term will be used throughout this book. However, we must recognize that value within process chains is manifested in two ways. First, there must be value potential, which is typically a configuration of resources that is expected to be able to satisfy needs and improve well-being. However, value potential is not enough, since ultimately the needs will need to be satisfied (and well-being improved), which is value realization.

One surprising outcrop of this is the observation that value realization of necessity takes place in the customers' process domains. For this reason, PCN Analysis requires studying and analyzing processes that take place in customers' process domains. This is quite different from common practice wherein provider firms only study processes that are within the boundaries of their firm. PCN Analysis emphasizes that it is as important or even more important to study parts of the process chain outside of those boundaries.

This chapter also emphasized the important concept that a successful PCN configuration is based on *mutual* realization of value, meaning that all entities that participate in a process chain do so because the participation somehow leads to improved happiness and well-being. As we analyze our process relationships with other entities we need to consider how value is realized by all parties, if we are to assure an optimal and sustainable process configuration. Attaining an optimal process configuration requires considering design alternatives, which is the topic of Chapter 5.

Chapter 5 – Strategic Process Positioning

Strategy is primarily about focus—about deciding what to focus on as well as what not to focus on. A firm cannot do everything for its customers, and those that attempt to are likely to dilute their competencies into obscurity. Therefore, firms need to decide what they intend to do and how they intend to do it, which defines their chosen offering. For interactive service businesses the offering is largely embodied in the business process design, and the strategy of a firm is primarily manifested by that process design. As we will see, deciding on a type of process design is a fundamental strategic decision.

One element of strategy is innovation. Business innovation is a decision leading to possible improvement. Improvement of what? Chapter 4 suggests that the ultimate goal of all business endeavors is improving the well-being (i.e., providing value) of stakeholders (customers, employees, stockholders, etc.). This implies that the focus of innovation should be centered on improving the value potential of a given offering, thus leading to increased value realization. In other words, the focus of all innovation is to meet more needs and enable more happiness of various entities.

The PCN framework unlocks a powerful approach to service process design and innovation based on exploring process configuration alternatives. Innovation can be introduced into process chains by repositioning steps or sets of steps across the regions of a process domain or across the entities of a process-chain network. It should be recognized that there are always process alternatives, with some being more practical than others in terms of costs and benefits. It should also be recognized that in many cases, service (or interactive processing) is one option, and independent processing is another. *Service—interactive processing—is a strategic choice!*

Process Design Options

Consider the process chain involved in providing sandwiches to hungry consumers. One key step in the process is "assemble sandwich" wherein an actual sandwich is created. Where can or should the "assemble sandwich" step fit in regions of a provider's or consumer's process domain? In fact, that step could be positioned about anywhere.

Figure 12 depicts positioning options for that "assemble sandwich" step. Option 1 performs the step in a factory, completely independently from customers. That step might be performed at a centralized location, perhaps far from customers both in time and space. (It is amazing what they can do with preservatives these days.) After that sandwich is assembled it is pushed down a supply chain through some logistical system until it gets at a point of purchase by consumers. In traditional manufacturing jargon this is called a "push" system.

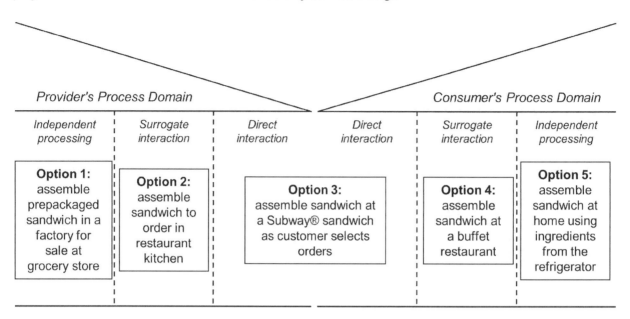

Figure 12: "Assemble sandwich" process design options

Option 2 has the firm assembling the sandwich based on a customer order, which order is a surrogate representation of a customer. The provider interacts with that customer resource (the order) which is surrogate interaction. With this option, the provider does not produce sandwiches to stock or inventory, but waits for an order before assembling a sandwich. In manufacturing language this is called a "pull" system, since each customer order pulls a quantity of production. Option 2 is more complicated than option 1 in that there must be a mechanism for receiving the customer order and for adjusting the process to accommodate the customer order.

Option 2 is also subjected to a serious time dependency. First, since the customer has already placed an order before production the step is very sensitive to time latency. In other words, the time from order to production and delivery must be quite fast, since the customer is waiting for the product. Second, it is difficult to manage the production schedule under option 2 since demand (customer orders) is likely to significantly fluctuate over time, whereas capacity of production might be relatively fixed. This means that the production capacity may be idle when there are no customer orders, such as in the middle of the afternoon, and then the sandwich production system may be stretched beyond capacity during times of high customer demand, such as lunchtime.

This challenging concept of "time-perishable capacity" means that (a) capacity utilization under Option 2 will likely be quite a bit lower than under Option 1, and (b) the producing firm needs to consider ways of making capacity more flexible and adjustable to fluctuations in demand. Under Option 1, capacity utilization is an internal decision based on process needs. Under Option 2, capacity utilization is limited by the availability of essential customer-provided resources. (This time-perishable capacity concept will be re-visited in Chapter 6.)

Option 3 is an interactive assembly process, as has been popularized by the ubiquitous Subway® Sandwich chain. Here the customer is actually in the sandwich assembly process, working with the provider in directing the sandwich assembly process. In this example the employee follows relatively standard procedures according to customer requests.

Option 4 has the customer initiate sandwich assembly at a provider's facility using resources owned by the provider. Here the customer has access to the provider's resources, including the facility (such as a buffet restaurant), equipment (forks and knives), and materials (bread and sandwich toppings). The customer uses those provider resources to assemble a sandwich that can meet the customer's specific needs. The firm is benefited by having the customer do much of the production work, assuming the customer is capable of performing that function.

Option 5 has the customer assembling independently from the provider. In this example the provider is an ingredient provider, such as a producer of bread and sandwich toppings. The customer has taken ownership of those ingredient resources (i.e., purchased them) and likely kept them in inventory (e.g., the refrigerator) until the time of demand. The customer then performs the "assemble sandwich" step, followed immediately by consumption (yum!).

Which of these five is the best process positioning option? That depends on the needs, expectations, interests, and skills of the customer segment, in conjunction with the capabilities of the sandwich firm. Although the five options each address the same hunger need of customers they are different operational configurations that provide different value propositions. The five process options each have different operating characteristics.

Principles of Process Positioning

The provider has specialized skills and performs specialized production. In other words, the provider is in the sandwich business. As such, the provider is willing to acquire specialized tools and competencies used in sandwich assembly, which represent a high fixed cost, but that cost can be spread over a lot of different customers. Therefore, the options in the provider's process domain are likely to provide superior economies of scale.

However, the customer may demand or desire control of the sandwich assembly process, making the provider's process domain less attractive. For example, the customer may desire to customize the sandwich assembly in strange and unique ways, which is easier to accomplish in the customer's process domain.

In some cases the customer only wants limited control, but wants the provider to assume much of the responsibility for the assemble sandwich step. Therefore, a more interactive option such as Option 3 might be desirable—letting the customer direct the assembly while the provider actually performs the assembly. However, this interactive co-production constrains the productivity of the provider and causes inefficiency. A surrogate interactive option might provide a better balance of efficiency and co-production.

These thoughts can be summarized in four basic principles:

Principle #1: Process inefficiency. In general, interactive processes are less efficient (from the perspective of the provider firm) than independent processing, with directly-interactive processes being the least efficient.   As Chase (1978; 1981) identified, operating efficiency is an inverse function of the degree of customer interaction. This relates to the concept of "customer intensity," which will be discussed in a later chapter and which is defined as the degree to which variation in customer input components causes variation in the firms processes (see Sampson 2010a, p. 116; Sampson 2010b, p. 38). Interaction leads to customer intensity, and the resulting variation hinders process efficiency. If efficiency is a goal, effort should be taken to reduce customer intensity by limiting how much of the process chain operates in the region of direct interaction.

Principle #2: Economies of scale. High fixed costs favor processing by specialized providers who can spread those fixed costs across more units of production. As will be demonstrated in the next section, customers involved in interactive processes usually have the option of performing certain aspects of the process independently—so-called "do it yourself" (Lusch, Brown, and Brunswick 1992). For example, a customer can hire a carpenter to build an addition onto his house or alternatively can purchase tools and attempt the project himself. Even though customers typically have a customization advantage by being their own providers (Principle #3 below), focused providers typically have a scale advantage. In particular, specialized providers can more easily justify incurring the fixed costs of obtaining skills and competencies.

Principle #3: Customization. Customization increases as process steps move closer to the customers' independent processing region. A firm can provide customization by moving steps from independent processing (e.g., make-to-<u>stock</u> manufacturing) to surrogate or direct interaction (e.g., make-to-<u>order</u> manufacturing). However, firms can increase customization even further by moving steps into the customer's process domain, allowing the customer to customize their execution of steps and use of resources. Indeed, the words "customize" and "customer" share the common root. Assuming they have sufficient skills and resources, customers can get more customized results by doing the task themselves since they are not constrained by practical or legal restrictions of hired service providers.

Principle #4: Surrogate positioning. Surrogate interaction is a tremendous tool for balancing the classic tradeoff between process efficiency and customization (Frei 2006). Changing an independent processing step to an interactive step or vice versa can be disruptive; and firms can use the surrogate-process region as a less-disruptive alternative.

Figure 13 shows these four principles with regard to personal income tax return preparation process options. The provider is a tax firm with tax filing expertise. The customer is a client that needs a completed income tax return. Option 1 has the greatest economies of scale—the firm can sell the book to millions of customers at relatively low variable cost. However, the book is a standardized offering, and Option 1 is the least customized option. The most customized option is Option 5, since the client has complete control over the tax return process, and can use any approach they desire (including illegal approaches, if the client is willing to spend time in jail). A weakness of Option 5 is that the client may not have the skills necessary to complete the tax return, at least not to the degree of a specialized service provider. Option 3 provides a balance of customization and economies of scale (esp. specialized skills), but at a cost of efficiency. Options 2 and 4 are more efficient than Option 3, and leverage the hybrid benefits of surrogate positioning.

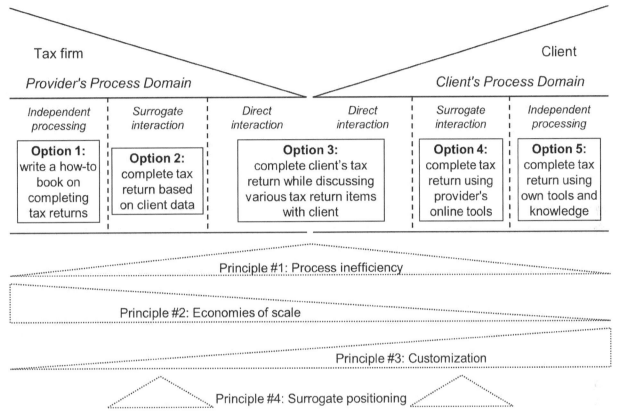

Figure 13: Personal tax accounting process options and principles

Strategic Process Positioning

The optimal processes positioning depends on what the provider is trying to accomplish in a particular offering to a particular customer segment (i.e., a group of customers with similar needs and potential for satisfying those needs). This process positioning is a strategic decision in that it defines what business the firm is in in terms of value proposition and requisite competencies. The process positioning also defines the relationship with customers in terms of roles assumed by the provider vis-à-vis roles required of the customers (which will be expounded in Chapter 9).

In general, the best process positioning depends on the desired value proposition of a given process, as depicted by realization of costs and benefits in the process (for both the provider and customers). For example, moving a process step from direct interaction to surrogate interaction may allow an increase in efficiency but may also decrease the responsiveness of the system to varying customer needs and abilities. If customers value efficiency then this could be a good process repositioning. If customers demand high levels of responsiveness to their unique needs it could be a bad process positioning.

Therefore, firms must understand the needs of their chosen customer segments, understand their corresponding competencies, and position the process steps accordingly. Good process positioning can lead to significant competitive advantage, and bad process positioning can leave providers on a path to dissolution. Chapter 11 will show how markets evolve in ways that make good strategic process positioning turn into bad strategic process positioning. The remedy to such strategic disruptions is innovation.

Enabling and Relieving Innovations

Richard Normann (2001, p. 73-74) discussed two major categories of process innovations, or what he called "value-space reconfigurations": **enabling innovations**, which enable customers to do things that were previously provided by others, and **relieving innovations**, in which a firm takes over activities that previously were done by customers. In the PCN framework, enabling innovations are visualized by moving process steps from the provider's process domain to the customer's process domain. Relieving innovations are visualized by moving steps the other direction (toward the provider).

Normann cites the Swedish retailer IKEA as an example of a firm that successfully executed an enabling innovation for strategic advantage (Normann 2001; Normann and Ramírez 1993). IKEA sells furniture in "flat packs" that are kits with materials and instructions that enable customers to assemble the furniture in their own homes with their own tools. Among other things, this allows IKEA to sell good-quality furniture at relatively low prices.

Figure 11 (from Chapter 4 page 39) showed a value proposition for a traditional "full-service" furniture retailer. Compare that with IKEA's value proposition as depicted in Figure 14. That PCN Diagram shows how IKEA differentiates by repositioning the "assemble furniture" step from IKEA's process domain to the customers' process domain. (It is often helpful to highlight steps involved in an innovation with double-border boxes.) This shift has various implications for the operating characteristics and value proposition, including:

- Improved firm efficiency: It is less expensive for the firm to "outsource" the assemble furniture step to the customers, leaving the firm with simply assembling the furniture kits.
- Reduced economies of scale: customers are less capable at assembling furniture than a specialized factory employee. IKEA manages this by providing simplified assembly that can be performed with basic household tools.
- Increased customization potential: customers can assemble furniture as desired, including adding extra paint or stickers or even not following instructions.

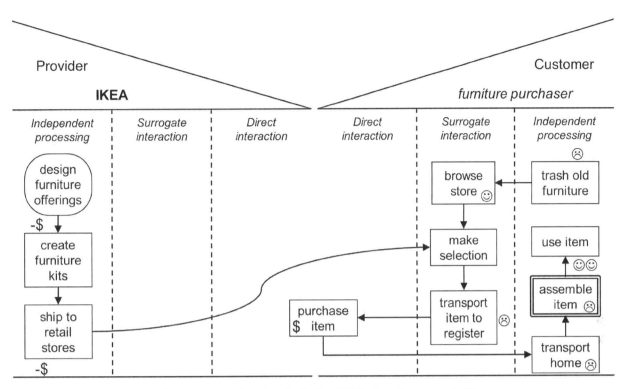

Figure 14: PCN Analysis for IKEA furniature retail

Another differentiating feature of IKEA is the decreased customer intensity from having less of the process chain in regions of direct interaction. The interactive firm shown in Figure 11 provides product advice that is valued by customers (☺) by employing experienced and costly (+$) labor. Compare that with IKEA's process shown in Figure 14, which has almost no steps in the region of direct interaction. In fact, by using self-check-out (surrogate interaction) the customer can avoid direct interaction altogether. Avoiding interaction further helps IKEA's efficiency and cost competitiveness.

Relieving innovations move steps the other direction, from the customer's process domain to the provider's process domain. Campbell, Maglio, and Davis (2011) describe relieving innovations in what they term *super service*, defined as providers performing tasks previously done by customers. They discuss home-delivery of groceries as a business-to-consumer (B2C) example, wherein the provider relieves the customer from having to travel to the grocery store. They describe vendor-managed inventories as a business-to-business (B2B) example, where producing firms manage inventories of products at their customer's locations.

Other examples of relieving innovations fall under the heading of **servitization**, which is when manufacturing firms (largely engrossed in independent processing) make a strategic process shift into related services (i.e., interactive processes). An example is a jet engine manufacturer, Rolls-Royce Aerospace, shifting from selling engines to leasing engines by the hour of use, and in the process relieving customers of engine maintenance and repair processes (Neely 2008). Servitization will be discussed more in Chapter 11.

PCN Analysis summary

This chapter emphasized how much flexibility there usually is in process configurations. There are often various process options for delivering a value proposition, each of which can provide a different set of operating characteristics. The key is identifying which process configuration is optimal given the need requirements from customers and the capabilities of providers.

To help our PCN Analysis this chapter introduced four fundamental principles of process positioning:

- Principle #1: Process inefficiency – Interactive processes are less efficient than independent processes.
- Principle #2: Economies of scale – Specialized providers generally have greater economies of scale than general customers.
- Principle #3: Customization – The potential for customization increases for process steps that are closer to the center of the customer's process domain.
- Principle #4: Surrogate positioning – Surrogate interaction can provide hybrid characteristics between direct interaction and independent processing.

We also reviewed how process configurations can be modified through enabling and relieving innovations. The goal is to select a particular process positioning in order to provide a particular value proposition. Once that is determined, we need to manage that value proposition to assure it is realized, which is the topic of the Chapter 6.

Chapter 6 – Managing Across the Regions

Recall from Chapter 4 that a **value proposition** is a formal or implied proposal about why any particular entity should participate in a particular process chain. Good service process management includes systematically managing the value proposition, assuring that the chosen value proposition is achieved. Poor service process management leaves the value proposition to chance.

As alluded to in Chapter 1, good management of interactive service processes is governed by different principles than good management of independent processing. This chapter will review important managerial distinctions according to the process positioning alternatives discussed in Chapter 5.

General managerial differences

Process steps in different regions of a process domain have different operating requirements. Figure 15 describes key operating characteristics across the five fundamental process regions, with examples given below.

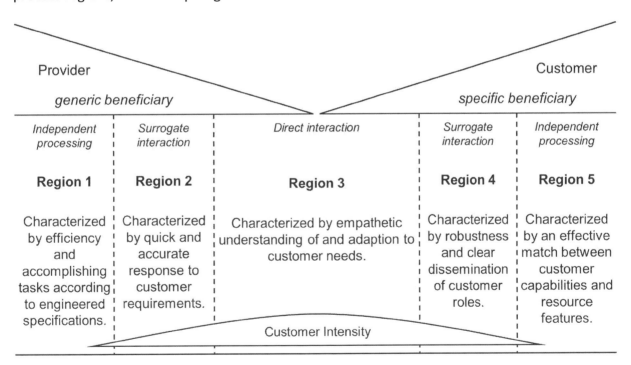

Figure 15: Managing the value proposition

Managing in Region 1: Internal operations

Region 1 (provider's independent processing) includes processes performed by the provider without interaction. For an electronics manufacturer this could be manufacturing products for later sales. For a bakery it could be baking goods. For a hospital or hotel it could be cleaning the facilities. For a software company it could be writing software.

The direction for steps in that region often comes from engineered specifications, meaning there should be standardized operating procedures. There are many powerful tools for managing processes that are positioned in Region 1, including Statistical Process Control (SPC), assembly line balancing, and inventory modeling methodologies. Those and other approaches are well documented, and will not be discussed here. In fact, most of the business process management methodologies developed over the past century were designed for processes in Region 1.

Managing in Region 2: The back-office

Region 2 (provider engaged in surrogate interaction) has the provider acting with some resource of the customer. Law firms do legal analysis and write legal documents based on customer information. Auto repair firms repair customers' cars. Banks process customers' transactions. Shipping companies ship customers' packages.

Firms operating in Region 2 desire some degree of efficiency, even in the face of varying customer requirements. To achieve this, customers may be required to provide their resources in a relatively standardized format, which limits the amount of variation the provider needs to deal with. For example, FedEx ships packages to almost any address, and must do it in a way that is efficient and avoids errors. One way to facilitate this is to provide customers with standard envelopes and boxes with standardized labels and standardized fees. This allows FedEx to operate in Region 2 with reduced variance in what customers provide, thus enhancing responsiveness while reducing errors.

Managing in Region 3: Personal interactions

Region 3 (direct interaction between provider and customer) hinges on the interpersonal and interactive skills of the provider's employees. As such, management of processes in Region 3 focuses largely on selection and training of those "contact" or "front line" employees. This is usually the region of highest "customer intensity" as depicted at the bottom of Figure 15. Customer intensity is the impact of customer variation on the providers' processes, as will be discussed below. The processes need to be sufficiently capable of responding to customer needs while staying within the bounds of provider capabilities.

Managing in Region 4: Self-service

Region 4 (customers engaged in surrogate interaction) is challenging in that it relies on the customer's capabilities to appropriately perform their process functions. Customers need to be both motivated and capable of performing the function. As will be expounded in Chapter 9, customers are being treated as "partial employees" of the provider, but must be managed quite differently from regular paid employees. Providers cannot usually send customers to training seminars to learn their roles in the process, it is not easy to certify the competence of customers at performing their co-productive roles, and it is usually not a good idea to fire customers who are unable to perform their roles. Instead, we train and motivate customers acting in Region 4 by subtle elements designed in the service system. Customer training will be discussed toward the end of Chapter 8.

Managing in Region 5: DIY

Region 5 is the so-called "do-it-yourself" region where beneficiaries act to produce their own benefit, independent from the providers. In this case, the providers are providers of resources that are given value potential through the provider's processes. Remember that value potential has meaning only insofar as it enables value realization. Therefore, managing processes in Region 5 largely comes down to resource *usability*.

A key to resource usability is recognizing that resource providers, specifically product engineers, are not the same as the specific beneficiaries (customers). Only in rare situations are customers the same as product engineers. They are not even the same *kind* of people. They do not have the same needs and capabilities. They do not have the same understanding of the resources. Managing DIY processes that occur in Region 5 largely come down effectively considering Human Factors perspectives in product development.

Managing Customer Intensity

Customer intensity was defined in Chapter 5 as "the degree to which variation in customer input components causes variation in the provider's processes" (see Sampson 2010a, p. 116; Sampson 2010b, p. 38). Customers vary. They vary in needs, requirements, motivations, capabilities, and so forth. Provider's processes can also vary, but usually not as much as customers vary.

Customer intensity indicates the degree to which a provider process varies in response to customer variation. High customer intensity means a provider's process is greatly impacted by customer variation. Low customer intensity means that customer variation has little impact on the provider's process. As suggested above, customer intensity differs from one process region to another, with the highest customer intensity typically being in the region of direct interaction.

Francis Frei outlined five forms of customer variation (Frei 2006):

1. Customer arrival variability—customers arrive and request service at random yet predictable times.
2. Customer request variability—customers vary in their needs and how they want them to be filled.
3. Customer capability variability—customers vary in what their able to do in a process.
4. Customer effort variability—customers vary in the amount of effort they are willing to expend in a process.
5. Subjective preference variability—customers vary in their expectations and perception of what they consider to be "good" service.

These forms of customer variation can have a major impact on the interactive operations of a service provider. If customers arrived at steady intervals, all requested the same thing, all were able and willing to do their parts of the process, and all defined "good" service the same way, then providing service would be easy—at least easier. Manufacturers that operate in regions of independent processing have the luxury of being buffered from customer variation. Frei points how disruptive customer variability would be to manufacturing operations; yet, customer variation is the norm for interactive service processes.

Process variation can be a good or a bad thing. When customer requirements vary, process variation may be required to meet customer needs. However, process variation hampers efficiency. Process variation limits learning effects. Learning curve theory suggests that standard, repetitive processes experience greater learning effects than varying processes.

Customer variation is. Barring a widespread adoption of human cloning, customers will inherently vary. A fundamental managerial question is how we deal with customer variation. Different strategies indicate different amounts of customer intensity.

A low customer intensity strategy involves reducing the impact of customer variation on the firms' processes. One way this is achieved is to buffer the customers from the firm through surrogate interaction. Moving process steps from Region 3 to Regions 2 and 4 can reduce the impact of customer variation. For example, when retailers move from brick-and-mortar stores (Region 3) to online stores (Regions 2 and 4), they reduce the amount of possible interaction by replacing flexible people with structured technology.

Alternatively, a high customer intensity strategy focuses on accommodating customer variation. One approach is through direct interaction, focusing employees on discovering and responding to customer interactions. This, of course, can be very costly and inefficient. An alternate is to utilize surrogate interaction by allowing customers to meet their own needs in their own way using resources from the provider. Chapter 10 will describe the introduction of self-serve retail that occurred near the start of the twentieth century. Prior to that, retail was very interactive, with employees retrieving items for customers, with the process being heavily influenced by customer requests. Self-serve retail moved the selection of products to the customer's process domain, making customers responsible for process variation and reducing the impact of that variation on the provider's operations (i.e., reducing customer intensity).

A key principle to remember is that customer intensity is typically highest in Region 3— direct interaction. Firms that choose to operate in that region need to appropriately prepare for process variation through flexible process design, employee training and empowerment, and so forth. Firms that desire lower customer intensity would typically move process steps to other process regions.

Specific managerial distinctions

The rest of this chapter will describe how specific areas of business management differ between interactive versus independent processing. As suggested in Chapter 1, the traditional approaches used in managing independent processing are much more developed and rigorous than the typical approaches used to manage interactive processes. PCN Analysis includes an understanding of how that traditional business management needs to be adapted for interactive processes.

Managing production imbalances: Inventory and Queuing

The operations of firms have productive capacity that is defined by available resources: labor, machines, component parts, and so forth. In almost every situation, demand coming from customers is variable and seemingly random, though often predictable. On the other hand, capacity is relatively stable as defined by the availability of resources. A big question is how to best meet variable demand with stable capacity.

With **independent processing**, the opportunities for matching capacity with demand are plentiful. One option is to set capacity at a peak demand level, show by the "Peak-demand capacity" line of Figure 16. That approach means that the firm is ready to handle any level of demand. The big problem with this approach is that at times other than peak demand the capacity might be underutilized. Providers that feel the great need to have high capacity utilization produce to inventory at times of lower demand, and as a result may wind up with more inventory than is demanded, which can be costly.

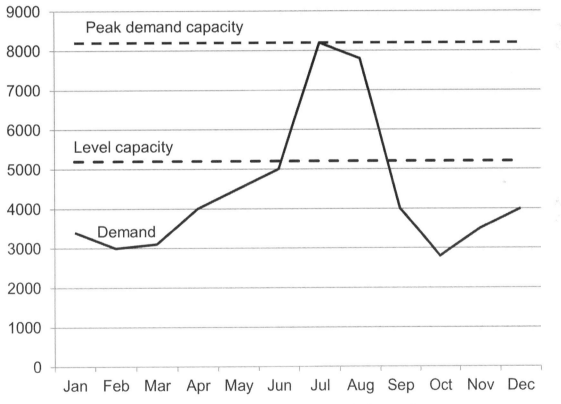

Figure 16: Matching capacity with demand

Therefore, with independent processing a better approach is usually to plan capacity at a stable level that is in-between peak demand and low demand, shown by the "Level demand" line of Figure 16. That way when demand is low (below capacity) the firm produces to inventory, and when demand is high (above capacity) the provider sells from inventory.

Of course, the effect of this is that the firm has to incur a cost to hold this inventory that serves as a buffer between stable capacity and fluctuating demand. These holding costs are directly incurred as an expense to the provider, and indirectly passed onto customers through higher prices. The science of "Inventory Theory" uses mathematical models to calculate the optimal amount of inventory to keep in order to satisfy fluctuating demand.

Another approach for dealing with fluctuating demand is to provide variable capacity that adjusts according to demand. This is much easier said than done. Capacity is typically acquired in "chunks" meaning fixed sizes with a fixed cost. Factories are built to a particular size, which cannot easily be reduced or increased. Machines need to be installed in factories, and the machine is either there or it is not there. Employees need to be hired one by one. As wonderful as it might be to have employees be "on call" and only paid when they are needed, the fact is their mortgages and grocery bills proceed at a constant rate. Hiring part-time employees from a temp agency will easily cost double the hourly rate of full-time employees.

For these reasons, variable capacity is usually not a great idea for independent processing. Of course, there is a common way for achieving variable capacity—although it is not technically independent processing: outsourcing production to a contract manufacturer. Contract manufacturers produce items based on the orders of customers. For this reason, contract manufacturing is technically surrogate interaction, with the manufacturer acting on the customer-provided order. Contract manufacturing makes wonderful sense when demand for the items being produced does not justify dedicated capacity, or when the ordering firm lacks the capability to manufacture items competitively.

This leads us to consider the problem of managing the imbalance between variable demand and relatively fixed capacity for **interactive processes**, especially those that are directly interactive. From Chapter 2 we established that the defining nature of services is that the provider's production process is dependent upon customer-provided input resources. This implies that are more limited capacity/demand management options for services.

For example, service businesses do not usually have the opportunity to produce in excess of demand, since production is *dependent* upon demand. For example, a lawn maintenance company has high demand during summer months but lower demand during winter months, especially if it is in a snowy region. It is not practical for the company to mow extra lawns in the winter months to meet high customer demand during the summer months. In other words, keeping finished-goods inventory in excess of demand is not a practical option.

Interactive service businesses can plan capacity for peak demand, but that leads to the same inefficiencies as described above for peak-demand manufacturing. Planning to peak demand only makes sense if the cost of insufficient capacity is great. For example, a hospital emergency room may plan for some approximation of peak capacity, but the result is a value proposition that is hopelessly inefficient and extremely costly.

Interactive service businesses that plan capacity for moderate demand do indeed see inventory, but it is not the finished goods inventory that comes from a factory. Instead, it is the **inventory of customers** waiting for their needs to be met. Customer inventory is similar to finished goods inventory in that it results from a mismatch between capacity and demand. Customer inventory is different in terms of the costs.

Fitzsimmons and Fitzsimmons (2004, p. 428) described various ways in which customer waiting is analogous to manufacturing inventories. Both incur holding costs, although the former is usually measured in minutes and the latter measured in months. Both require a storage location, although customer inventory may require more comfortable facilities than physical goods inventories. And both are an outcome of inadequate capacity planning, scheduling, and coordination. "Inventory management" in services includes deciding how to deal with excessive waiting, which includes psychological dimensions as discussed below (Maister 1985).

Customer inventory, or waiting lines, represents a direct cost to the customer and an indirect cost to the provider. Providers usually do not directly compensate customers for waiting, but the providers pay in terms of decreased customer loyalty and lost sales. The big problem managers have is that the cost of customer waiting is not directly represented on an income statement; therefore, naïve managers trivialize this important cost. The cost of finished-goods inventory shows up on financial statements as a holding cost expense, but the cost of customer waiting only shows up in reduced revenues in subsequent periods.

So, an important lesson in managing interactive service processes is to be sensitive to the costs of customer inventory that does not immediately show up on financial statements. The science of "Queuing Theory" can help managers estimate the customer waiting that will result from a particular capacity configuration. However, even queuing theory will not accurately describe the attitudinal impacts of customer waiting, which should not be underestimated.

These attitudinal impacts of customer waiting can actually be managed to the provider's advantage. Inventories of physical goods in a warehouse are neither happy nor sad, and incur monetary holding costs. The "holding cost" of customers waiting to be served is primarily attitudinal and emotional, and depends on the way in which the customers wait. Customers who are comfortable will experience a lower "holding cost" than customers who are uncomfortable.

David Maister described this concept in what has become known as **psychology of queuing**. Maister outlined eight concepts that impact the emotional impact of customer waiting (1985):
1. Unoccupied waits seem longer than occupied waits.
2. Pre-process waits seem longer than in-process waits.
3. Anxiety makes waits seem longer.
4. Uncertain waits seem longer than waits of a known duration.
5. Unexplained waits seem longer than explained waits.
6. Unfair waits seem longer than equitable waits.
7. The more valuable the service, the longer people will be willing to wait.
8. Waiting alone seems longer than waiting with a group.

These ideas can be used to reduce the cost of waiting by reducing the perceived wait time. The cost of customer waiting is not so much a function of actual wait time, but rather is a function of the time the customer *perceives* they are waiting. In some situations, the wait can be so pleasant that it is without cost. (My calls to our technical support services fit in this category. The hold music is usually much more pleasant than my conversation with the technician.)

There are non-customer inventories of materials and supplies in most interactive service businesses. However, for many interactive service businesses the management of supply inventories is a relatively trivial matter. The noted exception is retail and other service business whose primary offering is selling or renting/leasing physical goods. For most other service business the dollar value of the supplies is trivial compared with overall operating costs, even if the supplies are crucial to production. For example, law firms keep inventories of high-quality printer paper. Managing paper ordering does not require sophisticated inventory models, and having excessive extra paper on hand has little impact on the profitability of the firm.

It is so difficult to balance capacity with demand for interactive service businesses that providing variable capacity may actually be a practical alternative. You are much more likely to find part-time employees working in interactive service businesses. Most employees working in a packaged food factory will be full-time employees. However, many employees in restaurants will work part-time to meet demand peaks during traditional mealtimes.

Another approach to managing capacity/demand that is much more likely to occur for interactive service businesses is attempting to shift demand such as through temporary price adjustments. For example, airlines charge higher fares during high-demand seasons than low-demand seasons in an attempt to somewhat smooth demand. Too much demand during popular times can mean the loss of potential customers, and too little demand during low times means lost revenue opportunities. The concept of **time-perishable capacity** means that capacity for independent service processes cannot be preserved at times of low demand, which leads to our net topic: utilization and costing.

Managing utilization and costing

As described earlier, a manufacturing facility engaging in **independent processing** can smooth production levels and still meet fluctuating demand. One result of a level production rate is the ability to plan capacity that is slightly higher than the production level. This allows manufacturers to have relatively high utilization of resources such as labor and machines.

For example, a machine at a typical manufacturing facility might be operating 90 percent of the time during an operating shift. Firms may attempt to push utilization to 100 percent, but that level of utilization is likely to have problems due to breakdowns and required maintenance. Pushing employees to 100 percent utilization can also be dangerous. However, it would not be unusual for an employee at a manufacturing plant to be engaged in productive work for 90 percent of an eight-hour shift (not counting breaks).

When a machine or employee has high utilization it is reasonable to calculate the amount of cost that is incurred for each item being processed by that machine or employee.

For example, if an employee costs the provider $30 per hour and is able to assemble 60 headsets per hour then we can assume that each headset contains $30/60=$0.50 worth of that labor. This is called **activity-based costing**, since the resource activity is used to determine the cost.

Processing in the **direct interaction** region has very different economics. Because of dependency on variable customer demand, it is not uncommon for the utilization of interactive processes to be 10 to 20 percent! In fact, it is quite common.

Consider a bank teller. Bank tellers conduct transactions based on customer inputs and information. When there are no customers, bank tellers must work on activities not dependent on customer inputs, such as studying company policies or tiding their desks. If teller capacity (i.e., number of tellers) is set at a level high enough to keep customer inventories (i.e., waiting) at a reasonable level, then it is likely that the tellers will spend a lot of time waiting for customers.

What if we wanted to know how much teller labor cost to attribute to each teller transaction? Could we use activity-based costing? The problem is in accounting for all of the time the teller is not actually working on a transaction. If the teller's time is not fully utilized, and if the teller is paid an hourly wage instead of a per-transaction commission, then an additional transaction represents no variable cost to the bank.

Instead, we have to account for the idle capacity in our costing. It would be more appropriate to assess interactive service processes with **inactivity-based costing**, which recognizes how the cost of idle capacity is accounted for in the cost of production. This requires recognizing the impact of utilization on the costing of each item. An additional item of production does not incur additional costs, but provides additional contribution towards fixed costs.

For example, imagine two hotels, one in a city and another in a seasonal tourist location. The city hotel might have a relatively stable demand, involving travelers for business and pleasure. The tourist hotel might have larger fluctuations in demand according to the tourist season. It is therefore likely that the tourist hotel would have lower average room occupancy (utilization) across a year. If that was the case and if the fixed costs (building cost, labor cost, etc.) of the two hotels were similar, the monetary contribution required of each guest would be higher for the tourist hotel than for the city hotel, likely leading to a higher room rate. The inactivity of the hotel drives the cost allocation.

Marketing through Operations

The function of marketing takes on many definitions. For example, the American Marketing Association has defined marketing as "the activity, set of institutions, and processes for creating, communicating, delivering, and exchanging offerings that have value for customers, clients, partners, and society at large." That broad definition sounds somewhat like a description of PCN Analysis.

For **independent processing** such as manufactured products, marketing might assist with the design of products, but the actual creation of the offerings is more of an operations function. Marketing may establish product delivery relationships, but the actual delivery is more likely to be managed by logistics experts in the supply-chain function. Even the exchange of offerings, such as retail, often falls under the operations function of retail firms.

An aspect of business that is clearly the expertise and domain of marketing is communication, meaning communicating with customers and prospective customers in order to increase their likelihood of purchasing the offerings.

One method of marketing communication is advertising. Advertising is valuable because it gives prospective customers an idea of what to expect from a given offering. This may include expectations for product features, or expectations about how the product will meet customer needs.

Advertising is not the only source of information prospective customers use to make purchase decisions. They may also rely on word-of-mouth testimonies of other customers. Word-of-mouth information may be considered more reliable if it not subject to recommender bias. Consumers may be skeptical of recommendations coming from the provider, but more trusting of claims coming from friends of known character.

However, there is another source of information that is even more credible—a customer's own prior experience. If a customer tries a product and likes it, he or she is likely to repurchase even if trusted friends say they tried it and did not like it. Personal experience drives personal preferences.

Offerings that are produced through independent processing are often marketed through independent processing, meaning mass advertising. If product specifications are tightly controlled, the advertising should be able to accurately describe expected product features. As a result, customers can at least have some knowledge about how the product will perform, and may thus speculate that it will meet their needs.

For example, the purchaser of a computer may know that a 2.6 gigahertz processor is twice as fast as a 1.3 gigahertz processer, but may still wonder what that increase means in terms of productivity. In other words, the products may be easily measured and compared, yet the value in using the product may be subject to speculation.

Offerings that come through **interactive service processes** are more difficult to accurately describe through mass advertising. For one thing, the actual execution of the process will be influenced by the customer's inputs to the process. Mass advertising can describe service offerings in general terms, but experience is necessary to accurately know how the process will perform.

As a result, effective marketing of interactive service processes tends to be more *experiential*. This means not just describing the offering, but allowing the customer to experience the offering. A common way this is accomplished is through trial promotions. Customers might be invited to try out the service offering for a specified period of time before making their purchase decision.

For example, fitness centers like Gold's Gym often provide a free or low-cost trial membership. Internet Service Providers frequently offer six-month discounted plans. Banks often waive the first year fee for various banking cards.

Another key aspect of experiential marketing is that the communication of product features largely comes from the performance of employees that interact with the customers, or from the interaction the customers have with the provider's facilities. This means that the operations of the provider are being used as the means for marketing communication. For this reason, interactive service processes should be designed and managed to accomplish their marketing communication function.

An interesting way of thinking of this comes from my marketing-scholar friends Steve Vargo and Bob Lusche. In one of their seminars they talked about marketing *to* customers versus marketing *for* customers versus marketing *with* customers. In the PCN framework, marketing *to* customers means marketing through independent processing, with the communication subsequently being broadcast to customers. Marketing *for* customers means providing more customized marketing communication, such as accomplished by Customer Relationship Management Systems—which is largely surrogate interaction. Marketing *with* customers means involving the customers in the marketing effort, which is what we see in interactive processes. This idea will be revisited in Chapter 14 and Chapter 20.

Some services cannot be easily evaluated by customers even after they experience the service process. These services pertain to what will be called "divergent" processes in Chapter 8. Examples include healthcare, education, and legal services. The thing they have in common is uncertainty about what is good and what is not. Do patients actually know that they received good healthcare? Sometimes patients could die even with good healthcare, or live with mediocre healthcare. How do students know they have received a good education? Sometimes good attorneys lose cases, and bad attorneys win cases.

For services that are difficult to evaluate even after customers experience them must rely on "credence" marketing—which relies on some credible expert for evaluation. Healthcare providers and attorneys must qualify for a license to practice. Students typically rely on accreditation bodies and ratings services to assess the quality of education. The licensing boards, accreditation bodies, and rating services provide credibility to the providers.

Thus we see three approaches to helping customers make service purchasing decisions. First, tell customers about superior features, which works for most physical products but less for interactive services. If customer variation makes that impractical, then consider providing customers with an experience trying out the service. If uncertainty still renders that inadequate, consider using credible sources of information. These three options are known as:
- search properties (customers can search the information before purchase)
- experience properties (customers need to experience the service to assess), and
- credence properties (customers must rely on credible sources of information)

Again, physical products tend to possess search properties. Interactive service processes are more likely to have experience and credence properties.

PCN Analysis summary

This chapter summarized just some of managerial distinctions that occur across different regions of a PCN Diagram. These issues are summarized in Table 2, which is a continuation of the concepts from Table 1 (page 6).

Table 2: Summary of managerial distinctions

Managerial issue	Independent processing	Interactive processing
Matching capacity with variable demand	Finished goods inventory can be used to match capacity to demand.	Customer inventory (queues) help match demand to capacity.
Typical resource utilization	Can be high, perhaps 80% to 90%	Usually low, perhaps 10%-20%
Costing	Production cost can be attributed to individual items (Activity Based Costing)	Idle capacity needs to be accounted for (Inactivity Based Costing)
Marketing communication	Advertising can be effective when products are describable.	Process interaction requires experiential marketing, or, in some cases, credence marketing.

Chapter 7 – Measuring and Assuring Quality

The prior chapter reviewed general ways in which interactive processes are managed differently from independent processing. This chapter focuses on how we measure and assure quality.

The term "quality" has various definitions. All definitions of quality connote some degree of excellence according to some standard. As you might imagine, the standard of excellence differs—according to the region of processing.

In **independent processing**, quality is determined according to engineered specifications. We assume that products are designed in a way that they are fit for use by consumers; otherwise the value potential will not achieve value realization (and thus not truly be value potential). We also assume that the product specifications are grounded in sound engineering principles, giving products design attributes of reliability, reparability, and ease of production.

Once engineered specifications are known, the task becomes producing the products to conform to those specifications, which is an independent processing definition of "quality." Production managers have tremendous tools at their disposal for measuring and tracking that quality. Various automatic and manual measuring devices can be used to take measurements that can be tracked and analyzed.

Statistical Process Control (SPC) is a common tool for analyzing quality measurements. With SPC, average measurements and measurement distributions are studied over time in order to discover unusual variations in the process. The unusual variations are often called assignable variation, meaning that the variation can be attributed to some change in the process.

For example, a machine may fill soda bottles with 20 ounces of soda. The specification may be a fill of 19.5 to 20.5 ounces. Under normal conditions the machine is capable of keeping the fill between 19.8 and 20.2 ounces 95.7% of the time, which is well within the specifications. However, an SPC chart may show that five bottles recently had a fill of 19.7 ounces, which is still within the specifications but may indicate some has happened to let the fill process drift. If it is not checked it may eventually go out of specification. The operator may discover that a plugged hose is causing the fill level to drop, and may need to repair the hose to preserve the process capability.

If manufactured items are found to have defects (items out of specification) the alternatives include scraping the items or reworking them to correct the defect. If the defect is reasonably repairable then rework is a good option. Ultimately, the consumer who uses the product is not likely to know that the product was reworked once or many times, as long as the product is in good shape when he or she uses it to meet needs. The key is identifying defects before they get into the hands of customers.

Measuring and managing quality in independent processing is quite an exacting science, but with a little bit of art. On the other hand, measuring and managing quality in interactive service processes is far from an exact science.

Interactive service processes may have engineered specifications, which can be rendered futile by the involvement of customers. Chapter 6 reviewed ways that customers introduce tremendous variability into interactive processes, and that variability may be difficult to control. On one hand, customers may provide unreasonable inputs to the process, such as presenting a garment with a dried-in stain to a dry cleaner.[12] On the other hand, customers may provide unreasonable expectations for service providers that are well beyond what might reasonably be provided, like the elderly knee surgery patient who wants to be eighteen again. Even if the interactive process is performed exactly as planned, the customer may report that the process has failed.

The goal of SPC is to control process variation and identify sources of variation that can be eliminated. With interactive service processes, the primary source of variation is the customer, and eliminating the customer may have adverse consequences. Although some have attempted to apply SPC to interactive service processes, such can be precarious for reasons just mentioned. SPC will work in back-office surrogate interaction where variation coming from customers can be controlled somewhat. However, quality measurement that involves measuring customer opinions will always have variation—in the measurement itself.

Measuring interactive process quality is no easy task. Granted, it is easy to create a customer opinion survey (such as a comment card), but difficult to collect useful and reliable data. Customers often resist providing feedback, and providing attitudinal measurements is far from an exact science. Appropriate methods for service quality measurement are discussed in the article: An Empirically Defined Framework for Designing Customer Feedback Systems, by S.E. Sampson, in *Quality Management Journal,* 1999, vol. 6 no. 3, pp. 64-80.

Instead of striving to eliminate variation, interactive service processes need to be designed to accommodate customer-induced variation without adversely damaging the desirable operating characteristics. A **robust** interactive service process is one that continues to perform as designed even when subject to customer variation. Designing robust interactive processes requires tremendous attention to detail, including planning for numerous contingencies.

In Chapter 1 I told about a large group from my department that was having dinner at a local restaurant. During the dinner someone placed a tall stemware glass on the ridge between to tables that was covered by a tablecloth. The uneven tables caused the glass to tip over and shatter. Restaurant employees immediately cleaned up the glass and replaced the food of everyone in shatter-range of the glass. It was clear that this was not a crisis situation, but instead was something they had been trained for. (Not glasses shattering, per se, but any event that might disrupt a customer meal.) We were quite impressed with the rapid way they handled the problem, which demonstrated robust process design and relentless training.

---

[12] My wife, who is an expert, tells me that if you run a stained garment through a clothes dryer you will bake the stain into the cloth and it may never come out.

Inspecting quality in interactive service processes is a different game. For one thing, customer specifications generally trump any engineered specifications. A service provider might perform an interactive process flawlessly according to the normal plan, but the customer might still feel the execution was inadequate. Further, if a process defect occurs during an interactive process it is often not possible to fix it without the customer's knowledge.

Even attributing the cause of the defect can be precarious. The provider may think a process defect is caused by the customer, such as not following instructions. However, that customer failure demonstrates a lack of robustness in the process, and a more robust process would work even if customers did not follow instructions. On top of that, the customer may not care if the failure was customer-induced or provider-induced.

Customer failure prevention

Even a robust interactive service process is likely to have limitations in the amount of customer variation it can take before a failure. Well-designed systems will include mechanisms to prevent (or greatly reduce) customer actions that lead to service failure. A name for failure-prevention mechanisms is ***poka yoke***, which is the Japanese word for fail-proofing.[13] Service poka yokes can be used to prevent customers from errant actions.

For example, I once managed an online data system that collected research presentation information for large academic conferences. Customers were required to enter the title of their research presentation and information about all of the authors. An unacceptable number of customers would fail to enter all of the authors, causing subsequent complaints suggesting that the system must have somehow dropped some authors (which was not the case). The poka yoke solution was simple: On the web page where customers entered the author information I added the question "How many authors are on this research presentation?" When the customer clicked the submit button the system compared that number to the number of authors entered, and if different, requested that the customer re-check the author information. This simple mechanism virtually eliminated subsequent author omissions.

The following are some other examples of customer poka yokes:

- Automatic Teller Machines prevent customers from forgetting to retrieve their bank card by requiring them to remove the bank card before they are giving cash and receipts.
- Restaurants that serve food on trays sometimes make the hole into the trash receptacles slightly smaller than the tray size to prevent customers from throwing away trays.

---

[13] The term poka yoke originally meant fool proofing, which may imply that the person involved in the process is a fool. More recently the term has been assumed to mean fail proofing, which does not have that personal connotation.

- Health clinic patients sometimes mail out insurance and medical history information sheets to new customers before their first visits to reduce the likelihood prevent that they will arrive at the clinic without the necessary information.

    Of course, poka yokes' can be used to prevent provider errors as well; in fact, the concept of poka yokes originated in factories devoid of customer presence. Nevertheless, since customer actions are usually outside of the provider's process domain, and thus outside of the provider's span of control, poka yokes can be particularly beneficial when applied to customer actions.

    Figure 17 shows an example of a poka yoke used by Costco to prevent an awkward customer failure—forgetting to bring the membership card. Costco customers must have a membership card to make purchases. If a customer show up at check-out having forgotten his or her card, the situation could be quite embarrassing. Trying to provide a temporary card could damage the checkout efficiency. As a result, Costco assures that customers have their membership card at the time they enter the store.

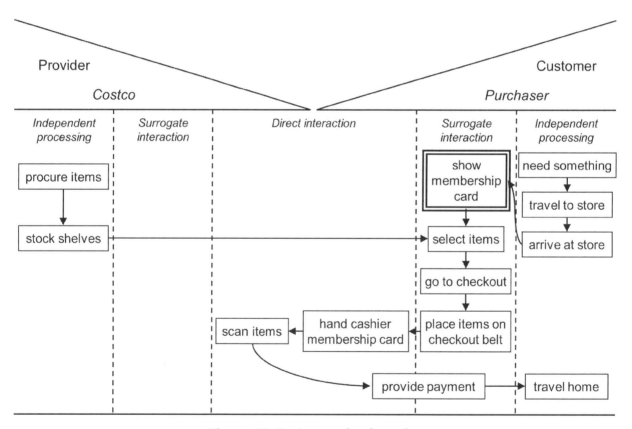

Figure 17: Costco card poka yoke

A Costco employee positioned at the entrance asks to see membership cards. However, it is quite obvious you do not need a membership card to get in—only to check out. I learned this by sequential attempts at avoiding showing my card. Initially I pulled my card out of my wallet and showed the entrance employee. Subsequently, I flashed the top of my card sticking out of my wallet. Then, I just showed my wallet. Then, I just held my empty hand out as though I had a card. Then, I just thought about my card as I walked through the entrance. In each case the Costco employee motioned me on, having verified that I was qualified to shop. I suspect that employee's job is to profile people who look like they might have forgotten their card, and remind them to bring their card, and that just having that employee stationed at the entrance reduces the incidences of forgotten cards.

The Costco card poke yoke is not unlike the carry-on luggage size-boxes in airport terminals. Those boxes tell customers the maximum size of carry-on luggage, although I have never seen anyone willing test their luggage by inserting it. (Perhaps they do not want to know that it is too big.) Nevertheless, the boxes serve to remind customers of requirements, and prevent surprises when customers are required to check their oversized luggage at the gate.

Service Recovery

Earlier in this chapter we two possible responses to manufacturing defects: scrap the item or rework it. With interactive service processes, scrapping the item might imply discarding the customer, which is probably not a good idea. The more reasonable alternative is rework.

Rework in interactive service processes often takes the form of "**service recovery**," which means that effort is taken to redo the part of the process that failed and to rectify the damage to the customer's attitude and loyalty. This may include providing compensation above and beyond the extent of process failure.

For example, my wife took our six children to the pediatrician's office for annual flu shots. A few days later a nurse from the office called my wife to report that the flu shot serum was an insufficient dosage and that the kids needed to come back for an additional booster shot. My wife's immediate response was asking, "Who is going to buy the ice cream?" The nurse did not know what that meant, so my wife explained that there was no way the kids were going to subject themselves to another flu shot without compensation. The nurse understood, and reportedly offered free ice cream to all of the kids who had to return for booster shots.

Unfortunately, a strategy of service recovery is almost futile due to the fact that the vast majority of interactive service process failures go undetected. This is based on a study that reports that only 4% of customers with a complaint report the complaint—the other 96% just leave with a bad attitude (TARP 1979; TARP 1986). The study also suggests that while satisfied customers are likely to tell others about their satisfaction, dissatisfied customers are much more likely to report their bad experience to others. In other words, even though quality is harder to measure and assure in interactive service processes, process improvement efforts must still be emphasized. (Process improvement will be discussed in Chapter 10 and other chapters.)

Dealing with problem customers

Even with well executed customer training it is conceivable—even likely—that customers are going to do things wrong and mess up the process. When the process fails to meet its value objective the knee-jerk reaction may be to blame the wayward customer.

However, I must defer to the legendary W. Edwards Deming who emphasized that the majority of quality problem (94% by his estimate) are due to bad systems instead of bad people (Deming 2000, p. 24, 315). He was referring to employees, but I think it applies to customers as well. My corollary to Deming's assertion is: Bad customers are rare, faulty systems are common.

Good service design not only assists customers in learning how to perform their requisite actions, but also helps avoid customer mistakes that lead to service failures (e.g., through poka yokes, as discussed above). It is incumbent upon the service designer to continually identify ways to improve the process and reduce the likelihood of customer-induced service failure.

This next statement may seem a little hard to swallow: *Problem customers who complain about the service system are golden!* I am referring to the customers who fail to perform as reasonably expected and subsequently blame the service provider. You know who I am talking about—the unreasonable customer that is asking for some type of apology or compensation, but you are sure he or she is completely undeserving. These customers are golden because they tax the service system and provide the means for improving the system for all customers. But that benefit only comes if they are taken seriously and their feedback is used to improve the system.

Let me give an example. A short while ago I got a phone call from a former student of mine (whom we will call Kent) who owns some very successful restaurants. He had received a two-page letter from a customer (whom we will call Chuck) outlining the reportedly poor service Chuck received at one of Kent's high-end restaurants. Apparently, Chuck went to the restaurant on Valentine's Day, which is the restaurant's busiest day of the year. Chuck thought the speed of service was slower than it should have been. The item Chuck wanted to order was no longer on the menu. At payment time Chuck tried to use some coupons that happened to be expired. It seems that Chuck wanted his money back.

I think Kent called me more for encouragement than for direction, since he started the conversation by saying "I know you told us in class that complaining customers are golden, but…." Kent knew what to do about Chuck's letter, but he seemed to be tempted to instead tell Chuck to take a hike. (BTW, Kent's restaurant happened to be the highest rated restaurant within 30 miles, was extremely popular, and probably had very few customer complaints.) I reminded Kent that he could either use Chuck's complaint letter as a basis for further process improvement and employee training, or, as an alternative, he could hire me to spend an hour with his staff discussing process improvement. I told Kent that I would charge him $500 for that hour, but discussing Chuck's letter with his staff would be practically free, and discussing Chuck's letter would probably be a better use of their time. At that point it seems like Kent was ready to take action.

As an epilog, when I had Kent on the phone I took the opportunity to invite him to speak in one of my Service Management courses a few weeks later. Interestingly, as part of his talk to my students he actually used Chuck's letter as an example. He read the letter and asked the class what he should do. He repeated the maxim that "complaining customers are golden." Then he told how he reviewed the letter with his staff so that they might identify ways of avoiding service speed problems on busy days, expectation problems due to changing menus, and problems with expired coupons. One of my students pressed him by asking "well, did you give Chuck his money back?" Kent nonchalantly responded that he sent Chuck an appreciative letter outlining how the restaurant might improve the system, including coupons for $150 (i.e., much more than giving Chuck his money back).

I must emphasize that the primary purpose for Kent's response to Chuck's letter was identifying ways to improve the service system. A much lower objective was to win back Chuck as a customer. Chuck was probably not part of that restaurant's target market of well-to-do patrons who eat out on a regular basis. This is a five-star restaurant and Chuck appears to be a student on a tight budget, probably trying to impress a date. Chuck is likely to only go to that restaurant on Valentine's Day or other equally congested days. The most compelling argument against winning back Chuck as a customer is the statistic cited previously that only 4% of customers with a complaint report the complaint—the other 96% just leave with a bad attitude (TARP 1979; TARP 1986). In other words, Chuck is in the vocal minority—the tip of the iceberg so to speak. As a single customer Chuck may not be worth the effort to retain. But as a basis for process improvement, Chuck is invaluable. The vocal Chuck allowed Kent to improve the process to avoid the 96% of related problems that go unreported—the 96% of the problem iceberg that Kent cannot see. Giving Chuck $150 probably underpaid him for the value Kent's organization got from his complaint letter.

PCN Analysis summary

This chapter summarized quality management issues that occur in interactive processes. Quality in regions of independent processing tends to be defined by conformance to engineered specifications. Quality in interactive process regions tends to be more customer focused, specified and evaluated by customer opinions. Providers need to account for customer variation in quality management efforts.

For example, customers may need to be trained on their roles that contribute to service quality. Even with conscientious customer training, it is still likely that customer-induced service failures will occur. Service designers should consider ways to reduce the occurrence of customer failures, such as with poka yoke mechanisms. Guidance for service system improvement can come from many sources (including Chapter 10 and Chapter 12), yet one of the best sources for improvement guidance is customer complaints. Even when customers seem to be at fault, their complaints can provide golden opportunities for process improvement.

Chapter 8 – Job Design

Table 1 (page 6) suggested that job design in regions of independent processing tends to be, "tightly defined with precise steps and cycle times." As discussed in Chapter 7, the processes in regions of independent processing can be engineered to exacting specifications and can be carefully monitored and controlled.

On the other hand, Table 1 suggested that job design for employees involved in interactive process are more broadly defined. This is because the interactive employees need to be able to accommodate tremendous amounts of customer variation. Broadly defined does not mean undefined. In fact it could mean quite the opposite. For a robust interactive process "broadly defined" likely means extensive and relentless job training.

Further, the *nature* of the job requirements and requisite training can vary dramatically. In this chapter we will review differences between process complexity and process divergence.

Process complexity versus process divergence

Managing process elements in any of the five regions of Figure 15 (page 51) requires competencies of the provider and/or the customer. The nature of competences depends on process requirements, and can vary dramatically. Some processes have easy requirements, and can be accomplished by relatively unskilled individuals. Other processes are more difficult, requiring greater knowledge and skill.

Two factors that directly affect process difficulty are complexity and divergence. However, complexity and divergence each have different implications for skill requirements.

Process **complexity** is the number of steps in a given process chain or segment. The complexity of a given process step is the number of sub-steps embedded within the step. Complexity is a relative measure more than an absolute measure, meaning that we probably cannot calculate a single number or set or numbers to represent the complexity of a process, but we can say that, "process A is complex, at least relative to process B."

For example, the process of completing personal income tax forms is amazingly complex, and can take many hours to collect all of the data and complete all of the forms. The U.S. Internal Revenue Service provides a one-page 1040EZ form for a limited set of filers. The process for completing form 1040EZ is much less complex than completing the regular tax forms.

Process **divergence** is the uncertainty about and decision ambiguity around the execution of a process or a process step. Divergent processes can be executed in a wide variety of ways but no clear rules that define how they are executed. The key element of divergent processes is in the skill requirements of the individual executing the process step. Divergent processes require some degree of expert *judgment*, which judgment comes from experience making decisions about the execution of the process or related processes.

For example, medical diagnosis and treatment is a divergent process. Although firms have attempted to develop highly complex databases of medical knowledge and expert systems that use the data to make decisions based on that knowledge, it is still a long way from being a substitute for an experienced physician. That medical diagnosis and treatment is divergent is exemplified by the method for becoming a medical doctor (MD). Most medical schools require students to attend a few years of classroom training, but faculty will tell you that the real way students are trained to be physicians is during residencies and clinical internships. These residencies typically involve 80+ hours of work per week interacting with patients and with other more-experienced physicians. There may be some general rules for making medical decisions, but process divergence relegates the most important decisions to an experienced physician's judgment.

Medical diagnosis is one part of a more complex healthcare process. Before a diagnosis the patient must make an appointment, check in, provide insurance information, pay a co-pay amount, complete a health history form, and so forth. Most of those steps can be completed by employees and customers with relatively little experience in healthcare.

Note that a given process can be both complex and divergent, but complexity and divergence are not the same thing. A process with high complexity might have a tightly-defined set of rules for process execution, meaning it has low divergence. Or, a process might have low complexity—even as simple as a single step—but have great decision uncertainty and thus high divergence. Figure 18 shows examples of air transportation processes of different types.

	low divergence	**high divergence**
low complexity	taking tickets; serving drinks	negotiating a union contract; responding to a flight system malfunction
high complexity	building aircraft; performing periodic preventative maintenance	designing an aircraft; merging the operations of two airlines

Figure 18: Air transportation process examples

Complex processes may require specialized skills, but if the process has low divergence then the requisite skills can be acquired through normal classroom training or individual study. The process executer simply needs to study the process steps in order to develop competence at executing the process. After a relatively short period of practice the complex process can become second nature.

The skill requirements are very different for divergent processes, since the skill cannot be easily acquired through classroom training or individual study. As suggested above, the only way to really master the execution of a divergent process is to have extensive experience in dealing with the uncertainty of the process. Eventually, the person sees such a wide range of process conditions that the person is able to make good process decisions even in conditions never before encountered.

Careers that involve highly divergent processes include CEO, entrepreneur, consultant, attorney, and NFL head coach. These jobs are relatively undefined, can have a wide range of outcomes, and usually require proven experience. Interestingly, they also pay a lot of money. When a process is divergent and the result of process decisions is significant, the cost of labor can be very high. For one thing, the experience requirement significantly limits the number of individuals who are qualified to perform the process.

Things are not quite the same for complex processes. Even the most complex processes can be run by people who have a reasonable amount of training and a nominal amount of experience. Or, they can be automated.

Think about how complex the process is of making a hand calculator. A basic hand calculator has perhaps 10,000 transistors etched into an integrated circuit, injection molded buttons with painted insignias, delicate springs or other mechanisms for button motion, a circuit board with display and other components attached with dozens of individual soldering connections. A hand calculator is an amazingly complex device, created with perhaps hundreds of individual steps. (Refining the petroleum to make the plastic pellets that are melted and injection into the keys is complex in and of itself.) Yet, that hand calculator can be purchased for one dollar ($1) at our local dollar store!

Complex processes that are not divergent can be performed by a wide variety of trained employees or automations. As a result, process complexity is much less expensive to handle than process divergence.

Of course, most processes have some degree of complexity and/or divergence. It is generally cheaper to hire employees for complex processes than for divergent processes. However, if the customer requires divergent processing, they are much more likely to pay high margins.

Airline illustration

An illustration of this economic difference is seen in the airline industry. Figure 18 listed some air transportation processes that would differ in complexity and divergence. What about the process of flying a jet airplane? Is it complex, divergent, or both?

In fact, the process requirements for flying jet airplanes has evolved over time. Some years ago, being an airline pilot involved divergent processes. Pilots had to make inflight decisions in all kinds of ambiguous situations such as lightning storms, head winds, system failures, and so forth. To become a jumbo jet airplane pilot required a small amount of classroom study and a large amount of "flight hours" developing the requisite experience.

In about the 1980s all of that changed, as exemplified by my experience on a flight between Idaho Falls and San Francisco that I took in 1984. It was a ski charter flight at the start of the season, meaning they had a load of San Francisco skiers to take to Idaho Falls for a week of skiing, but no one to take back to San Francisco until the following week. So, I happened to be the only passenger on that flight (I believe it was a Boeing 737).

After we took off, the flight attendant gave me a basket of peanuts and drinks and disappeared into the back of the plane for the rest of the flight. The cockpit door was open, so I meandered up and asked if I could watch. The captain folded down a third cockpit seat and invited me in (those were the days). For the next hour or so I chatted with the pilot and co-pilot about their jobs and becoming pilots. I was still thinking about career options, and this trip had become sort of a job shadow for me. They had plenty of time to chat with me because they were otherwise not doing anything else, except for the one time the air traffic control tower ask them to move to a different altitude. The pilot's response to that request was to flip a dial to the new altitude, then go back to chatting. The autopilot gradually lifted the plane to the new altitude and leveled off.

I learned that to become a jumbo jet pilot required a lot of flight hours, which is why many of the pilots are former Air Force pilots. I also learned that a 737 captain can earn as much as $250,000 per year, which peaked my interest. That salary comes after increased experience and ability to handle the difficult job of piloting such a complex machine.

It was only the last five minutes heading into San Francisco that they turned off the autopilot. At that point the diminutive co-pilot snapped to attention and piloted us to a safe landing. In my assessment those guys made a lot of money for about five minutes of work per flight. (Of course, they also have to take off and deal with rare events such as landing gear failure.)

1984 was also about the same time that the major airlines in the U.S. were heading down a path towards astronomical losses and numerous bankruptcies. The problem encountered by the major airlines was the expansion and popularity of the low-cost airlines such as Southwest. The low-cost airlines had streamlined processes that allowed them to operate profitably, but that is only part of the story.

One interesting realization of the low cost airlines is that aeronautical technology had advanced to the point where even relatively inexperienced individuals could be trained to become pilots. This was emphasized to me when my cousin in his mid-twenties attended a pilot training program at the nearby junior college and became a pilot for the very profitable Skywest Airlines. I was a little frightened to think that this kid and others like him might be my pilot, but I am kind of getting used to it.

What the low-cost airlines discovered is that the jet piloting process, while still being very complex, is not as divergent as it once was thought to be. As a result, they paid their pilots a reasonable salary that was a fraction of what the big airlines had been paying their pilots. The union contracts hanging over the heads of the big airlines was a major factor in their financial troubles.

Managing complexity and divergence

Unfortunately, it is not always easy to convert process divergence into process complexity. And, it may not be desirable, at least if you are used to charging for divergence. The ideal situation is to charge for divergence, but actually treat the process as complex! That may include automated procedures that otherwise would require judgment. However, eventually customers are likely to realize the process is simply complex (which is sort of an oxymoron), and competing providers are going to deliver the process at the lower costs allowed by complexity. For example, at one time electronics retail was treated as divergent, requiring experienced employees who could use their good judgment to guide customer purchases. The decline of brick-and-mortar electronics retail has corresponded to the increase of online sales and big-box stores that guide customers through purchase decisions with few or no experienced salespeople. Other examples of this concept will be reviewed in Chapter 11.

A key to managing complexity and divergence is *not employing divergence in processes where complexity is adequate*. Divergence is costly, both in terms of the skill set of employees and the stability of process delivery. Employee judgment is a tremendous source of process variation and can have a negative impact on quality and consistency. It is fine to let inexperienced employees "make things up" in trivial matters, but not where it has an adverse impact on service delivery.

On occasion I have read articles claiming that the key to effective service management is hiring the "right people" who are customer focused and can exercise their creativity in meeting customer needs. In most cases, that approach is necessary for providers that have poorly designed operating procedures therefore must rely on employee creativity and ingenuity. A better approach is to have well-designed systems that excel even with adequate employees— then train the employees in how best to do their jobs without having to rely excessively on their own creativity and judgment.

This may sound like a totalitarian approach to managing employees. Instead of thinking of it as controlling the actions of employees, think of it as developing good processes and decision rules and training employees on those processes and rules. Providing employees with **standard operating procedures (SOP)** will assist them in doing their job and likely reduce job stress. Assume that your employees want to do a good job and then show them how to do a good job. If the employees then act contrary to the SOP then you probably either need to revise the SOP (perhaps with their help) or revise the employees (i.e., get new employees). On the other hand, if you do not provide adequate SOPs and employees execute bad judgment in executing process steps then you should not be surprised.

This is usually not a big issue in independent processing where there is a clearer distinction between high-divergent processes and low-divergence processes. Divergent decision making is relegated to managers, engineers, or others who are paid for their judgment ability. Employees involved in production are told what to do and how to do it. Think of workers on a factory assembly line making auto parts. Instead of giving the production workers clear guidelines, imagine that management told them to just use their good judgment to guide the assembly process. The results would be disastrous.

It is quite a bit harder to provide employees with SOPs for processes that experience the tremendous variation that comes with customer interaction. Narrowly specified SOPs are likely to be derailed in the face of customer variation. Firms may be tempted to simply leave process decisions up to employees, but this can be to the peril of the process and the customers. The service nightmares described in Chapter 1 can all be attributed to either (a) poorly designed SOPs, or (b) having employees make process decisions that should have been defined by SOPs. The category of poorly designed SOPs includes failure to account for customer variation and customer emotional response. It is possible that some random employee can make up a process that delights a customer, but even that may raise customer expectations in a way that is not sustainable. Unless employee judgment is absolutely necessary, or of no consequence, firms are better off by providing well designed SOPs for interactive service processes than simply relying on employee judgment.

An example of getting it strait

A business that astutely exploits process complexity and divergence is orthodontics. Orthodontics has the economics of an illegal activity, but somehow has avoided alerting the government authorities.

For readers without teenage children, here is how orthodontics works. You take your child to the orthodontist for a "free assessment" and leave having signed a $2400 contract that will extend over the next two years. The first visit is worth the $100 you pay for it, since the orthodontist fits the child with braces, carefully considering all of the unique conditions of the child's teeth.

The next 22 monthly visits are where the questionable practice occurs. The monthly process, depicted in Figure 19, includes checking the child out of school, driving to the orthodontist's office, checking in, waiting in the waiting room, meeting with a technician, then finally, after all of this, spending up to five (5!) minutes with the orthodontist. Those five minutes are spent reviewing the patient's teeth and saying a few encouraging things to the child and parent. The orthodontist may also adjust the braces, although our orthodontist usually left that to the technician.

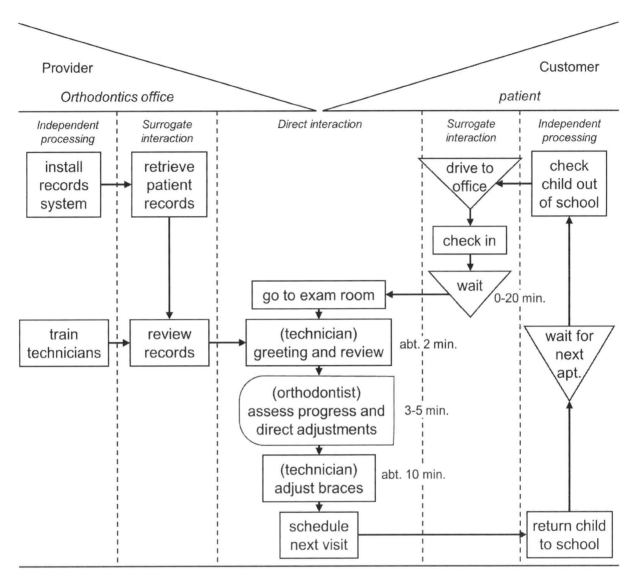

Figure 19: Orthodontics montly visit

A typical orthodontist will see perhaps 50 patients in a day—each at five-minute intervals. It is not rocket science to see that this comes to $1200 per hour! Even if you take out the cost of technicians and front-desk staff the orthodontist is operating a money machine. Not bad for just looking in a bunch of kids mouths.

The brilliance of the orthodontics process is that the highly-experienced orthodontist is only used in the divergent part of the process. All of the rest of the process is treated as merely complex, and is relegated to less-experienced (and lower-cost) labor, and technologies. (For example, the monthly reminders are largely delivered by automation.) Brilliant!

This example illustrates an important principle of process management: Identify process divergence and carefully match "judgment capacity" with "judgment requirements." Judgment capacity is the ability of an employee to exercise good judgment, as developed and demonstrated by prior experience. In a PCN Diagram we depict divergent steps with judgment requirements with rounded boxes like the "assess progress" step of Figure 19. In Figure 19 the "assess progress" step is only rounded on one side, suggesting that the judgement ability is on the part of the physician, not the patient. Other PCN Diagrams with divergent steps include Figure 7 (page 20), Figure 9 (page 26), and Figure 20 (page 80).

If your process requires divergent processing, more involved employee selection procedures should be employed, which is discussed in my prior book (Sampson 2001, p. 258-261). That book section also discusses substituting complexity for divergence, which can be a difficult but effective process strategy in some situations.

Training Customers

Up until now this chapter has been focusing on how employees acquire competencies. We must not neglect competencies that are required for processes that occur in the customer's process domain.

Customers typically need to be trained in-process, meaning in the process of experiencing and receiving the service. This is accomplished by including training elements in the service process and environment. Mary Jo Bitner (1992) discussed three types of elements of what she calls "servicescapes" – or environments in which customers receive service. They are:

- Ambient conditions – including temperature, air quality, sound, etc. This can be used to motivate the customers' participation in the system.
- Space and function – including layout, equipment, and furnishings. These provide an environment that facilitates the customers' performing their roles.
- Signs, symbols, and artifacts – items that provide customers with cues including signage or other items that signal how the service system is supposed to work. These provide directions to customers in what they should do and how they should do it, kind of like an in-process job description.

A great example of customer training is the IKEA process as was depicted in Figure 14 from Chapter 5 (page 49). There we saw that IKEA has a retail process that is largely self-service. This implies that customers need to be trained in their responsibilities. The following was my experience in the IKEA store near where I live.

Upon entering the store I was greeted by a large sign with an arrow pointing to the showroom, which was up an escalator. Next to the escalator was a bin of yellow shopping bags with a sign that says "Borrow a big yellow bag." On the way up the escalator is a sign that says "It's OK, you can bring it back!" letting the customers know that they can make impulse purchases with little risk.

The top of the escalator has a large map of the showroom with smaller maps to take along. Next to that is a sign touting "Make a list to find things faster" with paper shopping list forms and pencils to use, and a rack of paper measuring tapes to take and use. Other signs throughout the store describe delivery and furniture assembly services, which will be discussed in Chapter 13.

I needed a work chair, but rather than ask an employee for advice I consulted a large sign in the chair section titled "How to choose a work chair." The sign had three simple steps to consider in choosing a work chair. When purchasing a bed I asked an employee if they had a certain model in a specific size. The employee walked me over to the sign by the bed, looked at the sign and said "I guess not." IKEA employees are eager to help, but are not experienced interior designers, which is okay because the IKEA value proposition is not dependent upon divergent processes. Instead, IKEA employees are trained in helping customers help themselves.

Further into the store they had carts and trollies for customers to use to load up larger items. The journey through the IKEA showroom is quite intuitive, with signs at every step of the way. Also, the floor is marked with large arrows pointing the normal path through the store, which somewhat correspond with arrows on the map that customers pick up at the entrance.

Particularly intriguing was a "Planning table" with computers running home design software. A sign on the tables says, "You know better than anyone what you need. Do your own planning with the tools we offer here!"

Near the end of my visit I took my children to get a snack at the IKEA cafeteria, which has a large sign that queries and answers "Why should I clear my own table?" Nearby signs answer questions such as, "Why isn't there always an assistant when I need one?" "Why should I deliver my own furniture?" and "Why do I have to assemble the furniture myself?" These signs help customers learn and accept their process responsibilities.

IKEA has ambient conditions that are very inviting. The layout is organized and well described. The signs, symbols, and artifacts make the self-serve customer experience almost foolproof. They operate with a surprisingly few number of showroom employees—but even then the employees seem to spend a lot of their time standing around waiting for a customer question. As mentioned above, the job of these employees seems to largely be training customers on their roles in the IKEA process. An important principle is that all interactive service employees should consider their roles as customer trainers.

As obvious as these elements of customer training may seem, it is surprising how many service providers neglect or ignore their management. Some other furniture retailers have broken furniture arbitrarily distributed around a store that is difficult to navigate. A first step for improvement is to document customers' experiences (with more detailed PCN Diagrams) and identify what customers should be doing at each step and how the service environment either facilitates or distracts those customer roles. We can note those environmental cues on a PCN Diagram with annotations. Figure 20 shows an annotated PCN Diagram for IKEA (from Figure 14). That diagram reminds us that a map facilitates browsing the store, a pencil helps customers note the item they need, and a cart assists transporting items to registers.

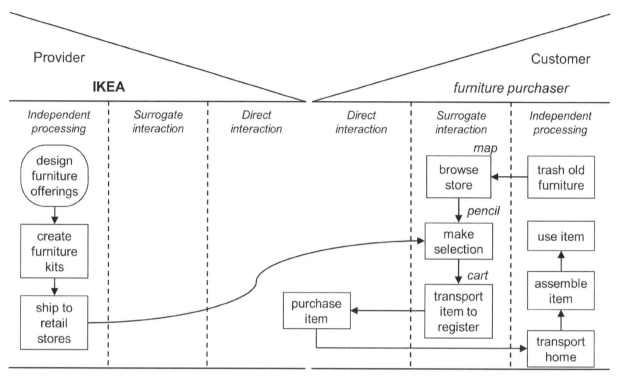

Figure 20: Annotated IKEA PCN Diagram

Managing the Control

In this chapter we have reviewed three general ways of specifying the job requirements for an interactive service process (or process step):

1. The provider (company management) controls the process by providing standard operating procedures.
2. The employee controls the process by using their own judgment for how the process should progress.
3. The customer controls the process by specifying how they think the process should proceed, which often happens with self-service.

These three options have been called the "service encounter triad," as depicted in Figure 21.[14] The idea is that there are three focuses for controlling interactive service processes: provider, employee, and customer. Although each of the three may have some control in a particular process chain, in a particular process step one or the other is likely to dominate. Which of the three is best certainly depends on the process requirements and desirable operating characteristics (such as was covered in Chapter 5).

As discussed earlier in this chapter, the most costly is likely to be employee control, since that typically requires hiring employees who have sufficient experience to exercise good judgment. Providers may want to control the process in order to limit variation and increase

---

[14] see Bateson, John E. G., "Perceived Control and the Service Encounter," in J. A. Czepiel, M. R. Solomon, and C. F. Suprenant (eds.), The Service Encounter, Lexington Books: Lexington, Mass., 1985, p. 76.

efficiency, but that may conflict with individual customers' desire for satisfaction of their unique needs. Customers might be able to control the process if they have sufficient competencies and motivation.

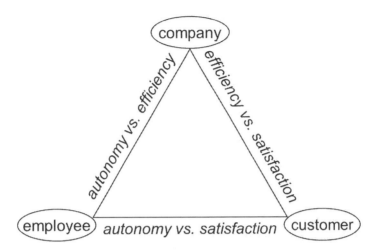

Figure 21: The service encounter triad

An important job design issue represented in the service encounter triad is the need for buy-in on the part of the entities participating in the process chain network. Figure 21 shows how they might have competing objectives, with company management wanting economic efficiency, employees wanting autonomy, and customers wanting satisfaction. It is important that the job design considers how management, employees, and customers each will accept the intended process control.

For example, I was recently booked on a United Airlines flight that was delayed for hours then finally canceled. We finally found out it was canceled from other passengers—the airline had failed to announce the cancellation to those of us waiting at the gate. It was late in the day and there were no other flights to San Francisco. After some effort I located a United employee and said I wanted them to book us in a hotel so that we could take a flight the following morning—my objective was satisfaction.

The employee said there was a company policy against giving hotel vouchers for weather-related delays (apparently it was raining in San Francisco, although the Delta flights had left for San Francisco without problem). However, the employee admitted that they are short-staffed, which probably contributed to their failure to notify the passengers of the cancelation, so she chose to exercise her autonomy in giving me a hotel voucher as well as meal vouchers for that evening and the next morning—even more than what I was asking for. That encounter worked out okay from my perspective, since my needs were satisfied and the employee was able to exercise her autonomy.

Interestingly, my flight back from San Francisco that next week also encountered serious delays. The United Airlines terminal in San Francisco was mayhem, with confusion about which delayed flights would depart from which terminals. (The weather was actually quite pleasant that day, both in San Francisco and Salt Lake City, the destination.) We finally departed and had a pleasant flight to Salt Lake City. I sat next to a sweet widow woman who was continuing to Grand Junction, Colorado, to spend Thanksgiving with her son.

We arrived in Salt Lake City minutes before her connecting Delta flight to Grand Junction was supposed to leave. The United agent at the arrival gate said the Delta flight was delayed in departing, so we raced through the airport (I was pushing her in a wheelchair) only to find that the Delta flight had left on time. We headed down to the United baggage counter. Once again it was late in the day, and I was expecting that they would put this sweet woman up in a hotel. The employee said the United flight delay was weather related (huh?), and company policy prevented them from providing compensation. I asked to speak to a manager. After about 20 minutes the manager arrived. I explained the situation. When the manager again said the flight delay was weather related I countered with "it was not." He asked who I was. I said I was a friend of the woman (a new friend, but a friend nonetheless). He told me to leave or he would call the airport police. I told him that he better call the police. When the police arrived (with a very large dog), we had a nice visit. The police officer told me I should not talk to the agitated United manager, but instead just assist the widow woman. Ultimately they gave her a $50 hotel voucher (not the entire hotel room amount)—she said she was okay with that, so I left.

These experiences demonstrate the conflict that can occur in the service encounter triad. In the first experience (flight to San Francisco) the objectives of the firm (don't compensate customers for weather-related problems) conflicted with my objectives for satisfaction and the employee's objective for exercising some degree of autonomy. Somehow the employee was able to override the firm in that case.

In the second experience (flight back to Salt Lake City) the first United employee expressed no desire to exercise autonomy, and the manager seemed committed to upholding company policy (even if it meant enforcing it by police action ☺). This hampered my desire for satisfaction (on behalf of the widow woman). The airline saved some money that day, but without customer buy-in will likely lose significant future revenues.

If the airline had more than a myopic view of service encounters they would design a flight-delay recovery process that plans for customer and employee buy-in to the decision control. An important aspect of PCN Analysis is considering the perspectives of various entities that participation in a given process chain.

PCN Analysis summary

This chapter reviewed some significant issues pertaining to managing the human resources involved in a process chain network. The human resource requirements and corresponding job design differs across regions of a process domain. Working in regions of independent processing requires different general skills than working in interactive processes.

PCN Analysis includes the concept of process complexity and process divergence. Process complexity is represented in a PCN Diagram by the number and detail of steps. Divergence is represented by rounded boxes for steps that do not have tightly defined specifications. In other words, divergent steps require some degree of judgment on the part of the person executing the step. That judgment typically comes from extensive experience, making employees with good judgment skills a rarer and more expensive resource.

A key element of PCN Analysis also covered in this chapter is the idea that customers usually perform a labor role in interactive service processes. Good PCN Analysis will consider the job design for customers, remembering that training customers is very different form training employees. Customers are often best trained in the process of service delivery. The complexities surrounding customer roles will be discussed further in Chapter 9.

As discussed in prior chapters, PCN Analysis includes identifying which process steps will occur in which process domain, which has implications for who controls the process. Design options include company control (through policies), employee control (through autonomy), or customer control (such as through self-service). One or the other might be more appropriate for a given process or process step. Effective PCN Analysis includes considering whether and how the various entities buy in to the given process design and control.

Chapter 9 – Managing the Customer Roles

This chapter reviews specific customer roles that can occur in interactive service processes, which Chapter 2 referred to as service supply chains[15]. These roles actually exist in all supply chains, including traditional manufacturing supply chains, although in different ways. The discipline of supply chain management largely involves identifying and coordinating the roles of the various entities. Figure 22 shows roles that exist in a typical manufacturing supply chain, including some of the following:

1. Suppliers—supply input materials and components.
2. Labor—provides the human effort in production.
3. Engineering—provides design specifications for products and processes.
4. Production—executes productive processes.
5. Product—the object of production.
6. Quality assurance—assures the quality of inputs and production.
7. Inventory—buffers rate gaps between stages of production and between production and demand.
8. Competitors—motivate the focal firm to improve performance.
9. Customers/consumers—select and pay for production output.

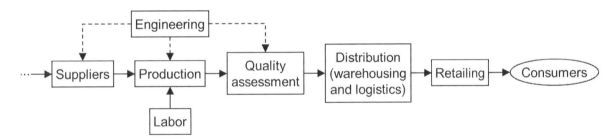

Figure 22: Typical supply chain roles

This list of roles is, of course, not exhaustive. These roles occur at various stages throughout traditional supply chains, and in some cases, the roles may overlap. However, in traditional supply chains the final role, customers, is generally distinct from the other roles:

1. Suppliers are upstream; customers are downstream.
2. Labor works within the focal firm; customers are exogenous.
3. Engineering is the function of trained engineers.
4. Production is often shielded from customers.
5. Products are what customers ultimately receive.
6. Quality assurance keeps defective products from reaching customers.
7. Inventory can be used to satisfy customer demand in a timely manner.
8. Competitors provide customers with choice.

---

[15] This chapter was largely taken from (Sampson and Spring 2012).

In traditional manufacturing supply chains, the customers—end consumers in particular—are beneficiaries of the various supply chain roles, but are only responsible for selecting, paying for, and using the outputs. In some cases, customers provide feedback that can be used for future production, or they may assume a marketing role by providing word-of-mouth recommendations to other prospective customers.

Although customers may assume expanded roles in traditional supply chains, PCN Analysis shows that customers do assume expanded roles in service operations. The Unified Service Theory (discussed in Chapter 2) asserts that expanded customer roles are the defining feature of service businesses. This chapter will review eight customer roles in service processes that relate to the traditional supply chain roles listed above.

1. Customers as Component Suppliers

Lovelock (1983) generically classified services based on what customer components the service provider acts upon. His four categories of services are as follows: (1) services that act on customers' minds (e.g., education); (2) services that act on customers' bodies (e.g., healthcare); (3) services that act on customers' physical possessions (e.g., television repair); and (4) services that act on customers' information (e.g., tax accounting). This classification scheme implies that service customers are component suppliers (of their minds, bodies, belongings, or information) to service businesses.

The "customer as component supplier" phenomenon occurs with B2B services as well as B2C services. Buildings are supplied as essential inputs to building cleaning services. Business problems and data are supplied as inputs to management consulting services. Copy machines are an essential input to copy machine repair services.

As suggested above, in traditional make-to-stock manufacturing supply chains (e.g., Figure 22), customers are customers and suppliers are suppliers. In particular, individual end consumers do not provide any distinct components to be used in the manufacturing of their products, and likely do not even know where or when the products were produced. If a manufacturer starts producing items based on each specific customer's specifications (i.e., custom manufacturing), the manufacturer transforms, to some degree, into a service process (Sampson 2001, p. 142).

2. Customers as Labor

Chapter 4 reviewed the concept of co-production, wherein service customers serve as labor to assist in the production of the service (Grönroos 2008). As mentioned in Chapter 6, service customers have been called "partial employees," indicating that they assume some—but not all—functions of regular employees (Mills and Morris 1986; Schneider and Bowen 1995; Xue and Harker 2002). A B2C example is the common practice of customers filling their own drinks at fast food restaurants. The large pharmaceutical distributor McKesson provided a B2B example when they installed computer terminals in client pharmacies, allowing pharmacists to check the availability of medicines without having to talk with a McKesson employee. Another perspective on customer labor is that some of the labor requirements of service firms are "outsourced" to customers, indicating a role shift (Sampson 2012).

Bitner, Faranda, Hubbert, and Zeithaml (1997) delineate two manifestations of customer-labor effort. First, they indicate that customers are productive resources, contributing to the productivity of the firm. Second, they describe how customers contribute to their own satisfaction and value, regardless of whether they have contributed to the productivity of the organization. Obviously, the ideal situation is when both can be achieved.

One example of how customer labor can benefit both service providers and customers is through the use of self-service technologies, which enable customers to perform functions previously assigned to regular employees (Froehle and Roth 2004). Chapter 6 pointed out that self-service is surrogate interaction in the customers process domain. Self-service is becoming increasingly common in many service business processes. Banks have shifted from tellers handling transactions to customers using ATMs. Years ago drivers started pumping their own gas. Airlines provide incentives for customers to manage their own check-in online. Retailers are increasingly providing self-check-out stations in place of human cashiers.

Self-service systems benefit providers through cost efficiencies, since customer labor is cheaper than paid labor. Providers also have increased scalability, since the available labor (customer labor) increases as demand increases. And, despite the costs of learning to use a self-serve system, customers benefit through increased control of the process.

3. Customers as Design Engineers

Customer focus groups may give general ideas to make-to-stock (push production) manufacturing organizations about product design, yet, with the exception of large-scale industrial customers, individual customers have little influence over product design. Production timing and required production efficiencies make it impractical for individual customers to participate in manufactured product design in most instances. It is even rarer for customers to influence manufacturing process design, since most customers have little or no knowledge of the intricacies of suppliers' manufacturing processes.

Chase and Aquilano (1995, p. 104) paint a very different picture for services: "Everyone is an expert on services. We all think we know what we want from a service organization and, by the very process of living, we have a good deal of experience with the service creation process". The implications of this supposed "customer expertise" is that service customers are very likely to have strong opinions about how the service should be designed, including opinions about the process by which it should be delivered. Some have espoused actively involving customers in new service development activities (Lundkvist and Yakhlef 2004; Matthing, Sanden, and Edvardsson 2004).

Customers act as design engineers in service processes from a wide variety of industries. Oliveira and von Hippel (2011) show how much of the innovation occurring in commercial and retail banking between 1975 and 2010 came from customers. When the insurance company depicted in Figure 5 outsourced the call center function, they certainly provided detailed specifications about how calls are to be handled. B2C examples are also common. Hair salon customers may be expected to specify the design of the finished product (i.e., hairstyle) and sometimes even the process (e.g., "use #3 clippers"). With the advent of "discount brokers" such as Charles Schwab and E*Trade, customers design their own investment portfolios. Even service operations as complex as healthcare involve some degree of customer-lead process design, as patients help configure treatment plans that fit their needs, capabilities, and resources.

Sometimes customer expertise may not be justified, such as a customer presenting service design ideas that are unreasonable, are against regulations, damage the cost structure of the firm, or otherwise cannot be implemented (Fitzsimmons and Fitzsimmons 2006, p. 204). In other cases, customers may have better design ideas than the service employees themselves, due to experience with the service and other service providers. Either way, when a customer presents design ideas to a service provider, that customer is assuming the role of a design engineer (Dubé, Johnson, and Renaghan 1999). Such customer involvement may be desirable or undesirable; either way, it is a reality.

4. Customers as Production Managers

In manufacturing, after products and the production process are designed, it is still up to the production manager to execute the process and create the products. Production managers receive direction from engineering, and make decisions about when to produce specific items and in what quantities. Manufacturing production managers typically base decisions on demand forecasts, inventory levels, and orders in hand, but otherwise seldom interact with customers (Frei 2006).

Again, we see a service operation distinction. As Namasivayam and Hinkin (2003, p. 27) state, "In contrast to manufactured goods where the consumer makes choices from products being offered and has no control of the products themselves, the service product is created during the service encounter, under the direction of the customer". In other words, to some degree, service customers assume a role of production manager.

A B2B example occurs when firms outsource IT functions, but keep the management of those functions in-house. A B2C example is the role parents assume in executing their families' visit to an amusement park like Disneyland. Disneyland is in essence a configuration of specialized workstations including rides, shows, and food outlets. Parents are responsible for managing the flow of their products (children) through the various workstations, striving to maximize productivity and avoid significant bottlenecks.

In some cases, customers may attempt to alter the service delivery to their liking. Even when customers fully comply with standard operating procedures, they still may make key operating decisions, such as the pace of the service and amount of attention to details. For example, in retail, customers determine how much time they spend in the facility, what types of questions they ask employees, how much knowledge they require to make a purchase decision, and so forth.

5. Customers as Products

In the case of so-called "human services," customers are the actual product (Lengnick-Hall 1996, p. 796). This pertains to Lovelock's first two categories of services: those that act on customers' minds and those that act on customers' bodies (Lovelock 1983). In some situations the customer-product also has some control over the production process, such as in education and healthcare. In other situations the customer-product is the passive recipient of processing, such as mass transit. Although the product of mass transit may be defined as "transportation systems for public use," ultimately the product that customers pay for is "customers delivered to their desired locations." In other words, the bus/train/plane is not the product—the customer is the product.

The customer-as-product effect is also seen in B2B services. For example, a firm may employ an investment-banking service to orchestrate an initial public offering (IPO). The investment bank may provide legal direction and underwrite the offering, but ultimately the "product" of the IPO is the firm itself that is being sold to investors.

6. Customers as Quality Assurance

It is an unfortunate fact that not all students manage the production of their education and not all patients manage their health in ways that allow optimal education or healthcare service quality. On the other hand, service customers can and often do assume an active role in quality assurance. Service customers provide specifications of quality. They measure and judge quality (Chervonnaya 2003). Chapter 7 pointed out that instead of measuring products or processes, service quality is primarily measured by customer feedback (Lengnick-Hall, Claycomb, and Inks 2000, p. 360; Parasuraman, Zeithaml, and Berry 1985; Sampson 1999).

The service customer role of quality assurance pertains not only to what service outcome is delivered but also how it is delivered (Kelley, Donnelly, and Skinner 1990). Service customers often have an active role in both process and outcome quality (Webb 2000). For example, a business owner may hire an accounting firm to conduct an audit of financial records. The accuracy of the records certainly will influence the outcome of the audit. The organization and completeness of the records will influence how well the audit process progresses. The business owner desires an audit that is defensible and also desires the audit process to go smoothly – the former representing outcome quality and the latter representing process quality.

Customers provide quality assurance functions in B2C services as well, as demonstrated by the prevalence of customer comment cards used across many industries. Service quality is commonly measured through customer feedback, and service quality is defined by performance relative to customer expectations (Parasuraman et al. 1985).

7. Customers as Inventory

Customer evaluations are not just about service quality, but also about process efficiency. Customer interaction has been cited as the primary cause of inefficiency of service operations (Chase 1978; Chase 1981), yet research has shown that customers value efficient service. As noted by Xue and Harker (2002, p. 254), "in terms of judging the efficiency of service delivery, a consumer often makes this judgment based not only on how long it takes the firm to complete its portion of the process but also on how efficient the consumer views the use of their resources, especially their time, to complete the service process". Customers do not want to be kept waiting before, during, or after the service delivery.

As described in Chapter 6, the primary reason customers are kept waiting in a service is because service capacity is insufficient and customer inputs arrive before the server is ready to handle those inputs; this same phenomena causes inventories to occur in manufacturing supply chains (i.e., goods arrive before the system is ready to process them) (Chopra and Meindl 2001, p. 52). Indeed, service customers are often inventory, waiting for themselves, their belongings, or their information to be processed. (See Chapter 6 for details about managing customer inventories.)

8. Customer as Competitor

With traditional supply chains, customers select from among competing firms (or from among the products of competing firms). With service supply chains, the customer is often the competitor (Bitner et al. 1997). This phenomenon is a form of service disintermediation, in that customers process their inputs without passing them through a service provider. The concept has also been called "internal exchange," wherein individuals or organizations satisfy their own needs without relying on an outside supplier (Lusch et al. 1992). Examples are numerous in both B2C and B2B settings: carwash customers can wash their own cars, business consulting clients can solve their own problems, airline passengers can drive their own vehicles, and so forth.

There are various motivations for internal exchange. As just discussed, using a service provider may involve unacceptable waiting. A customer may feel he or she has sufficient time and expertise to "do it yourself," may value the control that comes with self-service, and may receive cost-saving benefits. For businesses, internal exchange may bring similar benefits, especially if the exchange involves a good or service that is strategic to the firm.

In manufacturing supply chains, the customer-as-competitor phenomenon is manifested by manufacturers that vertically integrate, thus eliminating the need for one or more suppliers. At the consumer level, customers seldom compete with manufacturing suppliers. Manufacturers dominate consumer-competitors through major barriers to entry, including economies of scale, experience curves, access to the best sources of inputs, and so forth (Porter 1980). In developed economies it rarely makes economic sense for consumers to build their own goods when those goods are otherwise mass produced. (This is true for simple goods like pencils and complex goods like automobiles. A possible exception is foodstuffs—yet in developed countries few people grow their own food; instead they rely on food supply chains for components.)

With services, internal exchange is a viable option both for businesses and consumers. A primary reason for this viability is that the barriers to entry are lower, due to customer involvement in service delivery processes: customer involvement makes services quite heterogeneous, reducing economies of scale; customer involvement leads to customer expertise, as discussed previously; customers are suppliers of inputs to services and thus have direct control over those inputs; and so forth (Sampson 2001, p. 230). This important topic will be revisited in Chapter 11.

Customer role design alternatives

Each of these customer roles provides a design alternative for the service operation. As discussed in Chapter 5, each role can be enhanced through enabling innovations or reduced through relieving innovations, depending on the desired value proposition. This section shows how we can enhance or reduce *specific customer roles* in a service design.

To illustrate the management of customer roles, we will use an auto repair example. In the simplest sense, auto repair involves a customer bringing an inoperative car to a repair shop so that it can be repaired. However, even this simple interaction provides major process design alternatives. Consider the step of diagnosing the problem with car. An auto repair firm has diagnostics skills. A customer has an inoperative car in need of diagnosis. The "diagnose problem" step has at least the options shown in Figure 23.

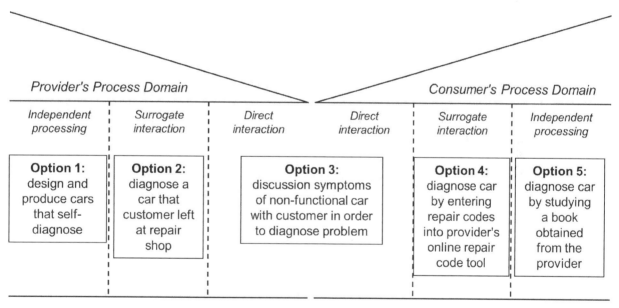

Figure 23: "Diagnose problem" process positioning options

Another way to consider process design options is by considering each of the eight expanded customer roles discussed in this chapter. Table 3 shows how each of the roles occurs in a typical auto repair process[16]. The table also shows how each of the roles could be enhanced (an enabling innovation) or reduced (typically by relieving innovation).

---

[16] This table was originally developed by Martin Spring, as published in (Sampson and Spring 2012).

Table 3: Design options for customer roles (auto repair)

Customer Role	'Typical' Base Case Role	Enhanced Role	Reduced Role
Component Supplier	Customer brings auto to the garage with vague description of symptoms of fault.	Expert customer provides extensive diagnostic information when repairs needed.	Customer doesn't provide anything to firm, but does repairs using self-help manual.
Labor	Customer drives auto to garage for repairs, also pumps gas, inflates tires and fills oil on routine basis.	Expert advisor talks customer through self-administered repair.	Garage tows/collects car from customer's home as well as doing repair work.
Design engineer	Customer exercises some choice e.g. brand or specification of replacement tires.	Classic car enthusiast knows more than the garage about the precise specification required.	Leaves all repair planning to the discretion of the auto shop.
Production manager	Customer manages the schedule for routine auto maintenance (oil change, tire rotations, etc.).	Customer books maintenance times online, buying a certain number of labor hours upfront.	Garage handles all routine maintenance, calling customer to schedule all maintenance activities.
Product	During repairs, customer is provided with face-to-face progress report and cost estimates, as well as doughnuts.	Repair customers could be advised/trained on practices to reduce need for repair, e.g. excessive braking leading to brake wear.	Customers required to provide minimal information and experiences no interaction or contact with garage staff.
Quality assurance	After repair work, customers see that vehicle works properly in normal use.	Customers watch repairs being conducted and provide feedback.	Intelligent tire inflation machine reads RFID chip on tire and auto and 'knows' the correct pressure, removing the need for customer QA of their own work.
Inventory	Some waiting in line when dropping car off for repair and collecting it.	Repair-while-u-wait as basic design of service (e.g. Kwik-Fit in UK).	Comprehensive collection and courtesy car provision to minimize waiting and inconvenience.
Competitor	Customer pumps own gas, inflates tires, refills coolant, cleans car inside and out.	Provision of kits and instructions for common tasks e.g. oil change.	Garage takes over minor routine tasks such as pumping up tires, washing and valeting car as part of total service package.

The desirability of enhancing or reducing each customer roles depends on the desired value proposition and/or the desired operating characteristics of the firm, and especially depends on the willingness and ability of customers to assume the roles. Enhancing a customer role includes assuring that the customers have sufficient motivation and skills to perform the role, which may include providing the customers with financial incentives and knowledge resources. Reducing a customer role also includes gaining customer buy-in, since reduced roles typically means reduced control and perhaps greater cost to the customer.

PCN Analysis summary

This chapter reviewed various roles that customers can and often do assume in interactive service processes, which correspond to non-customer roles in traditional product supply-chain roles. With any supply chain, if an entity fails to perform their role the productivity of the supply chain will suffer. That is why it is important in interactive service processes to analyze and appropriately manage customer roles. This chapter also showed how the customer roles can be used as a basis for strategic process positioning. Each role can be enable or relieved in order to improve a value proposition. This adjustment of customer roles can help us systematically identify opportunities for process innovation, which will be discussed further in Chapter 12.

Chapter 10 – Improvement through Lean Services

"Lean production" or "lean" is a very popular and important perspective on manufacturing management. Lean is traditionally centered on the goal of achieving high-volume production using minimal inventories. Under lean, most inventories are considered to be wasteful, and lean manufacturers plan their production so as to minimize inventories. This is largely accomplished by "pull production" wherein nothing is produced until it is needed. In other words, things are produce Just-in-Time (JIT).

In Chapter 2 we recognized that "Service providers inherently produce just-in-time (JIT), meaning producing according to demand, since the dependency on customer-resources precludes producing the service to inventory." In other words, service operations are *inherently* lean from an inventory perspective. By definition, service production occurs according to customer demand, as illustrated by the following examples:

- Auto manufacturers can produce cars at times of low demand and keep them in inventory until the time of demand—a non-service approach to meeting the transportation needs of customers. On the other hand, airlines can only produce customer transportation according to demand—transportation without demand is akin to kidnapping.
- Home appliance manufacturers can produce vacuum cleaners and keep them in inventory until the time of demand—again non-service approach to meeting carpet cleaning needs. Conversely, carpet cleaning services can only clean homeowners' carpets according to demand—cleaning homeowners' carpets without demand is referred to as "breaking and entering."

Lean has different implications for service operations other than inventory reduction. Note that lean is concerned with eliminating waste in general, not just eliminating inventory waste. Lean defines waste as anything that does not provide value to customers. Waste includes unnecessary waiting[17], unnecessary transportation, unnecessary processing, and avoidable defects. All of these can produce waste in service operations.

It is also important to note that lean is not about simply eliminating costs. Rather, lean is about preserving value, or even improving value, with an appropriate amount of resources. As such, lean may actually focus on getting the most value out of available resources.

Applying lean to service operations

The Unified Service Theory (see Chapter 2) implies that service operations are distinguished by their reliance on customer resources. The principles of process positioning discussed in Chapter 5 suggest that an optimal configuration of a PCN process depends on the requirements of a chosen value proposition. The customer intensity concept reviewed in

---

[17] According to the "customer inventory" concept from Chapter 6, reducing customer waiting could be considered a form of "inventory reduction."

Chapter 6 implies that interaction breeds inefficiencies. This implies that lean services are about obtaining an *optimal* process configuration to deliver a chosen value proposition without waste.

The distinctiveness of service operations centers on provider-customer interactions. Correspondingly, the distinctiveness of lean service operations should focus on managing interactions, which is a basic function of PCN Analysis. This can be accomplished through what I call the Four E's of Lean Services:

1. Enhance strategic interactions.
2. Eliminate wasteful interactions.
3. Enable customers to self-serve or do-it-themselves.
4. Extend offering outside the firm.

The following provides examples of each.

1. Enhance strategic interactions.

We define a "strategic interaction" as an interaction that contributes to the chosen value proposition. Determining a value proposition was discussed in Chapter 4 and includes identifying what specific customer needs are being addressed. Enhancing strategic interactions involves focusing on those interactions that contribute to the chosen value proposition, and making sure that the specific needs are being met in an appropriate way.

For example, Amazon.com began by selling books over the Internet, but over the years has expanded into selling home electronics, clothing, toys, home appliances, sporting goods, and so forth. If we carefully consider Amazon's value proposition – or what customer needs they meet – we see that Amazon distinguishes itself by providing *convenience*. Amazon dramatically reduces the effort to locate items, especially uncommon items, compared with brick-and-mortar shopping and even digging through multiple online stores.

I needed a replacement battery for an out-of-production netbook computer. The process I went through to place the order is depicted in Figure 24. Searching the Amazon.com website involved simply entering the netbook model number and "battery" in the search box. Amazon provided many battery options, most of which were actually sold by Amazon affiliates. (I do not think Amazon itself stocks batteries for old computers.) The customer process included the usual review of options, adding the item to a shopping cart, entering payment and shipping information, and confirming the order.

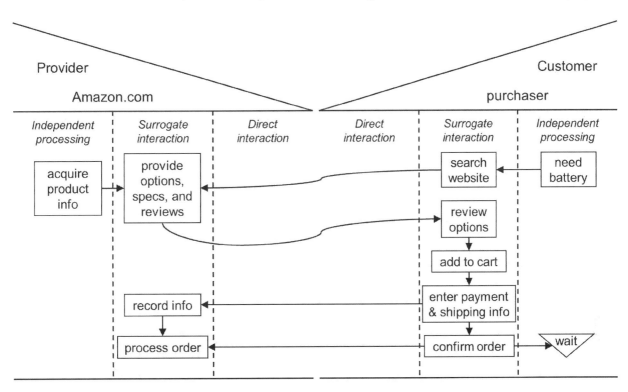

Figure 24: Placing an order on Amazon.com

Amazon enhances this order process and enhances the convenience benefit by their so-called "1-Click" ordering process, which is depicted in Figure 25. Under that process configuration the customer reviews options and then simply clicks the on-screen order button (labeled "1-Click Order"). The order is processed and the customer receives a confirmation email message. One-click ordering requires that the customer has previously entered standard payment and shipping information, and that the customer is logged in to the Amazon.com website. (Actually, Amazon.com is normally set up to keep the customer logged in at all times – I discovered this when my daughter ordered a book on my account without talking to me first. It was so easy that she had no idea she was actually placing the order.)

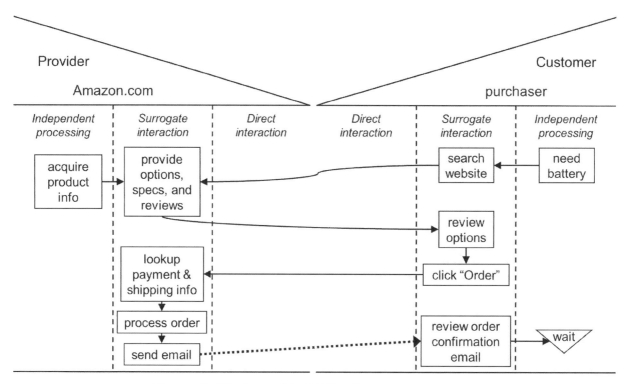

Figure 25: Placing a "1-click" order on Amazon.com

Again, 1-click ordering enhances the ordering process by enhancing the benefit (convenience) that underlies the value proposition. In this example the benefit includes eliminating the waste of having to re-enter or re-check information every time an order is placed. (Frankly, that is why I am afraid of one-click ordering: It is too easy! I am afraid it will lead me to impulse purchases.)

An approach to enhancing strategic interaction that is relevant in person-to-person direct interactions is **scripting**. Some direct interactions are standardized, such as the "may I take your order" conversation that takes place millions of time each day at McDonalds and other fast food restaurants. However, scripting can even be useful in more dynamic situations. Sometimes it needs to be **adaptive scripting**, meaning that the script is simply a structure of interaction that can be modified by the service employee as necessary.

For example, a restaurant in my community has a reputation for world-class service (i.e., world-class provider-customer interactions). The servers interact with customers to communicate offerings, answer questions, take orders, deliver food items, and receive payment. These steps are relatively standardized to provide efficient delivery and uniform quality of interactions (despite having employees who are not uniform in skill and personality). Yet, an even bigger key to the success of this restaurant are the procedural scripting of even uncommon interactions such as dealing with a mistake in an order, responding to a spilled drink, and assisting customers who need to go to the bathroom.

This last item probably needs more explanation. The owner of the restaurant (my former student) told me that his employees have a service standard which states that if a customer gets up from their seat, such as to go to the restroom, the employee should fold their napkin and place it on their chair before their return. This is a signal to the customer that the employees are aware of their needs even without communicating those needs.

One day I had lunch with some colleagues at a different restaurant owned by this former student. As retold in Chapter 1, two crystal glasses were broken during the meal. (One was set on a gap between two tables that were not evenly aligned, and the other was broken in toasting our guest of honor.) As I expected, the response of the employees was very systematic, as though they had been trained on how to deal with customers who break glasses. I do not suspect this was a common occurrence, but the employee response process was sufficiently scripted to have it be a positive experience for the customers.

Remember that enhancing means *increasing the value* of interactions, not just changing or automating the interaction. For example, some banks and other organizations replace human phone receptionists with automated PBX systems. I hate those things! All I seem to get from them is "I'm sorry, could you please repeat your command from the following options...." Installing the automated phone system saves labor costs, but does not enhance the interactive process, at least for my customer segment.

2. Eliminate wasteful interactions.

The second element of lean services is eliminating wasteful interactions, meaning interactions that do not contribute to the value proposition. Chapter 4 suggested that "If any step of a process does not contribute to either value potential or a value realization, it should probably be eliminated."

Eliminate sometimes means remove completely. In some situations eliminate means to simply eliminate the wasteful and inefficient nature of the interactions. The following is an example.

On busy days when there is no time to cook dinner, my wife sometimes suggests I pick up pizza on the way home from work. I like pizza, but I do not like the pizza ordering process, which is depicted in Figure 26. I call the restaurant and ask about their daily specials. After two or three times reviewing the specials and possible options I place an order, hoping that the order is some approximation of what I actually want.

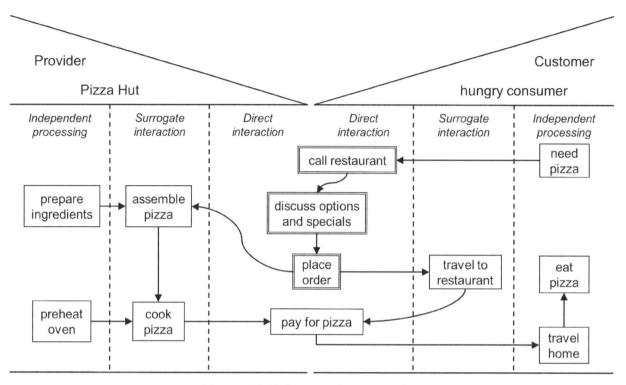

Figure 26: Take-out pizza ordering

To me, those repetitive direct interactions with the restaurant employee are wasteful. It would be more helpful if I could simply see the options and make my selection. That is what I would do in the restaurant, but if I place my order after I arrive at the restaurant I would have to wait for it to be prepared and cooked.

One way to eliminate the wasteful direct interactions is to substitute more efficient surrogate interactions. This could be done by allowing the customer to order via a website or mobile phone app, as depicted in Figure 27. The Pizza Hut restaurant chain introduced such an app in 2009. The app allows customers to see the pizza options, visually assemble a pizza on the phone's screen, and place the order with a nearby Pizza Hut restaurant.

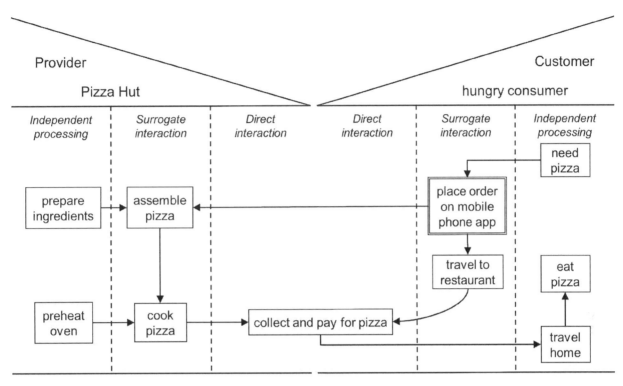

Figure 27: Take-out pizza ordering with phone app

This pizza example also illustrates our third "E" of lean services – enabling customers.

3. Enable customers to self-serve or do-it-yourself.

Chapter 5 discussed enabling innovations that involve moving process steps from the provider's process domain to the customer's process domain. These innovations can benefit the firm through increased efficiency (since customers provide their own labor), and benefit customers by providing increased control and potential opportunity for customization.

One strategy for enabling customers is self-service, which means that customers interact with the provider in a surrogate manner. Self-service retail is a classic example. In 1916 Clarence Saunders patented[18] an invention in which "The object of my said invention is to provide a store equipment by which the customer will be enabled to serve himself...." Prior to that time the retail employees were responsible for retrieving items as depicted in Figure 28.

---

[18] U.S. Patent No. 1242872 filed October 26, 1916.

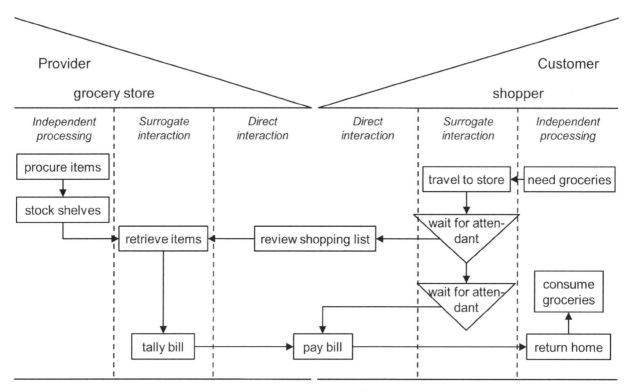

Figure 28: Traditional retail (pre-1916)

Saunders introduced his concept of self-service retail in his Piggly Wiggly retail chain that, despite pessimism by critics, set the standard for future retailers. That process, depicted in Figure 29, enables the customer to retrieve their desired grocery items. Benefits went well beyond simply reducing the retailers paid labor. Customers were able to have a more customized retail experience, including the ability to browse the store and study possible purchases without having to rely on store employees.

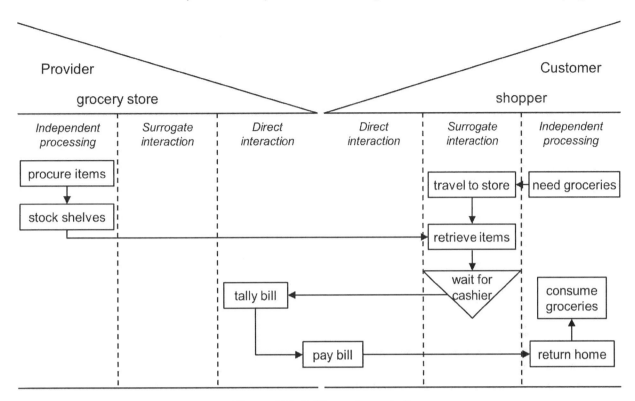

Figure 29: Self-service retail

A more recent trend in self-service retail includes even eliminating direct interaction at the time of check-out and payment, as depicted in Figure 30. Under that process configuration the customer can enter the store, select items, and pay without any direct interaction. When self-check-out technology was first introduced, customers seemed hesitant to participate and the equipment went largely unused. However, over time some customers have become comfortable using the technology, and eventually it may become their preferred mode of retail interaction.

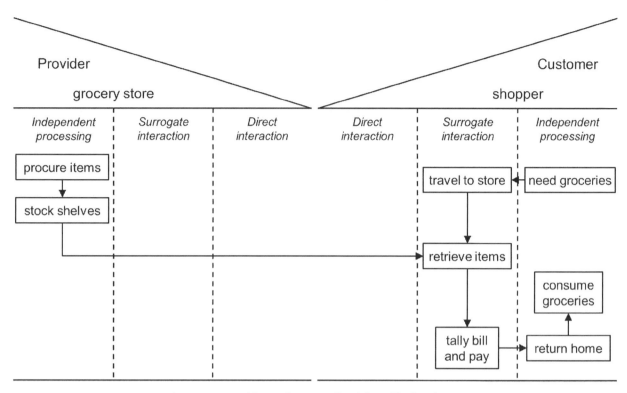

Figure 30: Self-service retail with self-check-out

The issue of customer adoption of self-service technologies needs to be addressed in all industries. When automatic teller machines (ATMs) were introduced by major banks in the 1970's and 1980's they were met with tremendous skepticism. However, over time the bank customers have become comfortable with that self-service technology, and ATMs have become practically ubiquitous.

When major airlines introduced online and kiosk check-in for flights the customers also needed to gain confidence in using the self-service technologies. As with retail self-check-out, the airlines have employees that are responsible for assisting customers in using the new technologies. In essence, these employees are responsible for *customer training*, as was discussed in Chapter 8.

One other way customers can be enabled to perform processes is to move process steps to the center of the customers' process domain, i.e., their independent processing region, which Chapter 6 called the "do-it-yourself" (DIY) region. An example discussed in Chapter 5 was IKEA, which requires and enables customers to assemble furniture themselves in their own homes (see Figure 14). A similar example is take-and-bake pizza, depicted in Figure 31, where the customer assumes full responsibility for the "cook pizza" step.

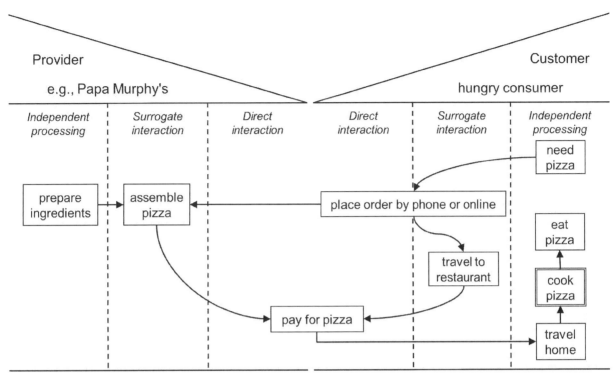

| | | Provider | | | | Customer | |
| | | e.g., Papa Murphy's | | | | hungry consumer | |

| *Independent processing* | *Surrogate interaction* | *Direct interaction* | *Direct interaction* | *Surrogate interaction* | *Independent processing* |

need pizza

prepare ingredients → assemble pizza ← place order by phone or online

eat pizza

cook pizza

travel to restaurant

pay for pizza

travel home

Figure 31: Take-and-bake pizza

The pizza benefit of DIY is not just economical (lower price due to lower production costs to the firm). One problem with the take-out pizza process depicted in Figure 26 is that while the customer is traveling home the pizza is getting cold. The customer must either eat the pizza immediately or reheat it (or eat it cold), which can take away from the freshness. The take-and-bake process configuration in Figure 31 allows the customer to take control of the cooking process. This allows customizing the time in which the pizza can be served. It also facilitates more customization of the pizza toppings before putting it in the oven.

4. Extend offering outside the firm.

As mentioned earlier, lean is not about providing less value with fewer resources. Lean is about providing a chosen amount of value with the appropriate (or optimal) configuration of resources. Although firms have *specialized* competencies, target customers are likely to have *general* needs. If customers have related needs outside of the firm's core competencies, then the lean approach would include identifying the appropriate process configuration for meeting those needs. As just mentioned, that may mean moving the process steps to the customer's process domain. Another alternative is to position the process in the domain of another firm with appropriate competencies.

This is Richard Normann's concept of "value constellations" or what I call "Service Value Networks," which is the topic of Chapter 13. Normann introduced the related concept of **density**, which he defines as the degree to which a mobilization of resources to satisfy a given need can take place (2001, p. 27). Value propositions that have high density meet a high amount of need by bringing together the appropriate combination of resources (including competencies) at the right time and the right place.

Density does not imply that providers should do everything for everyone anywhere. Instead, density implies that we have an appropriate configuration of entities, each with their unique competencies and resources, and that the actions of the entities are coordinated in order to "mobilize the creation of value in new forms" (Normann and Ramírez 1993, p. 66).

Interpreted from the PCN perspective, the concept of density means that we *reconfigure* (which is the term used by Normann) the processes represented in a Service Value Network (an extended PCN Diagram) to meet new needs in new ways.

An example depicted in Figure 5 is the auto insurance Service Value Network. Insurance companies specialize in managing financial risk associated with things like automobile accidents. When car owners have needs pertaining to an auto accident claim, they are likely to also have needs for auto repair. Although insurance companies could open a division of auto repair shops, auto repair is quite outside of their financial risk management competency. Therefore, insurance companies improve the density of their offerings by partnering with auto body and repair shops to meet more customer needs with the combined offering.

There are opportunities to extend the offering outside the firm in many industries. The following are a few examples.

- The British retailer ASDA offers a variety of services, including mobile phone services, financial services, home and life insurance, and so forth. These services are tightly branded as ASDA products, even though they are well outside of ASDA's retail competencies. We can be certain that ASDA has configured a Service Value Network to meet this variety of customer needs.
- Educational institutions provide students with classroom instructions, but students also have needs for books and food. Many campuses outsource bookstores and food service to contract firms that can better provide those services to students. For example, the Harvard Business School previously outsourced food service to Marriott and copy services to Kinko's.

Other examples will be described in Chapter 13. We will conclude this chapter by considering an application of lean service principles to healthcare.

Lean service in healthcare

Lean principles have been applied in healthcare, although the phrase "lean healthcare" sounds like somewhat of an oxymoron. The healthcare sector is ripe for the application of the four E's of lean services. We will consider a healthcare process that is similar to what was shown in Figure 9. Figure 32 is a repeat of that healthcare PCN Diagram for a parent that has a child with a sore throat. The parent drives to the health clinic, checks in, and waits to be seen by a nurse practitioner. The parent discusses the symptoms with a nurse practitioner and a throat culture is taken to determine if the cause is strep throat (thus requiring an antibiotic). The clinic lab analyzes the culture while the patent waits (possibly waiting at home -

independently). The clinic nurse reports the diagnosis and, if it is strep throat, calls in a prescription. The parent drives to a pharmacy, waits in line, shows ID, waits for the prescription to be filled, pays a co-pay amount, and goes home to administer the medicine to the sick child (who eventually feels better).

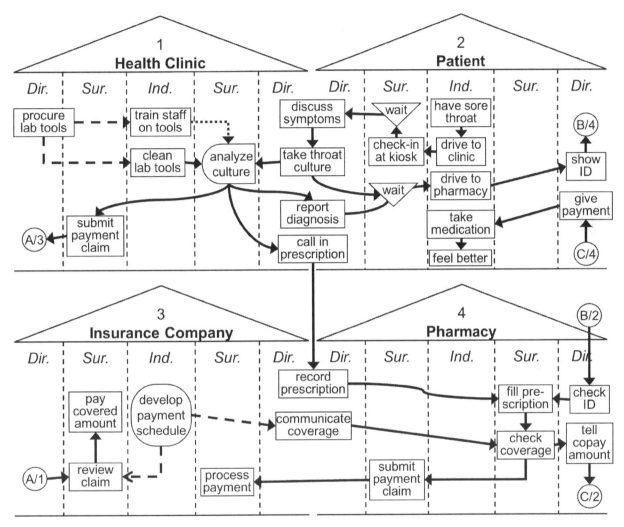

Figure 32: Healthcare PCN Diagram

Readers who have children and live in cold climates will recognize that this is <u>not</u> a lean process configuration. The parent spends a great deal of time waiting. This inconvenience is further compounded by all of the administrative steps to communicate information between the patient, health clinic, pharmacy, and insurance company.

The traditional process of Figure 32 fails to recognize that (a) *taking* a throat culture is not rocket science and does not require an advanced degree, (b) the parent may not be available to take a reply phone call at a particular time but would get a text message, (c) even when prescriptions are "called in" the pharmacies often do not begin filling prescriptions until the customer shows up, (d) patients often pay their co-pay amount from their Financial Savings Accounts (FSA) which requires completing insurance forms or using an FSA debit card,

A reconfigured healthcare Service Value Network is shown in Figure 33. Here, the parent has an inventory of throat culture sticks in the home medicine cabinet, and has been educated on symptoms of strep throat and use of the culture sticks. The parent takes the throat culture (by simply wiping the stick in the child's mouth), places it in the accompanying baggie, completes the attached information form, and drops it off at the front desk of the health clinic. The clinic analyzes the culture and emails the diagnosis to the parent.

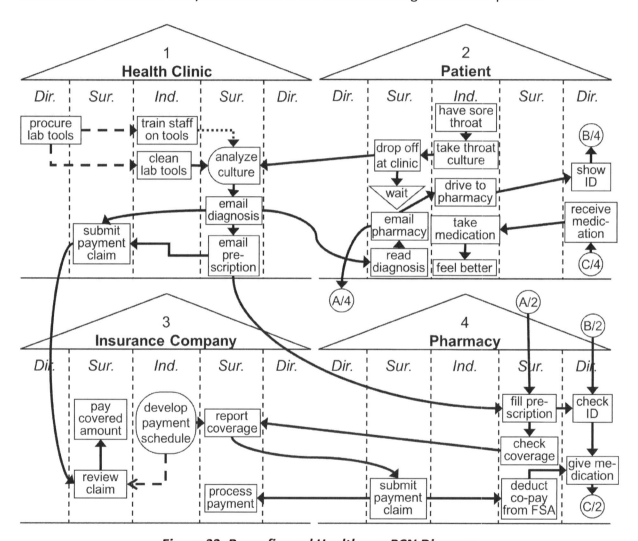

Figure 33: Reconfigured Healthcare PCN Diagram

If the diagnosis is strep throat, the antibiotic prescription order is emailed to the pharmacy chosen by the patient. The patient can also email the pharmacy to indicate that he or she intends to pick up the prescription on a particular day. (Alternately, the chosen pharmacy can confirm the prescription order received from the patient on the health clinic's secure website.) With order in hand, the pharmacy can fill the prescription, check coverage with the insurance company, bill the insurance company, and take the co-pay amount out of the patient's FSA. When the patient arrives at the pharmacy the prescription is already filled and paid for. The patient simply needs to show appropriate ID and leave with the medication.

This reconfigured lean offering has more value density because (a) it provides the appropriate resources at the right time, minimizing unnecessary waiting, (b) it makes sure the resources are at the places they need to be, (c) it has the entity best suited to do each step perform the step, and (d) it involves interactions in an efficient and effective way. These points correspond to Norman's four dimensions of improving density: time, place, actor (entity), and constellation (configuration of interaction) (Normann 2001, p. 28).

It is especially compelling to note how much less direct interaction there is in Figure 33 than there was in Figure 32. Direct interaction has an important time and place in service operation processes. However, and Normann points out, new information technologies enable new and improved process configurations. In particular, we can often improve the effectiveness and efficiency of interactive steps by utilizing surrogate interaction (Principle #4 from Chapter 5).

PCN Analysis summary

The lean perspective has strong application in interactive service contexts by focusing our attention on reducing waste and improving the value proposition. We reviewed four approaches that comprise the "Four E's of Lean Services," namely:

1. Enhance strategic interactions.
2. Eliminate wasteful interactions.
3. Enable customers to self-serve or do-it-themselves.
4. Extend offering outside the firm.

These Four E's emphasize that interaction should not occur simply for interaction's sake, but should appropriately contribute to the value proposition. PCN Analysis can help us identify areas where a process configuration may be reconfigured to improve process density, i.e., the range of needs met by the process chain network.

Chapter 11 – Servitization and Deservitization

Providers would like to position their offerings according to their core competencies, but things are more complicated than that. Some "full-service" providers have core competencies in direct interactive processes and command healthy margins. Sometimes these providers are the darlings of Wall Street and the subject of "Great Companies" books. Then something happens. They get slammed by new providers that enter the market with less experience and skills and providing a "poorer" customer experience. These new providers lack the direct interaction skills of the full-service providers, but dominate the market nonetheless.

Examples exist in many service industries. At one time, Thomas Cook, PLC, was one of the world's largest travel agencies, although recently their stock price has been trading at about 5 percent of the 2007 high. British Airlines reputation for exceptional service came with a 20 percent decline in passengers between 2002 and 2010[19]. Blockbuster, the largest video rental chain in the U.S., filed for bankruptcy in 2010. CompUSA was "The Computer Superstore" until 2007 when they closed 225 stores[20]. Other full-service retailers that are out of business include Sharper Image, Mervyn's California, Circuit City, and Borders Books.

One thing all of these companies had in common was a reputation for excellent service, meaning excellent interactions with customers. The front-line employees were well trained and able to help meet the needs of customers in a professional and personalized manner. I must confess that I actually enjoyed visiting a lot of these companies, whether I bought something or not.

Yet, the other thing these companies have had in common is being clobbered by new companies that provide *less* service. The growth and prosperity of these companies has been hampered by the middle-aged malady of deservitization.

Deservitization

Later in this chapter we will review the concept of servitization. But first we need to review the concept of deservitization, which is the natural tendency of business processes. **Deservitization** means reducing the level of service provided by a specialized provider, which means reducing the amount of interaction in the process chain connecting the two entities. Deservitization is caused by two parallel phenomena: service commoditization and service disintermediation.

Service commoditization

In general, commoditization is when an offering that comes from multiple providers is treated as practically indistinguishable from one provider to the next, which is to say that the

---

[19] Source: Wikipedia.com
[20] The Gutting of CompUSA, The New York Times, March 8, 2007,
http://pogue.blogs.nytimes.com/2007/03/08/the-gutting-of-compusa/

offering becomes a "commodity." The most common examples of commodities are food items. Corn and bean are commodities. Milk is a commodity. Wheat is a commodity.

Of course, "indistinguishable" has degrees. My wife, who is an expert homemaker and bread baker, will assure you that hard white winter wheat is superior to most other wheat, at least for baking bread. However, most people that encounter "4 cups flour" in a bread recipe do not care about the pedigree of the wheat.

Once a product becomes a commodity it is subject to being traded on an open price market such as the commodities market of the Chicago Mercantile Exchange. Traders buy and sell corn futures without any regard for the type or quality of corn. The entire purchase decision comes down to price, which is thus a function of estimated supply and demand.

Technologies can become commodities. Current examples include incandescent light bulbs and out-of-patent pharmaceuticals. The technology of incandescent light bulbs is quite standard, and name-brand bulbs seem to be no better than generic brand bulbs. Generic substitutes are especially prevalent with out-of-patent pharmaceuticals. Store-brand ibuprofen is the same chemical composition as the name-brand versions.

Food and technology products are not the only business offerings subject to commoditization. Interactive business processes (services) can also become commodities. This means that the process becomes so well known that it can be performed, for all intents and purposes, identically by a wide variety of service providers. The process is perceived by customers as being standardized, even if it is not.

Figure 34 depicts this process commoditization effect. The incumbent firms have a very responsive process that delivers "personalized" service. Each customer is treated as a unique entity with unique needs. The incumbent provider has depth of experience responding to needs in a timely and expert manner.

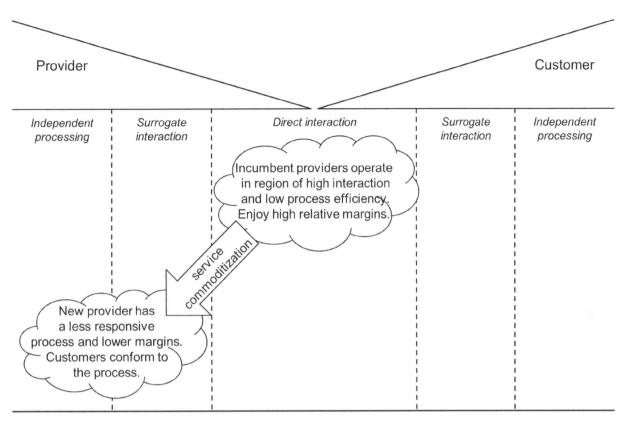

Provider

Customer

Independent processing

Surrogate interaction

Direct interaction

Surrogate interaction

Independent processing

Incumbent providers operate in region of high interaction and low process efficiency. Enjoy high relative margins.

service commoditization

New provider has a less responsive process and lower margins. Customers conform to the process.

Figure 34: Service process commoditization

Process commoditization occurs as providers learn how to hone in on customer needs without the need for expert front-line labor (the employees that interact with customers). They discover that customer needs are not as heterogeneous as once thought, and what previously was thought to be judgment-based processes (called "divergent" in Chapter 8) can actually be automated to a great degree, or at least reduced to sets of rules that can be acted on by less-experienced employees.

In other words, process commoditization results from the increased knowledge of providers about the process of delivering service in order to meet the needs of customers. It allows them to meet the needs of customers in a much more efficient way.

Process commoditization can be viewed as good or bad, depending on who you are and what you need. Most customers love process commoditization because it allows them to have their needs met at lower costs (both monetary and psychological). However, it means a loss of the "personal touch" that they may have been used to. Some customers truly may be unique in their needs, and process commoditization means they are left to patronize incumbent providers that are holding on to the interactive process positioning (until they sadly go out of business).

Process commoditization means that firms with interactive skills, such as highly experienced front-line employees, will lose the competitive advantage of those skills. These firms are able to absorb more customer variety than is necessary, meaning they have responsive capacity that is wasted. Unfortunately, the skills to provide a commoditized service are quite different from the skills to provide the customized interactive version.

For example, retail used to be a wonderfully interactive experience. Customers could engage knowledgeable employees in discussion about almost any type of purchase. I remember back in 1982 when I arrived at work one day and had forgotten my necktie. I crossed the street to Nordstrom where a delightful employee assisted me in picking out a tie that would meet my unique needs. It seems like she even helped me understand my needs, knowing all of the right factors to consider when purchasing a necktie. The necktie selection process was highly interactive and responsive to even my unknown needs.

Fast forward 30 years. These days when I need a tie I am likely to purchase it from a warehouse store called Costco. The necktie selection process involves me wandering around until I see the necktie rack, then picking the appropriate necktie out of a shipping box. Actually, it would be a package of 6 neckties, since Costco does not sell anything in normal quantities. Half of the neckties would suite my needs, but since it is half the price I would pay at Nordstrom I do not mind.

Some may argue that it is the product that has commoditized, not the process, but I would disagree. The products sold at Costco are quite distinguishable from products sold at other retailers, and Costco is known for selling premium brands, albeit at less-than-premium prices.

Another example of how Costco has contributed to the commoditization of retail is the outdoor spa (hot tub) that I recently bought from them. I previously went to a local hot tub showroom and met with a sales employee who was wonderfully eager to help me make a hot tub decision. At the time I was not very knowledgeable about the types of hot tubs there were available, about how difficult they were to install, and about what they typically sell for. This sales employee answered many of my questions, and provided brochures that answered other questions.

Since I am a Costco loyalist, I also consulted the Costco website. It turns out the physical Costco stores only stock hot tubs on rare occasions like promotional events. Nevertheless, the Costco website was very informative. It had diagrams of the hot tubs, which I needed to know since I was having it built into a new deck. It had videos of hot tub operation (featuring people who seem like they are having a good time). It had electrical wiring specifications. It also had a toll-free number to the manufacturer, which I called to ask about considerations for building a deck around the hot tub. (Answer: be sure and leave deck access panels in case the hot tub jets need to be serviced.)

The hot tub I bought from Costco was not a commodity – it was what customer reviews suggest is a high-quality hot tub. (And, it has 70 jets, whereas cheaper hot tubs have fewer.) What was a commodity is the process of gathering information and making a purchase decision. The showroom salesperson did not have as many answers as the Costco website, and where the website fell short a call center filled in. Basically, it was the same purchase process I went through when I bought my shed and other things on Costco's website.

Note that visiting the Costco website is not a lot different from visiting the stores. The customer experience at a Costco store is primarily surrogate interaction. Employees in the store are mostly unloading boxes to satisfy the seemingly insatiable needs of customers. If you ask them a product question they will simply direct you to the product packaging. (If you ask them if they have some item they will usually tell you where it should be on a shelf and say, "if it is not there, then we do not have it.") The only reason to directly interact with a Costco employee is if he or she is your friend, but even then it is awkward since chitchat will hinder their productivity.

Given the chance, I suspect the hot tub showroom employee would probably tell me that their hot tubs are superior to the one I ordered from Costco, but without supporting evidence. He would tell me that Costco would not be there if I had a problem with the hot tub, but that is not what customer reviews have said (that the manufacturer would get a local plumber to my house to get everything in working order). He might suggest that the satisfaction of my needs may be in jeopardy, but Costco takes anything back for a full refund if you do not like it. (We have even taken bananas back if they fail to ripen in a reasonable time.) I actually called Costco about this, and they said if I did not like the hot tub I just needed to drain the water and leave it on my street curb and a truck would come and pick it up.

Costco has commoditized the high-end retail process for my customer segment. I am sure there are other customer segments that are still willing to pay higher prices for a highly interactive retail process. My segment seems to be big enough to justify this strategic process positioning, given the massive crowds at Costco almost any day of the week. One advantage of using the highly interactive retailers is that there are usually not massive crowds.

If this disruption were not bad enough, service commoditization is often accompanied by the parallel concept of service disintermediation (the other element of deservitization).

Service disintermediation

Recall that service commoditization occurs because providers are learning more about the process of service delivery, and discovering ways of delivering the process with less interaction and more efficiency. Similarly, disintermediation occurs as customers learn more about the process of service delivery, and realize that they can perform the process steps in order to meet their needs in a more efficient and effective manner.

The term "disintermediation" traditionally means to remove an intermediary from a supply chain. For example, Oakley, the producer of sunglasses and sports equipment decided to start selling directly to customers through its website. This disintermediation involved bypassing the retailers who were intermediaries between Oakley and customers.

Service disintermediation is distinct in that customers reduce or eliminate the need to interact with service providers. Recall from Chapter 2 that service supply chains are bidirectional, meaning that the productive process goes from the customer (supplying inputs) to the provider (processing those inputs) and back to the customer (receiving the output).

Figure 35 shows a simplified PCN Diagram for a brake repair. The customer has a need, visits the provider, allows the provider to do the work, pays for the work, and drives away happy.

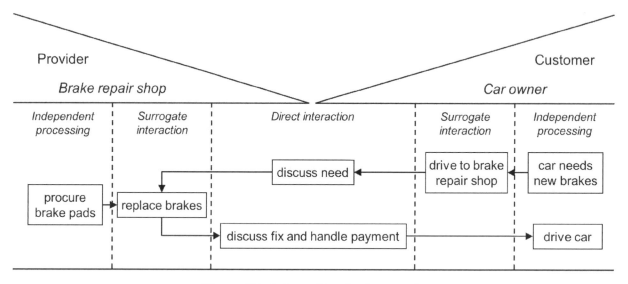

Figure 35: Interactive brake repair

There are actually two ways the brake provider can be disintermediated. In essence, the customer is purchasing brake pads from the repair shop, which purchased the pads from a distributor, wholesaler, or manufacturer. Product disintermediation would be for the customer to purchase brake pads directly from the supplier used by the repair shop.

Service disintermediation is different, since it focuses on the customer reducing or eliminating the process steps involving interaction with the provider. In other words, service disintermediation means that customers figure out how to do it themselves, either independently or with reduced (e.g., surrogate) interaction with the provider. This phenomenon of "customers as competitors" was introduced in Chapter 9, and will be expounded upon here.

Customers as competitors

Figure 36 shows an alternative for brake repair that involves service disintermediation. In that PCN Diagram the customer still starts with the car as an input to the repair process – the customer is the supplier of that key process input. However, the customer bypasses the provider by replacing the brakes himself or herself. Figure 36 shows how car owner can purchase brake pads from the brake repair shop, or from some other source (being independent from a relationship with the brake repair shop). The self-purchase of brakes is an example of product disintermediation. The do-it-yourself brake repair is an example of service disintermediation.

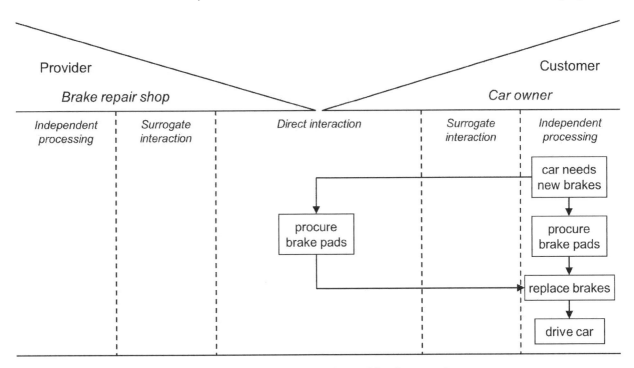

Figure 36: Disintermediated brake repair

In summary, service disintermediation means that customers are reducing or eliminating the amount of interaction with a provider that is required to meet their needs. It is motivated and enabled by customers attaining sufficient knowledge that they can perform process steps themselves with less reliance on specialized providers.

Customers typically like service disintermediation and it is usually their conscious choice. Customers realize they can get potentially higher quality at usually a lower price (both in variable monetary costs and in convenience) if they can figure out how to do it themselves. Examples are numerous:

- Customers are renting carpet cleaning equipment rather than hiring a carpet cleaning service.
- Customers are buying teeth whitening kits rather than visiting a dentist for teeth whitening.
- Customer firms are installing and configuring their own IBM computers rather than having IBM technicians install the computers.
- Customers are watching movies in their home theaters rather than visiting specialized movie theaters.
- The list goes on.

Interactive service processes are different from independent manufacturing process in many ways, not the least of which is economies of scale (see Chapter 5). That actually means that it is quite unlikely that customers will disintermediate providers whose value proposition largely comes from independent processing, such as mass-production manufacturers.

Customers, be they firms or consumers, seldom produce any mass-produced items for their own needs. The demonstrative examples are ubiquitous:

- How many law firms make their own paper?
- How many hospitals make their own wheelchairs?
- How many plumbers make their own tools?
- How many restaurants grow their own tomatoes?

This last example is an interesting one. I actually grow my own tomatoes, as do some of my neighbors. We call them "ten dollar tomatoes" because we are sure that if we tallied up the cost of plants, equipment, watering, and our weeding effort we would probably find that each tomato we harvest costs us about ten dollars. The great irony is that our harvest occurs just at the moment when local farmers are harvesting their mass-produced tomatoes, meaning that the price is the lowest of the year and the store-bought tomatoes are the freshest. We obviously don't do this for present economic reasons, but enjoy connecting with the soil and want a degree of perceived self-reliance.

But pretty much everything else that is mass-produced I leave to specialized providers.

Interactive service processes are different. Very different. Since customers are suppliers to the service providers they usually have the practical option of disintermediating the service provider and serving themselves.

Service providers hate being disintermediated, especially since customers can be formidable competitors. This concept is summarized in my previous book (Sampson 2001, p. 202):

> "With services, often the chief competitor is the customers who can provide the service themselves. Customers' typically have competitive advantage in controlling their inputs and providing maximum personalization (they get it exactly how they want it). Self-serving customers have fixed cost disadvantages due to low economies of scale, and quality disadvantages due to lack of specialization. They can have a variable cost advantage or disadvantages depending largely on the value of their time."

You can see that other book for more information about effectively dealing with customer competition. Customers acting as competitors is the basis for service disintermediation, which is an element of deservitization.

Impacts of deservitization

Recall that service commoditization and service disintermediation are parallel phenomena, and often (if not usually) occur together. They are both the result of learning, either on the part of specialized providers or on the part of customers. Both contribute to deservitization, which was defined above as reducing the level of service provided by a specialized provider, which implies reducing the amount of interaction in the process chain connecting the two entities. Figure 37 depicts these two effects of deservitization.

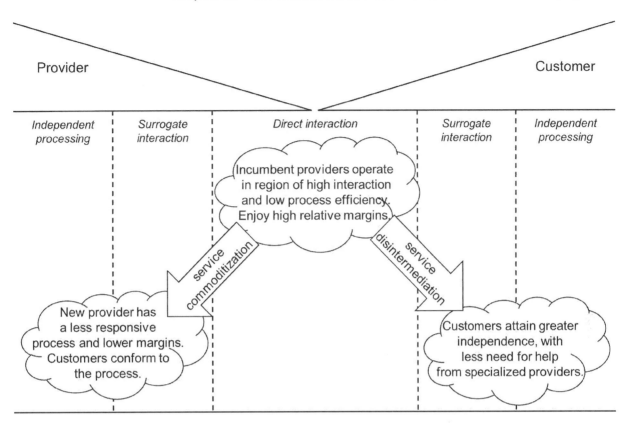

Figure 37: Two forces of deservitization

As suggested at the start of this chapter, deservitization is disrupting many service industries[21]. Travel agencies have deservitized from the agent-based processes of Thomas Cook, PLC, to the surrogate interactive alternative of Travelocity and the information-based alternative of TripAdvisor. Airlines with the interpersonal touch of British Airlines have struggled while the low-service alternatives like Ryanair have prospered. Interactive video rental firms like Blockbuster gave way to Redbox's interaction with a kiosk and Netflix's interaction with your mailbox, and now interaction with your video-streaming device (see Chapter 19). In auto insurance, interacting with your "good neighbor" State Farm agent has shifted to interacting with the Geico website (or remote call center). Instead of interacting with a friendly bookworm at Borders Books, people interact with the Amazon.com website to order books by mail, and now interacting with the Amazon e-book store or Kindle e-book reader. The list could go on and on.

At this point I feel compelled to insert some metaphysical theory. The two forces of deservitization are based on the idea that, over time, providers and customers are learning and becoming more knowledgeable and skilled. If that is the case, then the theory is that, in the

---

[21] Elsewhere, I have decried the use of the phrase "service industries" since, technically, a service is a type of process, and all industries possess both service elements and non-service elements (Sampson and Froehle 2006). In this instance, when I say "service industries" what I mean is "industries that are replete with interactive service processes."

absence of a counter force, deservitization will always increase[22]. This means that over time we will expect to see fewer and fewer interactive processes (between specialized providers and customers).

This theory is actually counter to what business schools have sometimes taught in the past. Not long ago there were a number of management "gurus" who held up the highly interactive service providers as the models for the future – Nordstrom in retailing, Ritz-Carlton in hotels, Singapore Airlines in passenger travel, and so forth. Those "full-service" (i.e. intensely interactive) companies are cool to study, but have been eclipsed by the deservitized providers in their respective industries.

Less we become depressed with the deservitization of industries, we should recognize that less interaction with specialized providers allows for greater time resources to spend interacting with friends and family. My theory is that in the future we will have less interaction with service providers in which the interaction is simply a means to meeting some other need, and have more potential opportunities for interaction with people with whom the interaction is a need-filling end unto itself, such as family and friends.

This does not detract from the fact that specialized service providers with competencies in interactive processes and accustomed to the high margins that interactive processes have provided in the past should be worried about deservitization. The remainder of this chapter will review strategic actions that can be taken to counter deservitization.

Servitization

I must admit that I made up the term "deservitization," but it is based on a word that has become popular in research literature: servitization[23]. Servitization typically describes firms that primarily operate in regions of independent processing, i.e. manufacturers, and find that their margins on manufactured products are squeezed (due to things like commoditization as well as competition by low cost labor regions of the world), so therefore attempt to extend their operations into interactive regions (services) in order to gain new revenue sources and perhaps improve margins (and profitability). In other words, servitization is a form of "forward integration," meaning that firms that produce things for customers move forward in the supply chain to more interact with customers in the use of those products.

Here is an example. For many decades, IBM was the premier designer and manufacturer of computer hardware and software. They had great margins on these products, even to the point that they could have their salespeople and systems engineers help customers figure out what system configuration they needed for free. If you are selling a bank a computer

---

[22] At one point when I was giving a research seminar on this topic an esteemed marketing professor raised his hand to argue that my underlying premise was flawed – that in his assessment consumers are not becoming more knowledgeable over time. Perhaps there is anecdotal evidence that consumers may be becoming stupider over time, such as the proliferation of Men in Black movies and Angry Birds collectibles.

[23] Since British researchers have led many of the discussions of servitization, it should probably be spelled "servitisation," which is how they spell it.

system for $10,000,000, it is no big deal if it takes a salesperson six months working with a customer to close the deal.

Then something unfortunate (to IBM) happened. Computer technology advanced to the point where new and less experienced firms could make comparable hardware (even to the point of being "IBM Compatible") at a much lower cost. In other words, the hardware commoditized. Things were even worse in software. Communities of users started producing "open source" software that did things similar to IBM software (such as manage huge databases) but not requiring payment for use.

Around the turn of the century IBM was in a horrible situation[24]. Their hardware and software margins were being squeezed on one side by low-cost hardware manufacturers and on another side by low-cost open-source software. Not one to take a beating without a fight, IBM made some bold moves, largely into services.

In 2002, IBM purchased the management and information technology (IT) consulting arm of PricewaterhouseCoopers (PwC), which they rebranded as IBM Global Services (IGS). IGS became a massive IT consulting operation, soon accounting for the majority of IBMs revenues. I must commend Sam Palmisano (then President of IBM) for his insight in purchasing the consulting services division rather than attempting to build it on his own. Why this was brilliant will be explained below.

Unfortunately, public financial documents reveal that while expanding into services helped revenue, it proved to be a drag on profitability. For some reason (also discussed below), the IGS division had much lower profit margins than the hardware and software divisions were producing. Servitization indeed is a mixed bag.

The perils of servitization

Things actually could have been much worse for servitization at IBM. Attempts at servitization can contribute to decline and demise of firms. Andy Neely, a professor at Cambridge University, published a report of a study that involved analyzing the strategic positioning of 10,028 firms based in 25 different countries (Neely 2008). He studied the reported positioning of firms over a period of a few years, and found that some firms moved into services (servitized) and other firms moved out of services (deservitized), with other firms keeping the same positioning over the study period. Some interesting findings include the following:

1. Servitization was quite a common trend. An amazing 30% of the firms classified as manufacturing had servitized over the study period.

2. Servitization often correlated with financial trouble. Manufacturing firms that servitized were 2.6 times as likely to have gone bankrupt as those that had not servitized.

3. Servitization correlates with profitability problems. He reported that, "while servitized firms generate higher revenues they tend to generate lower net profits as a percent of revenues than pure manufacturing firms."

---

[24] I tried to get precise dates on the IBM crisis, but the Wikipedia page on IBM seemed to be tremendously doctored and reads like a company sales pitch.

Servitization is clearly no panacea. PCN Analysis gives us some clues as to why this is the case. First, servitization means moving from regions of higher efficiency to regions of lower efficiency (see Chapter 5). It should not come as any surprise that operating in regions of direct interaction has a much higher cost structure than operating in regions of lower interaction. The deceptive thing is assuming that revenues that can be commanded in regions of direct interaction (with all of that cool expertise and customization) should increase at an even greater rate through servitization. That is a bad assumption, since forces of commoditization and disintermediation are still at work limiting the revenue potential.

Second, just because firms have expertise in a particular industry or technology does not mean they have expertise in interactive processes. For example, General Motors (GM) knows a lot about designing and manufacturing automobiles. Mobile phones are popular, so GM thought it would be great to build mobile phones into cars and bundle it with a bunch of interactive services (branded as "OnStar"). GM was servitizing by attempting to not only manufacture cars with phones but also continue an interactive relationship with customers through OnStar. For all intents and purposes, OnStar was a boondoggle. The failure GM had in delivering OnStar was not in their competence designing a phone into a car, but in thinking that their auto-related competence in regions of independent processing would translate to auto-related competence in interactive regions of a process domain.

In fact, my belief is that success or failure of servitization has more to do with acquiring skills in interactive processing than with exploiting skills in the industry area (like automobiles). This is why I commend Sam Palmisano for purchasing PwC to form IBM Global Services, rather than redeploying the tremendously skilled IBM labor force (largely engineers of various types) to the service processes. IBM engineers were surely brilliant in understanding computer technology, but not necessarily adept at interactive processes. (I am resisting the urge to insert an engineer quip. I do have the highest regard for engineers, but more for their technical skills than their social skills ☺.)

Back to the GM OnStar example, I happened to be speaking at a manufacturing symposium in Europe a few years ago on this particular topic. I mentioned the GM OnStar example, not realizing that an executive from GM was in the audience. After my talk he asked me what GM should have done differently. I responded that I thought that when GM wanted to move into services, instead of using a manager who knows the automobile business they would have been better off hiring a manager that had expertise in managing interactive processes, such as a former manager from Marriott who may know nothing about the automobile business but knows a lot about managing interactive processes. Reiterating, success in making a servitization transition is more dependent upon interactive skills than industry skills.

A final reason why servitization is often perilous was alluded to in Chapter 1, namely that the tools for analyzing and designing effective interactive service processes are embryonic compared with the tools for analyzing and designing physical products. Physical products are designed by trained engineers who have advanced degrees in engineering and have powerful design tools at their disposal like Computer Aided Design (CAD) technologies, prototyping tools, testing tools, and so forth. Designing interactive service processes has been highly unscientific, at least until now.

Servitization is both attractive and risky. The good news is that if your firm can pull it off, it can provide a significant competitive advantage. In Chapter 18 I will review a prominent example of a firm that successfully servitized and gained significant strategic advantage (and an astronomical stock price). We conclude this chapter by mentioning how subsequent chapters will address the deservitization dilemma.

Other ways of countering deservitization

Earlier in this chapter I theorized that, "in the absence of a counter force, deservitization will always increase." One of the best counter forces is to increase the skills and knowledge contained in an offering through innovation. When innovation is coupled with patent protection, the potential for delaying commoditization and service disintermediation is heightened. Systematic approaches for developing service innovation will be discussed in Chapter 12. Also, the strategic action of forming a Service Value Network can be an effective strategic response, and will be covered in Chapter 13.

PCN Analysis summary

This chapter recognizes the dynamic nature of strategic process positioning, recognizing that an optimal process design under one market condition might be inappropriate under subsequent market conditions. PCN Analysis includes identifying where process positioning has been in your industry and where it is going or could be going. We recognize that industries evolve both by the increased knowledge of providers and the increased learning of customer segments. As customers become more knowledgeable they tend to become less dependent upon specialized service providers, assuming the customers are not otherwise dependent upon the economies of scale that specialized providers have. Interactive service processes rarely have the economies of scale that independent manufacturing processes possess, implying that interactive service processes are especially susceptible to disintermediation and deservitization.

Another aspect of PCN Analysis is identifying how a firm can respond to industry changes that influence strategic process positioning. Incumbent firms with processes in the region of direct interaction may find themselves at a process disadvantage to firms designed more around surrogate interaction. For example, interactive retailers like CompUSA and Nordstrom may be at a disadvantage to retailers like Costco and Amazon.com that depend more on surrogate interaction. Identifying the best strategic process positioning should depend more on market needs than the firms' competencies.

Chapter 12 – Systematic Service Innovation

Up until now we have talked about using process positioning and customer roles as levers in designing interactive service processes. The decisions have surrounded increasing or decreasing the customer's co-productive roles in order to attain an optimal combination of operating characteristics.

A particularly beneficial application of this is coming up with process innovation ideas. I am afraid that sometimes service innovation is treated as an unconstrained think-outside-the-box brainstorming activity with few principles to guide the thought process. I am always surprised at the number of innovations that I hear were discovered quite by accident. Like the engineer who worked for Raytheon who was working on a military radar device and found that the candy bar in his pocket melted when he stood in front of the radar emitter—leading to the development of the microwave oven (and possibly to brain damage for that engineer).

It is better when innovation-seekers have structure methodologies for identifying innovation opportunities. Metaphorically, petroleum companies searching for oil have methods for identifying regions of the earth with a higher probability of containing extractable oil. These methods are at a much lower cost and effort than just drilling a bunch of holes hoping for a gusher. Likewise, service designers should have methods for identifying particularly promising process design alternatives before trying them out.

Preparing for innovation

The systematic approach to service innovation that we will discuss here may seem elementary, but it works. We begin by identifying fundamental process chain elements that are necessary to deliver a desired offering. This includes identifying steps that would be included in a basic PCN Diagram. As an illustration, let us return to the pizza example that was discussed in prior chapters, where we have seen at least three different process design options for pizza:

- Figure 8 shows the process design for a sit-down pizza restaurant.
- Figure 26 shows the process design for take-out pizza.
- Figure 31 shows the process design for "take-and-bake" pizza.

These are three different offerings with three different value propositions. For specific customer segments, each has been shown to be quite successful. However, there are many other potential process configuration options, each providing different value propositions. The next step of structured process innovation is to enumerate other process configuration options.

For simplicity in this discussion, we will consider just two steps of the pizza process: assembling the pizza and cooking the pizza. Figure 38 shows five different process configuration options for each of those two steps.

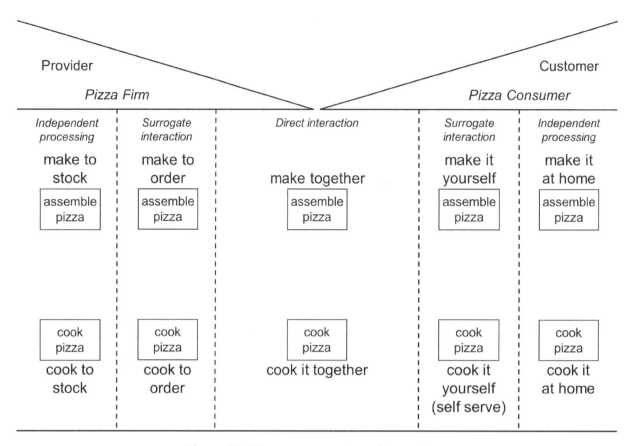

Figure 38: Pizza process step alternatives

The pizza could be "made-to-stock" meaning the pizza firm makes the pizza without any interaction with customers or information from customers. Make-to-order pizza is assembled in the back office according to specifications provided by the customer. "Make together" means the customer and the provider's employee interact to accomplish the process step. "Make it yourself" has the customer assembling the pizza, in this case by using resources owned by the provider. The right-most pizza assembly option is for the customer to make it at home using resources the customer previously acquired.

Figure 38 also shows process positioning options for the cook pizza step. Considering just these two steps, how many design configurations could be created? There are five options for assembling pizza and five alternatives for cooking pizza, suggesting that there may be as many as 5x5=25 configuration alternatives.

For example, Figure 39 shows two configurations. Configuration (1) has the provider assembling the pizza to order and cooking it to order, which is the configuration used in the sit-down restaurant (Figure 8) and the take-out pizza operation (Figure 26). That configuration provides a reasonable degree of customization–such as allowing the customer to select pizza options from a menu with personal tweaks like "hold the anchovies." There may be less customization in the cooking, other than differences for think or thick crusts.

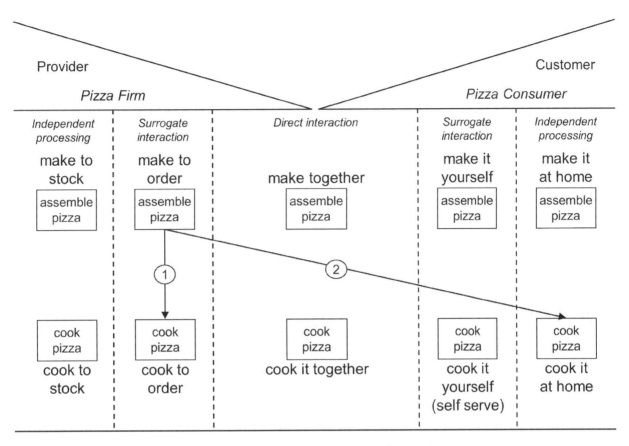

Figure 39: Two pizza process configurations

Configuration (2) is the take-and-bake pizza process as illustrated in Figure 31. This configuration allows the customer to have more customization about when and how to cook the pizza. The customer can cook the pizza at his or her convenience. The customer can cook the pizza in an oven, on a grill, or over the coals of a campfire. The pizza can be cooked lightly or, like I often do, charred to produce a hearty amount of carbon. This cooking alternative provides the customer with more control over the cooking process, but supposes that the customer has sufficient knowledge, skills, and equipment to complete the step.

There are even more possible configurations, four of which are depicted in Figure 40. Configuration (3) has the pizza assembled and cooked with no input from customers, as exemplified by the Little Caesar's Hot-n'-Ready pizza, which at this writing sells for an amazing $5 for a large pepperoni pizza—emphasizing the economy of scale and corresponding cost benefit associated with independent production. Configuration (4) demonstrates a highly interactive option comparable to the Subway Sandwich® mode of operation. (If you have not tried the custom pizza at Subway you should, it is great—and interactive!)

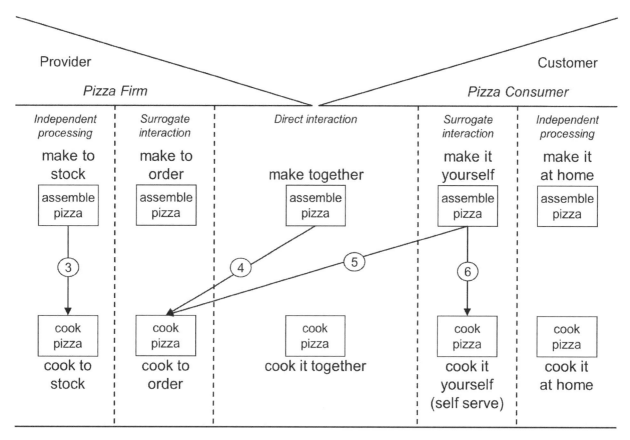

Figure 40: More pizza process configurations

Configuration (5) is akin to a Mongolian barbeque, which gives customers the option of assembling their food from a bar of components, and then having it cooked by trained employees. (Allowing customers to cook their own food on the provider's hot grill is probably an injury lawsuit waiting to happen.) In my estimation, configuration (5) is superior to configuration (4) when customers are picky eaters, as my six children have sometimes proven to be. It is nice to let the kids pick their own toppings, reducing their propensity to whine, even though they may favor items with less healthful attributes.

I have not seen configuration (6) in any pizza offering, but have experienced it at a Shabu Shabu restaurant in Tokyo. Shabu Shabu is a delightful Japanese food that involves a small cauldron of hot water (over a gas burner) for each customer, and trays of vegetables, spices, and thinly sliced meats. This configuration is in the customer's process domain, implying tremendous opportunity for customization but also assuming the required process competency is sufficiently accessible to target customers.

(My experience in Tokyo demonstrates that I was perhaps not in their target customer segment. When the speak-no-English server staff realized that I did not know what I was doing, they brought me an instruction card translated into English. I still did not know how to use the various spices, so after another period of my floundering, a Japanese waiter sensed my frustration so took charge of my cauldron and completed the assembly and cooking of my food.

It was late in the afternoon with few other customers in the restaurant—at other times it may have been impractical for the waiter to shift these process steps to the restaurant's process domain.)

But there are even more process configuration options! (Sorry for sounding like a Ginzu knife infomercial.) Figure 41 shows a couple of additional pizza process configurations. Configuration (7) is the staple of poor college students: pizza from the grocer's freezer, such as the ever popular DiGiorno or Red Barron brands. These frozen pizzas are produced through the epitome of mass production, with unbelievable economies of scale.

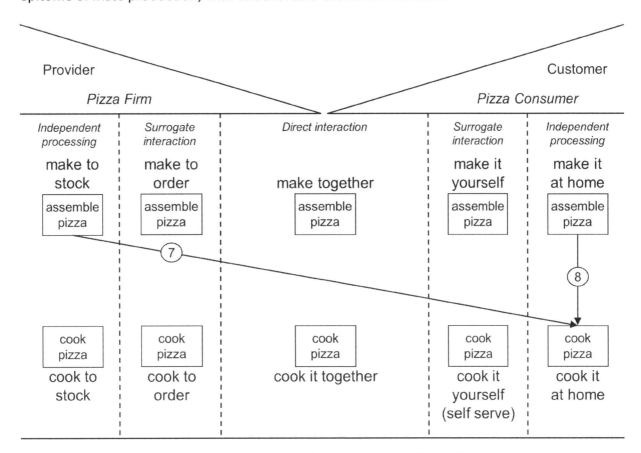

Figure 41: Even more pizza process configurations

Configuration (8) ensures provider efficiency by requiring the customers to assemble their own pizzas. In this case, the provider may sell pizza kits that contain typical components and assembly instructions. The Papa Murphy's pizza chain recently introduced "Mini-Murph" pizza kits targeted at kids. (Perhaps again recognizing that there are benefits to allowing sometimes-picky kids to control the composition of their food, and have fun in the process.)

According the process positioning principles from Chapter 5, configurations (7) is superior to configuration (8) in terms of economies of scale, but (8) is superior in customization. Having both operating characteristics in the same offering could be a tremendous innovation. But how could we accomplish that?

Finding innovation

Not long ago I was teaching PCN Analysis to students in my undergraduate Service Management course. Three of the students—Ryan Carnell, Rachel Su'a, and Clarke Holdaway—chose pizza restaurants as their course analysis project. After reviewing an incumbent process configuration they presented a form of the innovative process depicted in Figure 42.

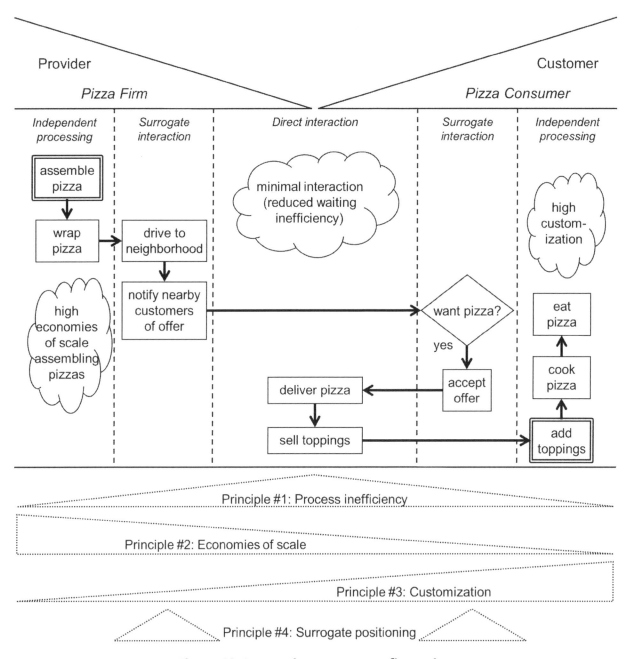

Figure 42: Innovative process configuration

The idea was that the pizza provider would assemble the basis of pizzas in a centralized location with common sets of toppings or no toppings at all. They would wrap the pizzas to keep them fresh for delivery. The firm, which already owned delivery vans, would then drive stacks of pizzas to select neighborhoods in the surrounding communities. A smartphone application controlled by the driver would notify the smartphones of subscribing customers in close proximity to the truck (or to where the truck was going), announcing "a fresh pizza is two minutes away! Do you want it?" The subscriber could tap a pizza-shaped onscreen button on their smartphone signaling their interest in the pizza.

Within minutes the driver would arrive at the customer's door, delivering the pizza and selling small packages of toppings.[25] The customer would then add toppings as desired, cook the pizza, and then eat. Brilliant!

Good innovation is not unconstrained brainstorming

I must point out that I penalize students who treat innovation as random thinking-outside-the-box brainstorming. Students that turn in work with that type of brainstorming get low grades, and if they complain I respond "it is not clear what you got out of my course, since you could do that type of random brainstorming without anything you would learn from the course!" I require that my students study structured innovation based on sound process design principles such as those covered in this book.

In fact, Ryan, Rachel, and Clarke got a good grade for their pizza process analysis project. Figure 42 highlights some of the astute application of process design principles. The assemble pizza step was moved to independent processing, providing high economies of scale and allowing for use of high quality ingredients and a reasonable cost. The team reduced interactive processing steps, which reduced inefficiency and accompanying customer waiting. This configuration brilliantly infuses the potential for impulse purchasing into a fresh pizza delivery process, since customers can order a pizza and receive it in mere minutes. The van drives to select neighborhoods without waiting for the customer to call.

The process allows high customization where it matters most—in when and where customers eat. The team originally was going to assemble a common assortment of pizzas through independent processing, but during their project presentation it became obvious that splitting the add-toppings step from the assembly step would allow toppings (the primary element of product customization) to be added in the customers process domain—providing maximal customization!

PCN Analysis summary

In seeking service process innovations, this chapter discounted unconstrained brainstorming in favor of principle-guided innovation that includes:

---

[25] The small bags of toppings part was my idea, in case it detracts from the other parts of this brilliant innovation. The other thing that struck me about this innovative process design is the potential for analyzing the habits of customers in different neighborhoods. For example, if a dorm room of colleges students tends to order combination pizzas on Friday afternoons, the van could plan a run to that location on Fridays.

1. Identifying the fundamental steps required to provide a given offering.
2. Identifying incumbent process configurations, including feasible alternatives exhibited in related (or even unrelated) business.
3. Considering the value effect (costs and benefits) of various configuration alternatives (as discussed in prior chapters).
4. Coming up with a configuration that achieves appropriate operating characteristics at various segments of the process chain. (Again, see the principles from Chapter 5.)

This approach to innovation requires first gaining a solid understanding of the principles of PCN Analysis as covered in earlier chapters of this book. PCN Analysis also provides a foundation for identifying process innovations by helping you visualize and understand your processes, competitors processes, and related customer processes, so that you can explore how innovative process changes might impact the value proposition.

Chapter 13 – Building a Service Value Network

Although we often study service operations in terms of interactions between dyads of entities—such as a provider and a customer—we must not forget that service operations are always part of networks of entities, or what Chapter 2 called Service Supply Chains. Chapter 10 mentioned that Richard Normann calls them "value constellations" (2001; 1993). I prefer to call them "Service Value Networks," implying that they are networks of entities that are configured to interact in a way to provide mutual value.

Getting beyond the dyad

The first step in managing a Service Value Network is to understand the network. This includes understanding the participants in the network and understanding their roles in the process. It also includes understanding where value potential is formed and where value is realized.

For example, Figure 43 shows a PCN Diagram for an industrial linen service that provides bed sheets, towels, and tablecloths to client hotels. The linen firm actually owns the linens and leases them to client hotels. The firm has route drivers that visit each client hotel on a set cycle to retrieve soiled linens and take the order for the subsequent linen delivery.

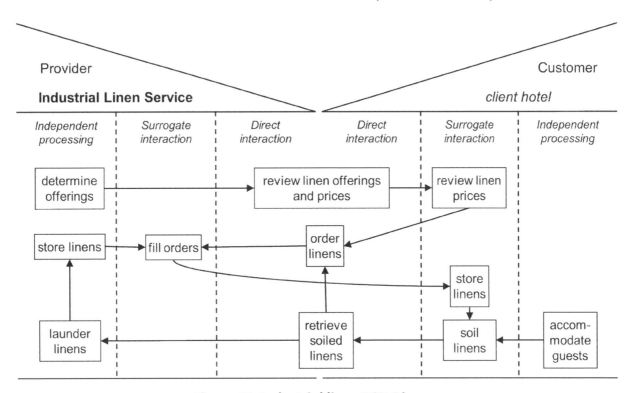

Figure 43: Industrial linen PCN Diagram

One problem that this linen firm encountered (it is an actual firm) was that the client hotels were sporadic in their use, storage, and ordering of linens. It was estimated that some clients had as much as nine months of inventory of linens even though the route drivers visited each client hotel on at least a monthly basis. Another problem is that the linen firm charged according to how much clean linen was delivered, but had no practical way of identifying if the same amount of linen was subsequently returned.

In searching for a solution to these problems, it must be recognized that the client hotel's demand for linens is directly related to hotel guests' demand for the hotel. In other words, there is some benefit in considering the interactive process between guests and the hotel.

Figure 44 shows a PCN Diagram for interaction that takes place between a resort hotel and a guest. Admittedly, it is a simplified example for illustration purposes. The guest identifies a travel need and books a hotel room. At a later time the guest arrives at the hotel. (The dashed line between booking the hotel and arriving at the hotel signifies a loose temporal relationship.) The guest checks in at the hotel then goes to his or her room. This is a beachfront hotel, so the guest grabs a towel out of the bathroom and goes to the beach. The towel is sandy, so the guest leaves it on the beach before going to the room to shower. The hotel subsequently replaces the towel in the room and eventually orders more towels.

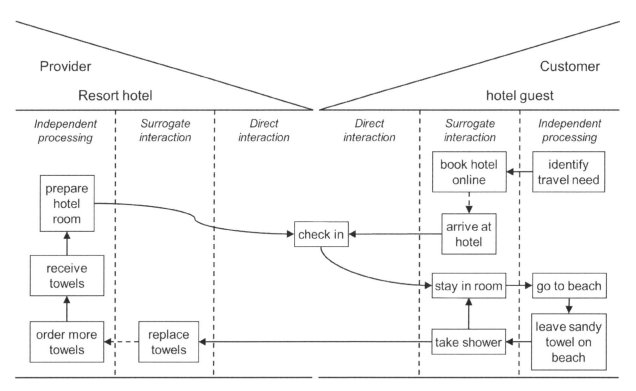

Figure 44: Resort hotel PCN Diagram

Figure 44 reveals at least two important issues. First, the hotel has booking information some time in advance. That booking information will correlate with demand for towels. If the linen firm had access to that demand information, the linen firm could potentially take over the hotel's responsibility for ordering linens – a relieving innovation. Or, the linen firm could provide the hotel with a tool that would help them plan their linen orders according to future room bookings and current inventory of linens – an enabling innovation.

Second, in this study we actually observed that hotel guests were using towels in a way that the linen firm did not intend them to be used – as beach towels. This resulted in damaged or lost towels. Further, the white bath towels were not as large as a typical beach towel, meaning that the guests' experience on the beach was not as good as it might have been.

A possible response to this beach issue is for the linen firm to provide client hotels with a set of larger beach towels that could be checked out to guests at the hotel front desk. Requiring guests to check out and return the beach towels to the front desk would reduce the incident of towels being left on the beach. The hotel could offer this as an additional guest perk, or they could charge each guest a small rental fee.

This simple example was meant to demonstrate the importance and value of considering the types of interactions in which entities are involved in a Service Value Network. Often the reason we have interaction between entities at one part of a network is to facilitate value realization (meeting of needs) at some other part of the network.

Figure 45 shows a PCN Diagram that includes the three entities from the prior two figures, as well as a linen manufacturer. The linen manufacturer may be involved in providing the beach towel offering. Alternatively, the linen firm may contract with a different linen firm to provide the beach towels, one that is more capable of dealing with colored linens.

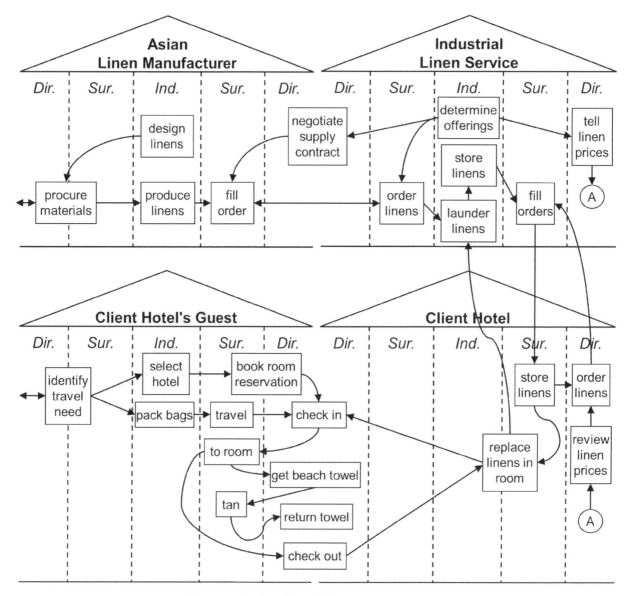

Figure 45: Combined linen PCN Diagram

Establish a Service Value Network

A central idea behind Service Value Networks is that they involve multiple entities. In other words, establishing a Service Value Network does not imply that the focal firm expands their operations to meet broader aspects of customer needs. Instead, it is more practical to establish a Service Value Network by engaging the competencies of other entities and providing them to customers as a beautifully integrated offering.

In fact, the firm that establishes a Service Value Network may not even provide any component competencies to the value proposition, but may instead have competencies in integrating the competencies of other firms. This is what Richard Normann called becoming a

"Prime Mover" (2001, pp. 26-36). Process chain integration skills are actually quite rare, and the firm that is able to use them can have great competitive advantage and make good money.

An example of a Prime Mover in the vacation travel industry is GetAwayToday.com. In Chapter 11 we discussed how traditional travel agencies have been subjected to deservitization, with interactive agencies being supplanted by less-interactive alternatives. A travel agency that has effectively overcome this problem is GetAwayToday, based in Ogden, Utah.

GetAwayToday specialized in family vacation travel, mostly to southern California. They have tightly orchestrated partnerships with hotels, transit companies, food and entertainment providers, and of course Disneyland. The vacation packages they provide are amazingly seamless experiences.

When I contact GetAwayToday either via their website or over the phone, they handle all of the major features of my travel. I often book my own flights, since I may be using frequent flier miles. GetAwayToday will arrange flights and rental cars. Actually, GetAwayToday contracts with a company called WTTE Travel that provides client branded travel services. Learning about WTTE took some careful investigations, but most customers would have no idea that the flight and rental car bookings services were provided by an entity other than GetAwayToday.

GetAwayToday is the Prime Mover in a tightly orchestrated Service Value Network, as depicted in Figure 46. The vacationer is presented with a unified value proposition. Everything fits. Not only am I instructed in everything I need to know about my booked vacation, but the service providers in southern California seem to know everything about my needs. One hotel used on a recent GetAwayToday vacation actually had a large sign in the lobby welcoming GetAwayToday customers, and they always know exactly what I have purchased, such as included parking, breakfasts, and park shuttles. This is quite amazing, given the vast array of hotels that are part of GetAwayToday's Service Value Network.

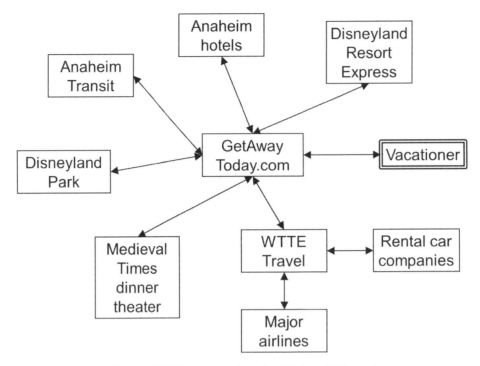

Figure 46: Vacation Service Value Network

Besides coordinating all of this interaction between vacationers and various service providers, GetAwayToday delivers another important Prime Mover function – to monitor the Service Value Network and make adjustments as necessary. This is exemplified by the phone call I received the first day into my recent family vacation. I was walking through Disneyland when my mobile phone rang. It was a GetAwayToday employee calling to make sure everything was going okay with my vacation thus far. All I could report was slight variations in the weather, which the employee could not do much about. I suspected this is more than a typical "courtesy call," but is actually a data gathering mechanism for monitoring and maintaining a relatively complex Service Value Network.

Selling a product versus selling a network

Chapter 4 discussed the relationship between value potential and value realization. Manufactured products have value potential, but that is only real if it leads to value realization, which is dependent on processes of use. The processes of use are usually in the customer's process domain. However, the use of manufactured products often requires competencies that are outside of the customer's process domain, or at least outside of the customer's area of interest. Customers may need to access a network of service providers in order to realize the value of a product.

For example, the value of an automobile is in meeting transportation needs, but that requires fuel replenishment, periodic maintenance, requisite insurance, and occasional cleaning. Most automobile owners rely on gas stations for fuel replenishment, auto repair shops for periodic maintenance, insurance companies for requisite insurance, and car washes for occasional cleaning. As Chapter 11 pointed out, customers can do many of these things for themselves, but often favor using specialized providers.

Companies that sell manufactured products can gain strategic opportunity by linking customers to service providers that meet related product needs. One way to do this is through servitization, which Chapter 11 pointed out can be perilous. An alternative is to establish a Service Value Network around the products, which means acting as a Prime Mover to coordinate partner competences into an integrated offering.

IKEA does this in a tremendous way. Chapter 5 discussed how IKEA sells furniture kits and requires the purchasers to assemble the furniture themselves. Not only that, but IKEA requires customers to pick up the furniture from the warehouse store and transport it home. Sure, IKEA's operations could be expanded to include those services, but they have chosen not to. However, IKEA provides all of those services through a Service Value Network involving other providers. IKEA has prominent signs in their stores that say "You pick it yourself but you don't have to," "You deliver it yourself but you don't have to," and "You assemble it yourself but you don't have to." In requesting these services, IKEA passes the requests onto service partners that specialize in the specific functions. The result is a seamless offering that meets a wider variety of customer needs, but without taking IKEA away from its core competencies.

An essential element of bundling a Service Value Network with manufactured products is coordinating the network so that it indeed functions as an integrated offering. A weak Service Value Network is one that is little more than a service-provider referral service. A strong Service Value Network maintains central control and responsibility of the Prime Mover throughout the customer experience. Costco provides an example.

In Chapter 11 I mentioned that I purchased a hot tub from Costco. Use of the hot tub requires at least interaction with (a) the trucking company that will deliver the hot tub, (b) an electrician who will install the wiring to the hot tub, (c) a deck contractor, who will build the deck surrounding the hot tub, (d) a pool supplies firm that will sell me chemicals for use in the hot tub, and (e) a plumber who will service the hot tub should anything go wrong.

Costco provides the delivery service and the repair service. However, Costco does not directly provide those services, but outsource them to the hot tub supplier. It is unlikely that the hot tub supplier (apparently a company called Strong Pools and Spas, Inc. based in Pennsylvania) has its own trucks, but outsources the delivery to common carriers. It is even more unlikely that the supplier employs plumbers throughout North America for repairs, but contracts with local plumbers when a warranty repair is needed.

Nevertheless, when that delivery truck shows up in my driveway, I as the customer consider myself to be dealing with Costco. If anything goes wrong with that delivery, such as unloading it on top of my lilac bush, you can bet Costco will hear from me. If I call to report a mechanical problem under warranty and the plumber shows up and only makes the problem worse, I will hold Costco responsible, even though the plumber was likely hired by the hot tub manufacturer, or by a warranty service firm.

The point is that Costco is not selling just a product—they are selling a Service Value Network that facilitates product use. The product purchase does not end my customer relationship with Costco for that item. Lesser retailers would disavow responsibility once the purchase is complete, directing customers with problems to the appropriate manufacturer. Again, Costco is not just selling products; they are selling a network that facilitates product use.

As mentioned in Chapter 11, when making the hot tub purchase decision I considered a high-priced local company, who I expect would have personally handled any subsequent problems. Of the moderately priced models from general retailers (like home improvement warehouses) I chose Costco largely because of a review I read that was written by a *dissatisfied* customer. This customer, "spauser" from San Diego, purchased the same model of hot tub and had all kinds of problems with it. After great frustration trying to resolve this with the manufacturer, spauser returned the hot tub to Costco. (Again, Costco will actually pick up delivered items that are returned from your house.) Other customer reviews were quite positive, but the spauser review showed that even in a worst-case scenario Costco would assume responsibility for the Service Value Network.

Again, I don't consider this to be as much about Costco's return policy as it is about how they effectively manage the Service Value Network. Retailers who outsource services to network partners and offer generous return policies but fail to manage the network are likely to be inundated with costly returns. You can bet that when a customer returns a hot tub to Costco, or anything else for that matter, they study ways to improve the network and avoid problem recurrence.

One thing Costco did not do for me is assist with installation. Other retailers like Home Depot and Lowe's provide installation services, or rather links to local contractors who work as branded partners. Costco provides a range of other services, such as those listed in Table 4 (from http://shop.costco.com/services/index). I do not believe that any of these Costco services are delivered by Costco employees, which would be operating in Costco's process domain. They are elements of a Service Value Network that Costco can sell individually or bundle with products.

Table 4: Costco service offerings

Consumer Services	Insurance Services	Business Services
Costco Auto Program	Auto & Home Insurance	401(k) plans
Boat & RV Loans	Personal Health Insurance	Business Phone Services
Checks & Forms	Mexico Travel Auto	Credit Card Processing
Costco Member Prescription	Insurance	Checks & Forms
Program	Business Health & Dental	Payroll Services
Identity Protection	Insurance	Electronic Health Records
High Yield Savings Account & CDs	Business Prescription	Domains, Websites &
Mortgage & Refinancing	Insurance	Online Solutions
Online Investing	Individual Dental Plan	Water Delivery
Vehicle Repair Protection		QuickBooks Online
Water Delivery		Business Stationery

Selling a network offering for competitive advantage

In 1993, Richard Normann went so far as to suggest that being a Prime Mover was the key competitive competency of the future, and forming service constellations would provide significant competitive advantage (2001; 1993). Unfortunately, he did not live to see this principle dramatically realized by companies such as eBay, Facebook, and Amazon.

eBay began as an auction website, but had really become a retailer—one that does not actually sell anything but rather facilitates transactions between buyers and sellers. A large part of eBay's business is "buy it now" which avoids auctions altogether. The magic of eBay is the efficient way it links buyers and sellers in a Service Value Network.

Facebook is a social network, but also a Service Value Network that links customers with service providers such as multiplayer game companies, genealogy experts, and photo editing services. Facebook has become the "face" of many small companies who way not have their own websites but use Facebook as their website.

Perhaps the most dramatic example of a recent Service Value Network is Amazon. Amazon began as an online book retailer, but has since moved into selling everything from A to Z. The original book business was built on the idea that an online book retailer could stock many more different books than a local brick-and-mortar retailer. However, Amazon has since learned that the number of books they could stock pales in comparison to the number of books stocked by numerous "affiliates," including mom-and-pop bookstores around the globe. Amazon handles the customer interactions and payments—the affiliates handle the fulfillment and shipping. Amazon is truly a Prime Mover.

It has been suggested that the Amazon Service Value Network involves as many as two million associates.[26] Customers who purchase items on the Amazon website are given the option of selecting which affiliate actually provides the item. These affiliates are sellers of books and about anything else under the sun. (I wanted a bag that I could use as carry-on luggage on Ryanair, which I bought from an Amazon affiliate located in the UK.)

Amazon has expanded their Service Value Network in various ways, as shown in Figure 47. Amazon sells music that comes from music providers. Amazon has recently begun offering LivingSocial-type of daily deals in specific locations. Amazon assists authors (like myself) develop books that can be distributed worldwide.

---

[26] http://amazonaffiliate.wordpress.com/2008/07/30/how-many-affiliates-are-registered-with-amazon-associates-program/

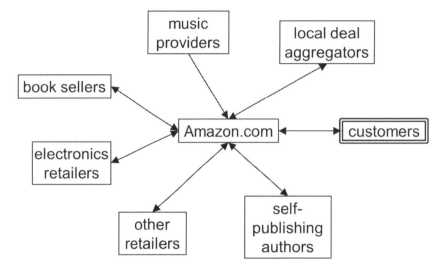

Figure 47: Amazon Service Value Network

The Amazon Service Value Network may seem like simply retail, albeit online, but it is more than that. Traditional retail sells products that come from numerous suppliers, but does not link the customers up with those suppliers in a bidirectional relationship (i.e., an service relationship). If a customer buys a bicycle from Walmart, the interactive process is purely between the customer and Walmart. On the other hand, when a customer buys a bicycle from an Amazon affiliate they fulfillment and shipping take place between the affiliate and the customer.

This is illustrated in Figure 47 by the bidirectional arrows between Amazon and affiliates. The exception is the music providers, who simply provide Amazon with music that Amazon sells—a traditional retail model. Granted, Amazon does have warehouses to stock items, but over time this will be less important as Amazon allows fulfillment to be accomplished by affiliates.

This example hopefully illustrates the competitive advantage that can come from the Prime Mover function. As you would imagine, being an effective Prime Mover is no trivial matter. Key competencies that can assist Prime Movers include understanding the processes that tie organizations with various competencies together, which is PCN Analysis[27].

PCN Analysis summary

This chapter emphasized how PCN Analysis ultimately is about studying networks of entities that share processes in order to provide value to process participants, including customers. The greatest process networks are those that provide an integrated offering, meaning that a group of related needs can be easily met by the PCN configuration, which we call a Service Value Network.

---

[27] I tell my students that I am a bit surprised at how successful Apple has been even before my book and materials about PCN Analysis have been published ☺. Seriously though, the advantage of now having PCN Analysis is that it provides a structured way of understanding process design factors that contributed to Apple's success.

Attaining an effective Service Value Network is no trivial matter, and is the work of the entity that Normann calls the Prime Mover. Being a Prime Mover requires significant skills in understanding the complexities of customer needs, the process requirements to meet those needs, the sources of competences that match those requirements, and how those sources of competencies might be integrated. These are all functions of PCN Analysis.

Chapter 14 – Using PCN Analysis Across the Organization

The purpose of PCN Analysis is to help managers in documenting, designing, analyzing, and reconfiguring processes of all types. As suggested in Chapter 1, service design is generally not relegated to the domain of an engineering department. In fact, it is best when service design involves the unique perspectives and distinctive competencies of various functional areas within organizations.

The following are ways various functions can contribute to and benefit from service design based on PCN Analysis.

PCN Analysis for Marketing Management

Marketers are concerned with how offerings will be received by target markets. For physical products that are produced and consumed in providers' and consumers' independent processing regions, marketing is a well-defined science. The potential market reception of physical products can be explored through market research studies. Customer panels and focus groups can be presented with product alternatives and asked to report on purchase intentions. Methodologies such as conjoint analysis can be used to assess the value that specific products provide in a product offering. Marketing campaigns can be devised to emphasize high-value features of products and can build the perception of product value through association. For example, I do not know if Nike shoes are any better than competing shoes, but the fact that basketball stars endorse them makes sports fans feel better with Nike shoes.

Service marketing, or the marketing of interactive service processes, is somewhat more difficult. As described in Chapter 6, service marketing tends to be experiential, implying that the marketing function is implicitly tied to the operations of the firm. Marketers for independent processing firms such as manufacturers can describe products to customers without ever setting foot in a factory floor. Service marketers cannot adequately convey interactive service processes to customers without understanding the nature of service delivery, which is facilitated by PCN Analysis.

In fact, marketers are probably the most qualified group to identify areas of customer value, as describe in Chapter 4. PCN Diagrams can help describe process alternatives to potential customers and assess customer responses to process reconfigurations—which is a service form of conjoint analysis. This may include exploring the implications of increased customer engagement, such as by moving process steps from a firm's process domain to the customer's process domain. With some basic explanation a process can be described directly with a PCN Diagram. Alternatively, the PCN Diagram can be explained in a textual scenario that potential customers would then evaluate.

PCN Analysis can also help marketers assess and plan the process configuration of their own efforts. Chapter 6 referred to Vargo' and Lusch's three approaches to marketing: (1) marketing *to* customers, (2) marketing *for* customers, and (3) marketing *with* customers. Marketing efforts that focus on mass advertising are performed in regions of independent processing, and constitute marketing *to* customers. Using so-called Customer Relationship Management Systems (CRMS) to provide customized advertising campaigns is an example of marketing *for* customers (i.e., for specific customer groups). Marketing through interpersonal interactions between "front line" employees and customers, and engaging customers in the marketing efforts, are examples of marketing *with* customers. Each approach is appropriate in different contexts, and PCN Analysis can provide clues of how best to design marketing activities.

PCN Analysis for Human Resource Management

Human Resource Management (HRM) involves "the management of an organization's workforce, or human resources. It is responsible for the attraction, selection, training, assessment, and rewarding of employees, while also overseeing organizational leadership and culture, and ensuring compliance with employment and labor laws." (Wikipedia: "Human Resource Management"). The traditional HRM focus has been primarily or exclusively on employees of the provider.

HRM is different for regions of interaction, where customers both complicate and contribute to the "human resources" available to the process. As described in Chapter 8, employee job design is less concrete in regions of direct interaction, owing to the process uncertainty that is introduced by customer involvement. That chapter described how job design and employee training for interactive service processes can be difficult and sometimes neglected, leaving individual employees to make decisions about process execution on the fly, based on their own judgment. With divergent processes this may be necessary, but with merely complex processes it is precarious. Consistent execution of directly interactive processes usually requires that providers provide significant efforts in employee training. What better basis for that training than PCN Analysis, which can be used to communicate standards of process execution and contingencies for process failures.

PCN Analysis can also help HRM professionals train employees in their specific roles in service delivery processes, and how their roles relate to customer roles. The nature of job design is very much influenced by the process region the job spans, which has implications for employee selection criteria. Also, work measurement and compensation can vary dramatically depending on the process configuration.

PCN Analysis also facilitates a more *avant garde* aspect of HRM: managing the customer workforce. For interactive service processes, customers are a key productive resource that can make or break the profitability of the firm. Chapter 8 described how training customers in their roles requires different approaches than training employees, and requires understanding what is required of customers and how customer actions fit within an overall business process. Again, PCN Analysis can be a great tool in this effort, helping focus HRM professionals on aspects and opportunities for enhancing customer roles (see Chapter 9).

PCN Analysis for Strategic Management

Strategic management "entails specifying the organization's mission, vision and objectives, developing policies and plans, often in terms of projects and programs, which are designed to achieve these objectives, and then allocating resources to implement the policies and plans, projects and programs." (Wikipedia: "strategic management") Strategic management includes identifying strengths and weaknesses of firms, and looking for suitable market opportunities and threats.

Again, much of the science of strategic management is inherently grounded in physical product companies that operate largely in regions of independent processing. Customers are considered to be the external market that consumes product offerings. However, companies that are largely engaged in interactive processes must recognize that customers are part of the production system. As such, the policies/plans/projects/programs that come from strategic management should consider customers as endogenous, or within the system.

PCN Analysis can provide great direction in strategic planning for interactive processes. The fact that firms have competencies in independent processing does not imply that they would have competencies in interactive processes, even if it is in the same industry or process chain. Chapter 11 asserted that "just because firms have expertise in a particular industry or technology does not mean they have expertise in interactive processes." Chapter 6 through Chapter 8 described how different process regions require different managerial skill sets. Informed strategic management should include discussion about the ability of a firm to operate in various process regions.

Also, much of the strategic direction of firms involved in interactive service process comes in the form of determining a process relationship with customers, which is the strategic process positioning idea outlined in Chapter 5. Strategic planners can use PCN Analysis in considering the strategic implications of various process configuration alternatives. This should not just include analysis of the firm's current or desired process positioning, but also the process positioning of alternatives (market threats).

Further, for interactive service processes strategic planning should include considering customer-driven process alternatives, which was discussed in Chapter 9 under the title "customer as competitor." Chapter 11 explained how customer competition, manifest in self-service and do-it-yourself processing, is major threat to many traditional interactive industries such as banking, retail, travel and tourism, etc. Subsequent chapters will describe how customer competition has traumatized the strategic positioning of firms from industries such as education (Chapter 15) and entertainment (Chapter 19). PCN Analysis can assist the strategic planning in those industries by describing industry trends from a process and customer value perspective, and even suggest how displaced strategies might be rectified.

PCN Analysis for Operation Management

The traditional area of Operations Management (OM) has focused on the concerns of repetitive production in regions of independent processing. Topics have included inventory management, production scheduling, and quality assurance. In recent years the focus has broadened to consider the operations of related entities under the heading of Supply Chain Management (SCM). Whereas OM is concerned with optimizing the configuration of a firm's production processes, SCM is concerned with optimizing the configuration of a related group of firms processes that each contribute to the production and distribution of products.

The less-known area of OM known as Service Operations Management (SOM) focuses on production processes involving customer interaction. Interestingly, the field of SOM has tremendous overlap with the field known as Service Marketing. This alludes to the fact that the effective management of service operations requires understanding customer behavior, which has traditionally been the domain of marketers. Since customers are participants in service processes, the effectiveness (efficiency, productivity, etc.) of service operations is dependent upon understanding and managing customer roles (see Chapter 9).

Chapter 2 pointed out that SOM is inherently a form of SCM, referring to service operations as "service supply chains." As such, SOM requires understanding the process relationship between multiple entities (at least a provider and a customer). Chapter 13 emphasized how interactive service processes span multiple entities in a Service Value Network. It is essential that operations managers involved in interactive service processes understand how the production process spans the network of entities, which can be tremendously aided by PCN Analysis.

Ideally, SOM professionals should be service system integrators, or what Chapter 13 referred to as "Prime Movers" (Normann 2001, pp. 26-36). This means they need to have a broad understanding of the firm's interactive and independent processes as well as of the related processes along the process chains with which the provider firm is involved. This requires understanding traditional operations, customer interfaces, and supply chains that extend outside of the firm. This can also mean understanding the processes of suppliers, suppliers of suppliers, and so forth. Integration requires identifying what information needs to be shared across the process chain, and how the integration should best be implemented, measured, and controlled. Again, PCN Analysis can aid this challenging effort.

PCN Analysis summary

Although PCN Analysis has been introduced as a tool for service design, in fact the value of PCN Analysis can and should permeate organizations, especially those that are heavily involved in interactive service processes. Various functional areas within organizations can benefit from increased understanding of current and potential process configurations. PCN Diagrams are an effective way of formalizing and communicating process configuration alternatives. The analysis includes understanding how management differs depending upon the particular process configuration.

I personally believe that PCN Analysis is within the comprehension reach of most managers, even those who are less familiar with a process or network perspective. Although PCN Analysis is non-trivial, my experience with training and applying PCN Analysis to diverse audiences show that it reveals useful insights with relatively little effort. Increased effort can provide increasingly powerful insights. The subsequent case study chapters will show examples of insights in common industries.

Chapter 15 – Higher Education case study

Higher education in the U.S. has expanded tremendously in recent years, largely due to growth in distance learning and for-profit institutions. For example, between 2005 and 2010 the number of public and private non-profit institutions of higher learning declined by 2 percent, yet the number of for-profit institutions increased by 34 percent[28]. In 2005, 899,869 students enrolled in for-profit schools, which more than doubled to 1,893,712 in 2010.

This growth represents a fundamental shift in the way higher education is delivered. Many for-profit schools and traditional universities now deliver education through online distance learning. The explosive growth in online learning is a classic illustration of the deservitization effect discussed in Chapter 11.

Even the successful for-profit schools are feeling the pressure. One of the biggest, the University of Phoenix, announced in October of 2012 that they would be closing just over half of their physical classroom locations, shifting the students to online programs[29]. The closures were part of a company plan to "re-engineer business processes and refine its delivery structure"[30] (which is a fancy way to describe deservitization).

In this chapter we will review the deservitization of higher education and show how it can provide a superior value proposition to certain customer segments. Indeed, some authors have suggested that higher educations is on the verge of a major disruption, with traditional institutions that have costly labor and costly interactions being supplanted by more efficient education providers that use technology to delivery education in a way that is more customized using surrogate interaction. This is supported by a major 2010 U.S. Department of Education study that found that "Students in online conditions performed modestly better, on average, than those learning the same material through traditional face-to-face instruction."[31]

For face-to-face instructors (like me) who find this education deservitization trend alarming, I will finish of this chapter by showing how traditional education providers can stave off the deservitization by changing their offering.

Traditional Higher Education

Traditional higher education comes in many forms, from individualized laboratory training at one end of the spectrum to large-lecture courses on the other. Universities under

---

[28] Jaschik, Scott, The Growth of For-Profits, *Inside Higher Ed*, January 18, 2011, http://www.insidehighered.com.

[29] Prior, Anna, University of Phoenix Closing 115 Locations, *The Wall Street Journal*, October 18, 2012, p. B7.

[30] Apollo Group, Inc. Reports Fiscal 2012 Fourth Quarter and Year-End Results, *BusinessWire*, October 16, 2012, retrieved from http://www.fool.com/investing/businesswire/2012/10/16/apollo-group-inc-reports-fiscal-2012-fourth-quarte.aspx.

[31] Evaluation of Evidence-Based Practices in Online Learning, U.S. Department of Education Office of Planning, Evaluation, and Policy Development, September 2010, p. xiv.

budget constraints often resort to large-lecture courses to improve efficiency of instruction. Figure 48 depicts the process of a typical lecture course. The provider is the university, or more specifically the university professor. The customer is the student (although I prefer to think of my students as the product and the recruiters as the customer).

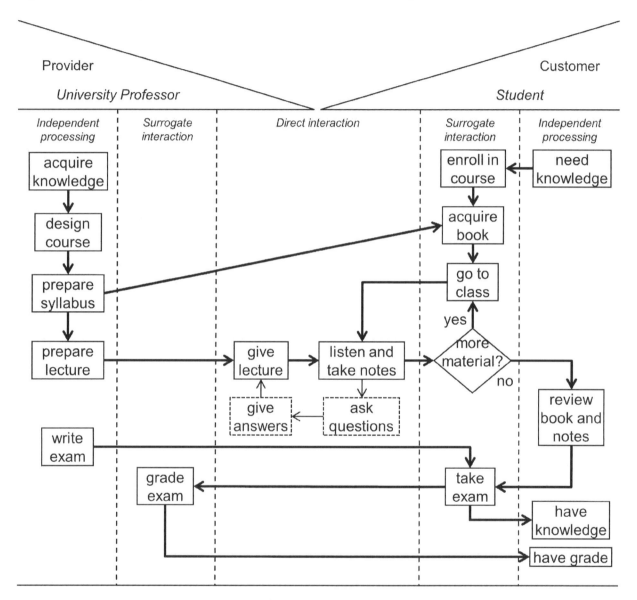

Figure 48: Traditional lecture course process

In this case, the professor is employed by the university as a topical expert. He or she acquires knowledge through years of study, designs courses, prepares syllabi that describe the course design to students, and prepares lectures.

The student, needing knowledge, enrolls in the course, acquires the course book (listed on the syllabus), and goes to class. In a lecture-pedagogy the student primarily listens and takes notes while the professor gives the lecture. If the class size allows, the students may ask questions for clarification, and the instructor gives answers. In large-lecture classes involving hundreds of students in-class questioning may not be practical; some classes provide recitation sessions staffed by Teaching Assistants who can answer questions.

At the end of the semester, or at junctures during the semester, the students review the book readings and class notes in preparation for an exam. The ultimate result is that the student has knowledge and gets a grade that counts towards graduation.

The process depicted in Figure 48 has a certain amount of inefficiency due to the requirement for the professor and the student to co-locate during class sessions. If the class size is so large that it precludes in-class questions, there could be great benefit by recording the lectures and allowing the students to listen to the lectures at a desired time and place.

This is in fact what a world-class instructor, Norm Nemrow, put to practice some years ago. Norm taught a very popular and engaging Introduction to Accounting course at BYU. He taught the course is a lecture hall that seated 844 students, and was able to keep the students attention and interest in what some may consider a not-so-exciting topic.

But Norm knew he was not going to be around forever, so he obtained a media development grant and developed a set of video CDs that covered his course topics. When played on a computer, the CD material has a window that shows Norm lecturing on the topic and another window showing example problems or other illustrations.

It was discovered that students loved the Norm Nemrow CD as an alternate way for covering course material. In particular, the students could play the lectures at double speed if they wanted to (or half speed for that matter) and could rewind and review lectures as many times as they wanted. The CDs also provided assessments of learning and a glossary of terms.

The process for this Norm Nemrow course is roughly depicted in Figure 49. Although Norm retired from BYU in 2011, he lives on in students' lives through the accounting CD. Further, the CD set is marketed to universities around the world, and reportedly has a broad following.

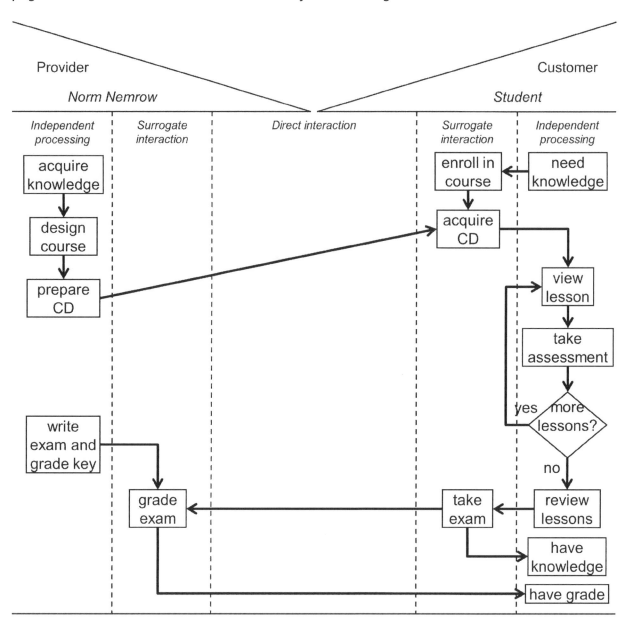

Figure 49: Media-based course process

The process of Figure 49 is superior to the process of Figure 48 in terms of both efficiency and customization. Moving the viewing of the lecture into the surrogate interaction region of the students' process domain gives the student more control over that part of the process. The quality of the material on the CDs reduces the need for students to ask questions. Further, BYU provides an accounting lab that is staffed by Teaching Assistants that can help individual students and answer questions. The disadvantage of the Figure 49 process might be the missed camaraderie of meeting with a bunch of other students, and perhaps not being able to see Norm "live" and in 3D (at least not yet 3D). But the students do not seem to mind.

Many schools set up online discussion forums for students, which may provide some feeling of belonging.

On to online education

The Internet has had a tremendous impact on the delivery of higher education. Online learning (Figure 50) is a slightly different from media based learning (Figure 49).

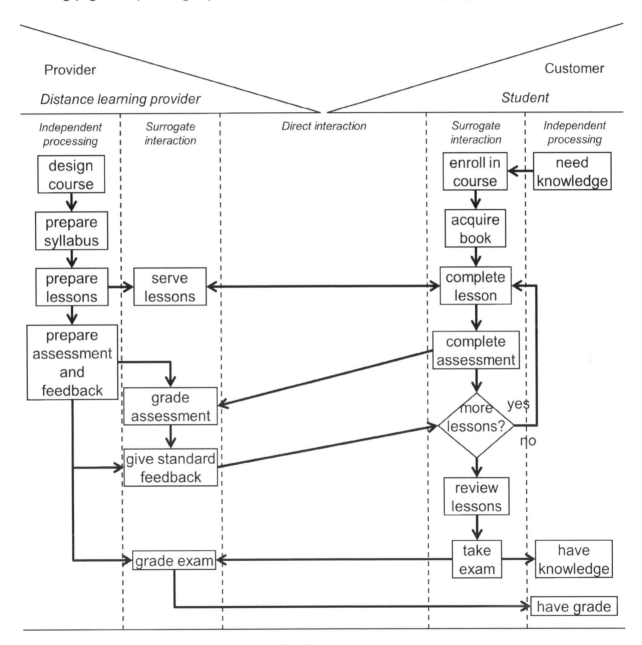

Figure 50: Online learning course process

First, the lessons are served interactively, requiring each student to log in to the system. Tying the access of lessons to the provider's process domain does a couple of things for the provider. It allows the provider to control the access to the content. With Figure 50 the students can easily share the CDs or sell/give them to other students, decreasing the revenue for the provider. The more interactive process of Figure 49 requires each student to have his or her own login ID and password.

Of course, students could share login credentials, but that may limit their ability to take tests and get a grade. Requiring each student to log in also has the benefit of tracking progress of students to know if students are on schedule. Delivering assessments interactively also helps track student progress. Providing deadlines for assessments can also motivate timely completion of lessons.

It is no wonder that for-profit schools like the University of Phoenix have less emphasis on classroom learning (e.g., Figure 48) and more emphasis on online learning (Figure 50). Online learning is a prime example of Principle #4 from Chapter 5: Surrogate positioning. Chapter 5 points out that surrogate positioning is an effective way of balancing the classic tradeoff between process efficiency and customization. The distance learning process exploits surrogate positioning to provide a custom experience that highly scalable.

It is also no wonder that the U.S. for-profit education industry is growing leaps and bounds, even while growth in public and private non-profit education is flat or declining. By my estimation this could largely be because government education grants are calculated based on interactive process designs that are quite inefficient, but for-profit educators are delivering education through surrogate-interactive methods that have different economies of scale. The government is paying for the old system as the new system is being delivered.

Education for the masses: Wikipedia!

When I was a cub scout back in the dinosaur age I had a scout leader who said his pastime as a kid was to read the encyclopedia. As nerdy as that sounds, I gave it a try and found it to be a fascinating intellectual journey. In those days my learning was guided by letters of the alphabet. At one point I probably knew a lot about things that start with the letter D but not much about things that start with M.

Probably my favorite website on the Internet is Wikipedia. Newton Minow, former Chairman of the Federal Communications Commission, reportedly called television a "vast wasteland."[32] If such is the case, then the Internet is a vast wasteland on steroids! Minow did say that, "When television is good...nothing is better," but pointed out that there is also a lot of broadcast trash. Similarly, there are good things on the Internet—things of such high value that they are almost without peer. In my opinion (at this writing), one of these is Wikipedia.

---

[32] Newton N. Minow, "Television and the Public Interest", address to the National Association of Broadcasters, Washington, D.C., May 9, 1961.

Despite some criticism for Wikipedia being unreliable, it has great processes and great ability to sort out the truth from the speculation. We can consider how Wikipedia comes into being, as roughly depicted in Figure 51.

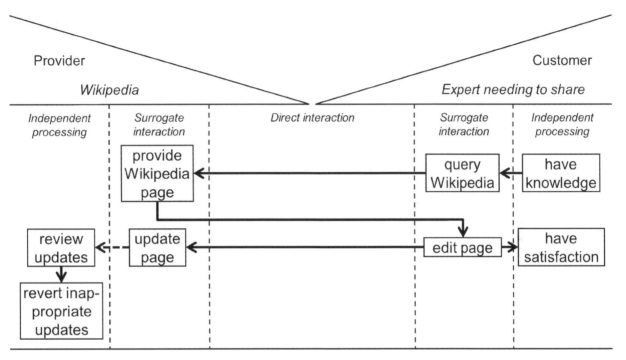

Figure 51: Wikipedia development process

From one perspective, Wikipedia is a means for knowledgeable people to share their knowledge, even if somewhat anonymously. Experts with knowledge call up any entry page, or create a new entry page, and share whatever knowledge they would like. This seems like it could result in mayhem, but Wikipedia provides various mechanisms for control.

For example, pages pertaining to a particular topical area are occasionally reviewed by topical editors. These topical editors are usually volunteers, and must be qualified as experts on that particular topic. The Wikipedia system (some software called MediaWiki) actually keeps logs of all changes, allowing the topical editors to easily revert inappropriate content contributions.

In fact, just about anybody can revert or change any inappropriate content. Entries that are victims of vandalism or commercial postings (spam) might be locked down by editors, meaning that only registered users (or only editors) can make changes.

Further, editors are effective at tagging entries that need corrections. For example, the tag {{Unreferenced}} causes the following message to appear at the top of the article: "This article does not cite any references or sources. Please help improve this article by adding citations to reliable sources. Unsourced material may be challenged and removed." In that way, editors may enforce the various rules governing contribution to Wikipedia.

The beauty of Wikipedia is in the way lifelong students like me can access the information, as depicted in Figure 52. I am continually coming across things that my curiosity drives me to learn more about. I keep a Wikipedia app on my smartphone, and select an entry to learn more.

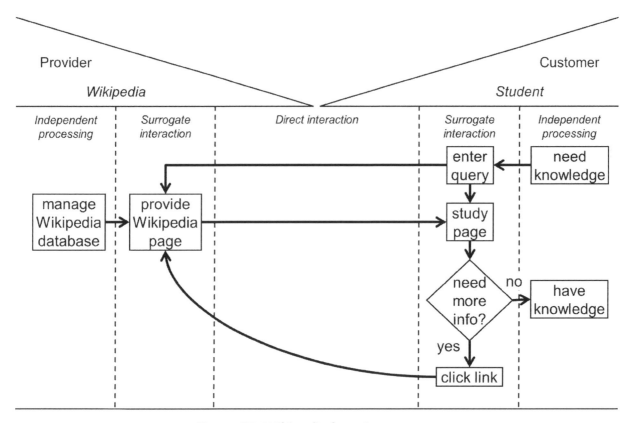

Figure 52: Wikipedia learning process

Wikipedia is tremendously well indexed, and each article has numerous cross references to other articles or external sources of information. Learning about one thing often leads to learning about something else. For example, when I took two of my children to the musical Wicked, I wanted to review the characters with them before the play. I could not remember some of the names of the characters, so went to Wikipedia. That article reminded me that the musical is based on a novel. A different article described ways that the musical departs from the storyline of the book. Another article described how Sherwood Schwartz came across the book on vacation, and what he had to do to finally get it to the stage. Fascinating!

The advantage of the Wikipedia process design is tremendously efficient while still maintaining a customized experience (again, Principle #4: Surrogate interaction). It is extremely self-paced, and leverages the economy-of-scale effect of having a centralized repository.

But is Wikipedia a suitable basis for higher education? I have heard about the one-laptop-per-child (OLPC) movement to get inexpensive laptops in the hands of disadvantaged people in developing nations—each one loaded with subset of the Wikipedia knowledge base. That could be great for learning, but not for providing a solid resume item.

Knowledge repositories like Wikipedia can become part of a formal higher education through the development of a Service Value Network. Chapter 13 reviewed how Service Value Networks can involve the competences from various service providers to provide an integrated service offering.

Figure 53 depicts a simple Service Value Network. The student (1) approaches an education provider (2) such as a for-profit college. The education provider develops programs, although may not develop actual educational materials. Instead, the education provider relies on the services of a knowledge repository (3) for the course content.

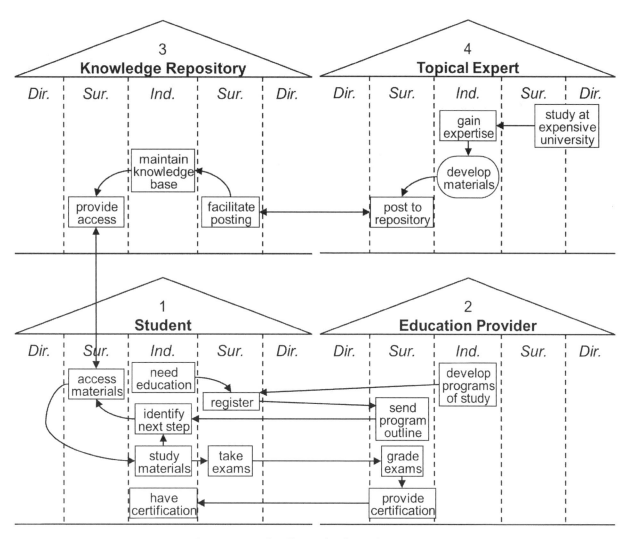

Figure 53: Distributed education process

Knowledge repositories might include Wikipedia or Wikiversity, which is the sister-website to Wikipedia in which authors publish their own educational material without relying on the crowd-sourced contributions of others. Also, many traditional textbook publishers are establishing online knowledge repositories comprised of book chapters, multimedia materials, and assessment tools.

The education provider draws on available knowledge repositories in developing courses of study. Students that register for a particular program are given an outline and instructions. At each stage of the process the students access the knowledge repository, which may be branded to the education provider (reminding the student that they are dealing with the education provider).

The education provider serves as a Prime Mover in this network (see Chapter 13). The education provider might involve other organizations with distinctive competencies to contribute to the value proposition. For example, the education provider might partner with organizations that certify skills in specific industries.

Western Governors University (WGU) is an example of an institution that has organized a network of service providers. WGU does not develop their own courses or employ instructors, but utilizes the course development and delivery provided by publishers such as Pearson and McGraw-Hill.

Each WGU student is assigned a "student mentor" who coaches students in their education process. These mentors do not necessarily have expertise pertaining to specific courses in a program, but have understanding of WGU processes and likely have certification as a professional coach.

As students complete programs they complete competency testing, which again, WGU outsources to other service providers. WGU coordinates with certifying agencies for specific career fields. They also engage independent contractors to grade students written materials.

This Service Value Network is depicted in Figure 54, which is a simplification. The full WGU network includes relationships with education funding providers, interactive discussion services, and so forth. The power of the WGU offering is in the way it organizes a variety of competencies that help students in various steps of their education process.

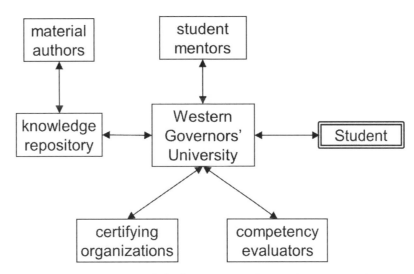

Figure 54: Simplified WGU Service Value Network

The perils of deservitization

Educational institutions that have resources and competencies for delivering interactive on-campus education may feel somewhat threatened by the onslaught of distance learning. Some are trying to redeploy their skills by having instructors of live classes port their course materials over to online learning system. That may help reduce the problem of an antiquated model for education delivery, but does not solve it.

For one thing, universities that have their professors switch from being course instructors to being online education authors are at a competitive disadvantage to firms that have even greater economies of scale. Professors who work in regions of direct interaction (e.g., Figure 48) have limited economies of scale. When they move their efforts to regions of independent processing (Figure 49 and Figure 50), other providers with greater economies of scale are likely to dominate.

Imagine a regional university that teaches accounting courses, which they realize they could do more effectively through online learning. The invite their professors to develop online versions of their courses that their students can take. However, they realize that the great Norm Nemrow already produced superior accounting materials at a great cost, which are being sold by http://www.accountingcds.com and used worldwide. Regional universities with brick-and-mortar campuses may be competitive in the days of direct-interaction education, but normally do not have an economy-of-scale advantage in independent-processing development of education materials.

This can be explained further through an analogy. A local Italian restaurant called Ottavio's was known for excellent tomato soup. The restaurant did quite well selling soup (and other items) to local customers, and was not at all threatened by an even better Italian restaurant located hundreds of miles away. In 2009, the owner decided to close the Ottavio's restaurant and instead opened Primavera Foods, which manufactured tomato soup for sale in grocery stores around the nation. Suddenly he was competing with tomato soup manufacturers worldwide, including the venerable Campbell Soup Company. It is unknown whatever happened to Primavera Foods.

This analogy suggests the fate of brick-and-mortar universities that try to retool as online learning providers.   When shifting from interactive processing to independent processing, those with the greatest economies of scale have clear advantage. The large fixed cost of developing a high-quality online course must be offset by a large customer base.

Developing a resistance to deservitization

An alternative to retooling for independent processing is to focus on an education market and pedagogy that is more resistant to deservitization. What if brick-and-mortar universities could provide value through direct interact that could not be replicated by online learning models?

An example of just such a pedagogical approach is the so-called "case method" employed by the Harvard Business School, the Darden School, and other graduate business schools. The case method is somewhat of an art and a science, and is roughly depicted in Figure 55.

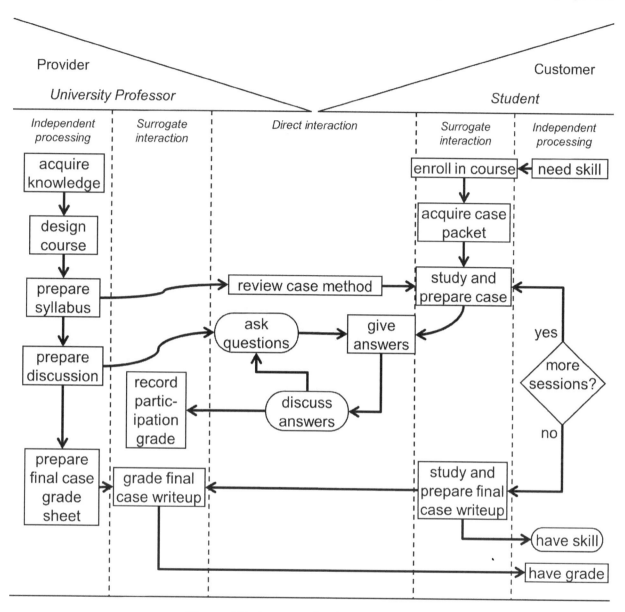

Figure 55: Case method course process

The professor acquires knowledge, designs courses, and prepares syllabi as usual. The syllabus tells students which cases will be studied, and may provide instruction about the case method. Students who are not familiar with the case method need to be instructed in the case method, since it is quite different from other ways of learning they may have experienced in the past.

A business "case" is basically a story of an actual business situation, including relevant (and some irrelevant) data, diagrams, and exhibits. A typical case might be ten to twenty single-spaced pages long, half of which might be data tables. Students prepare cases by reading them, performing appropriate analysis, and trying to identify a possible plan of action.

Students are often assisted in this effort by a set of case questions included in the course syllabus.

The most unique aspect of the case method is in the interactive delivery. As shown in Figure 55, the professor begins by asking questions of the students, and the students are expected to provide reasonable answers. The most exciting phase of this questioning is the initial "cold call" where an arbitrary student is asked to lead off the discussion by answering a nebulous question like, "what would you do?" The cold called student is expected to spend perhaps 10 minutes describing a plan of action, before having it scrutinized by the rest of the class.

Expert case teachers usually spend a very small portion of the class time talking, other than asking appropriate questions of the students. The instructor uses the questions to somewhat guide the discussion and help the students "discover" important principles.

At the end of the class session the instructor may or may not summarize what was actually learned during the case discussion. The learning coming from the case method is not so much the facts of knowledge pertaining to business management, but rather the ways of possibly thinking about problems that are somewhat ambiguous and do not have well defined solution rules.

Does this sound familiar? In particular, think back to the Chapter 8 discussion of complexity and divergence. The reason the case method is resistant to deservitization is because it relies heavily on the divergent process abilities of both the instructor and the students.

The Divergence Difference

The case method is orders of magnitude more difficult of a pedagogical process than traditional teaching. What could be so hard about asking students a bunch of questions? For one thing, the questions are based on prior student comments about the case, which could be all over the board, so to speak. The skilled case teacher never knows how students will direct the discussion, but astutely is able to keep the discussion on track without over directing. The key is helping the students discover principles themselves, and the learning is about this discovery process.

Notice that the "ask questions" and "discuss answers" steps of Figure 55 are rounded to show divergence. These steps are very different from the "answer questions" step from Figure 48, which is more likely to be complex. In other words, answering student questions as part of a lecture typically requires selecting the appropriate fact from a vast array of facts (and presenting it in an intelligible manner). That vast array of facts suggests that answering student questions can be a very complex process, but not necessarily dependent on the experience-based judgment of the instructor.

This, alas, is what makes the case method somewhat immune to deservitization—the reliance on interactive divergent processes. Of course, this presupposes that students value learning about making decisions in ambiguous environments, which happens to be a fundamental management skill.

One limitation of the case method is that it relies not only on the experience and judgment of the instructor, but also relies on the experience and judgment of the students. Students are expected to answer questions and provide discussion that draws on their own experience in industry. For that reason, managerial work experience is a major admissions requirement to case-method MBA programs.

I have successfully used a related method that works with less-experienced undergraduate students, as well as more-experienced graduate students. This method, depicted in Figure 56, requires students to prepare presentations of assigned topics (often from articles about the application of business principles). The students are organized into presentation teams and are given assigned topics.

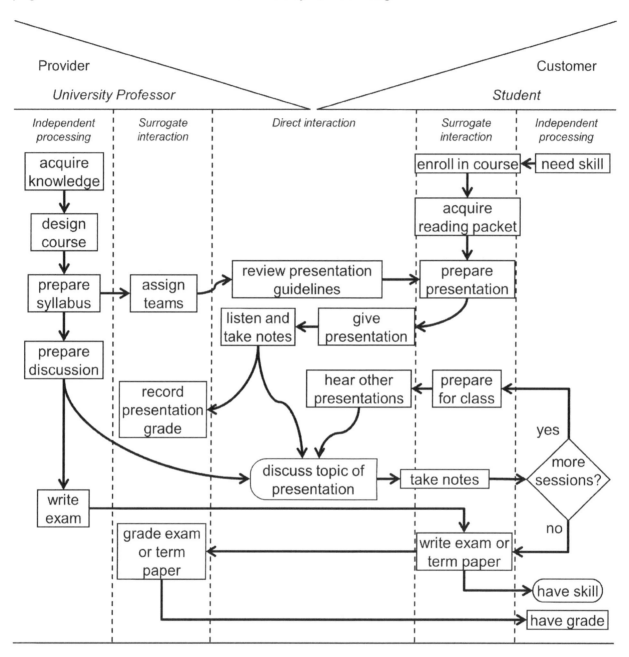

Figure 56: Team presentation course process

In this pedagogy approach, student teams give 15-30 minute presentations at the start of a class session, which serves functions of a cold call in the case method. I require that the students provide real examples of the assigned topic that are different from the examples given in the assigned reading. Often the students will develop a mini-case example as part of their presentation.

As with the case method, much of the course grade is based on the way each student and team contributes to the class discussion. Also, the discussion of the topic builds on the case discussion, which requires divergent thinking on behalf of the instructor. Throughout the course the students are expected to develop critical thinking skills through their contribution to the discussion of presentations.

This approach is not perfect, but does emphasize the experiential learning that comes from direct interaction. The focus is more on the process of discovery than on rote recitation of facts. I have seen that some students complain that they would rather than I just tell them the facts and principles rather than rely on a less-experienced team of students followed by less structured discussion. (Those students would also hate the case method.) Students that catch the vision and get engaged report that the course is a landmark educational experience.

Chapter 16 – Healthcare case study

By some estimates, healthcare represents about 17.4 percent of the U.S. Gross Domestic Product.[33]   Healthcare is big business, and getting bigger. There are various issues that might explain the massive growth of healthcare, including innovations, aging populations, and the massive growth of the junk food industry.

PCN Analysis reveals additional insights into the explosion of healthcare. Chapter 9 discussed the principle of commoditization, which suggests that over time all offerings commoditize as consumers become more capable. Are consumers more capable at taking care of their own health? Probably. However, the antidote for commoditization is innovation, and few industries have greater expenditures on research and development (R&D) than healthcare.

The result of this tremendous innovation is ever increasing opportunities to deliver value to customers (i.e., meet their health needs in increasingly superior ways). For example, consider refractive eye surgery. Radial keratotomy (RK) was developed in 1974 by a Russian ophthalmologist, which involved corneal incisions with a diamond knife. In 1987, the photorefractive keratectomy (PRK) was introduced as one of the first laser-assisted eye surgery techniques. Laser-assisted sub-epithelial keratectomy (LASEK) was introduced in 1996, which avoided the need to remove the outer surface of the cornea. In 2003, Epi-LASIC was introduced as an automated form of LASEC that has less chance of damaging eye cells and is less painful. As you might imagine, each iteration of healthcare technology comes with tremendous expense, numerous patents, and heightened demand.

Most of these innovations have stayed in the healthcare provider's process domains. Very few healthcare innovations involve moving process steps to the customer's process domain. The means by which patients deliver their own healthcare has not changed at a dramatic rate. Think about major do-it-yourself healthcare innovations. In 1920, Johnson & Johnson introduced the band-aid adhesive bandage. In 1950, Bayer introduced the Bactine antiseptic. In 1976, Warner-Chilcott introduced a home pregnancy test (e.p.t), the first in the U.S.[34] Most of the common over-the-counter drugs patients use have been popular for decades.

The healthcare industry may have a culture of elitist expertise that would cause resistance to enabling customers to meet their own needs.   The financial and legal incentives are for healthcare providers to do all they can to meet patients health needs, with less incentives to empower customers. Chapter 10 gave an example of reconfiguring a healthcare process to empower the customer, but it was purely hypothetical.

An example of innovation in the patient's process domain is the Shouldice Hospital located near Toronto Canada. Shouldice specializes in external hernia surgery, and ten full-time

---

[33] Michael B. Sauter, Charles B. Stockdale, "Countries that spend the most on health care," 24/7 Wall Street, March 29, 2012, http://www.foxbusiness.com/industries/2012/03/29/countries-that-spend-most-on-health-care/

[34] http://history.nih.gov/exhibits/thinblueline/timeline.html

surgeons perform over 7500 of these operations each year. This PCN case study will compare traditional surgery to the Shouldice process.

Traditional hernia surgery

Figure 57 shows a simplified PCN Diagram for traditional hernia surgery, mostly focusing on the patient experience. The process is highly interactive. In the first part the patient sees the surgeon for diagnosis. If the surgery is warranted it is scheduled. Then the patient shows up on the scheduled day, is admitted, prepped, taken to the operating room, put to sleep with anesthesia, operated on, wheeled to recovery room, recover, then sent home. It is quite obvious in this process that the patient is being acted upon. There is very little that the patient does for himself or herself, other than putting on the gown.

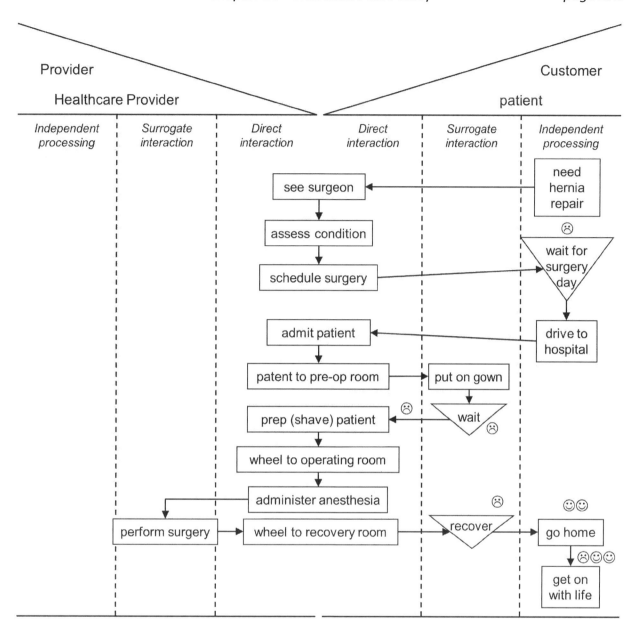

Figure 57: Traditional hernia surgery

Figure 57 hints at the value proposition from the customer's perspective. There is not much about this process to smile about ☺. The most joyous part of the process is going home. The rest of the process is not the most enjoyable. This definitely isn't Club Med!

The cost structure of this process is equally deplorable. Notice how most of the steps occur within the region of direct interaction, which is the area of maximum inefficiency. Figure 57 did not show all of the independent preparation steps performed by the service provider such as hiring and training staff. But it does demonstrate that the customer is allowed to do very little in the way of surrogate interaction, which contrasts with the Shouldice process.

The Shouldice Experience

Shouldice Hospital prides itself in having what a reporter from the American Medical News called "a country club" appeal.[35] I will describe the Shouldice process in three PCN Diagrams. The first part is depicted in Figure 58. When a patient thinks he or she has a hernia needing an operation, the patient requests and downloads a diagnosis questionnaire from the Shouldice website. The questionnaire form asks about the patient's health condition, hernia symptoms, and medical history. Patients can email, snail mail, or fax back the completed questionnaire.

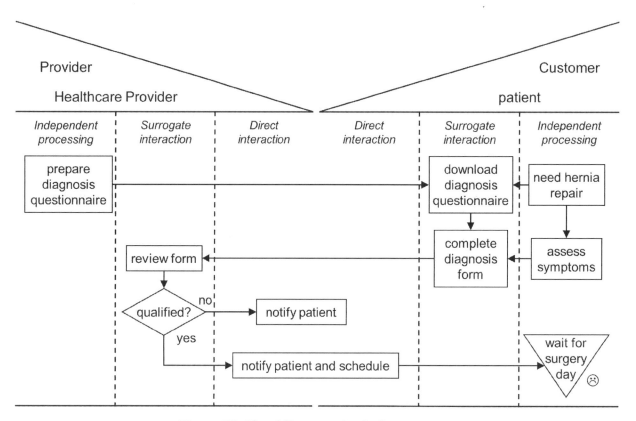

Figure 58: Shouldice part 1 – before surgery

The initial diagnosis is therefore accomplished by surrogate interaction, as Shouldice employees review the form to determine qualification. If the patient does not qualify for the Shouldice procedure, such as morbid obesity or other high-risk factor, the patient is left to find other healthcare solutions. Otherwise, the patient is scheduled for a day to arrive at the Shouldice hospital.

Figure 59 shows what happens the day the patient arrives, which is the day before the actual surgery. Most patients are scheduled to arrive in the early afternoon, allowing them to

---

[35] Information for this section is taken from the Shouldice Hospital website as well as an article titled "Shouldice Hospital—A Cut Above" from pages 60-61 of *Operations and Supply Management: The Core* (Second Edition) by Jacobs and Chase, published by McGraw-Hill (2010).

possibly fly in that day from New York or other regional location. After patients arrive they are examined by a physician to assure that they indeed qualify for the procedure (since the prior diagnosis was based on the patient's self-reported information).

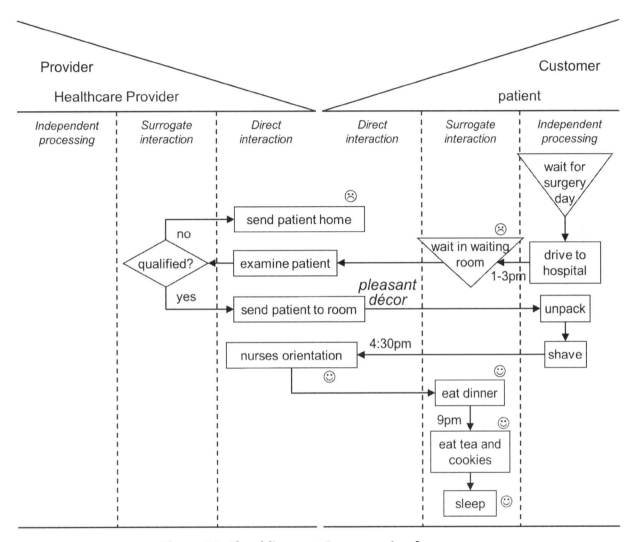

Figure 59: Shouldice part 2 – preparing for surgery

The patient is then sent to a pleasantly-decorated room that is comparable to a nice hotel room. The patient unpacks their luggage, since they will be there for three days. Immediately we see co-production taking place! The patient is responsible for shaving the surgery area according to instructions (which is probably a lot less awkward than having some young nurse do the shaving).

At 4:30 in the afternoon all patients have an orientation meeting with the nurses. Figure 59 has this marked with a ☺ because it is a great opportunity to calm the patient's fears about what will take place both in the surgery and in recovery. There is also a tremendous effect of comradery about being in the meeting with other patients in a similar situation.

After the orientation the patients have a nice dinner together in a well apportioned dining room. (Pictures on the Shouldice website suggest it is nothing like stereotypical hospital food.) The patients can then return to their room, or stroll around the gardens on the 23 acre Shouldice property, then return to the dining hall for tea and cookies at 9:00pm.

This 9:00pm social meeting is important, because it gives the patients the opportunity to meet patients who have undergone the surgery in the prior two days. The patients can tell the new patients what to expect, which is likely to be reports of how well they are doing with their recovery. Finally, the patients head back to their rooms for a good night sleep.

The morning of the surgery, depicted in Figure 60, shows the patient being woken up at the crack of dawn (or earlier than dawn, since this is in Canada). The patient is administered a pre-op sedative, which makes the patient more relaxed but otherwise awake and attentive during the surgery and subsequent recovery. The patient is taken to the operating room (O.R.).[36]

---

[36] It is not clear from the published materials whether the patient walks to the O.R. or is taken in a wheelchair. However, the published case emphasizes that patients walk from the O.R. to the recovery room, so we would suspect that they also walk to the O.R.

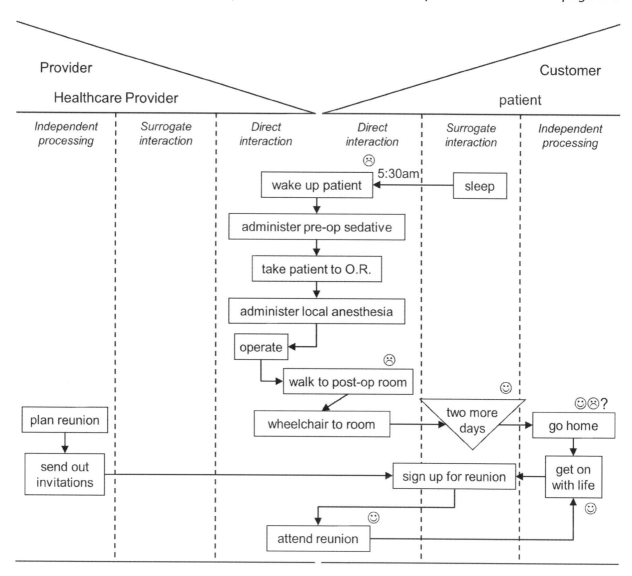

Figure 60: Shouldice part 3 – surgery and recovery

The patient is administered local anesthesia and operated on. (Note that in Figure 57 we depicted the surgery as surrogate interaction, since the patient is asleep and not actively participating in interaction. In Figure 60 we depict the operation as direct interaction, but in the provider's process domain.)

After the operation the patient is invited to *walk* to the post-operation room (with help from the physicians), and reportedly 90 percent of patients accept the offer. A director of nursing gave this explanation:[37] "While we use wheelchairs to return them to their rooms, the walk from the operating table is for psychological as well as physiological [blood pressure,

---

[37] From Harvard Business School case: Shouldice Hospital Limited (Abridged) by James Heskett and Roger Hallowell, p. 3.

respiratory] reasons. Patients prove to themselves that they can do it, and they start their all-important exercise immediately."

After a short period of recovery, the patient is returned to their own room for two more days. These are a very active two days of recover. The patients are expected to do a prescribed series of exercises. They are also expected to attend the daily 9:00pm tea and cookies events, to share their experiences with new patients, and probably to build friendships.

Figure 60 shows mixed emotions associated with returning home from Shouldice. For many patients this may have been one of the most relaxing and sociable vacations they have been on in a long time. "Getting on with life" is depicted as positive, since Shouldice patients have much lower hernia recurrence rates than typically comes with a hernia operation.

One would think that "get on with life" is the end of the Shouldice process, but company promotional materials emphasize that a Shouldice patient is a patient for life. For example, the surgery comes with free annual hernia check-ups if desired. Also, as depicted in Figure 60, patients are invited to annual reunions of former Shouldice patients. These reunions have been held for decades, and have attracted as many as 1500 patients at a time.[38]

It should be no surprise that Shouldice's customer loyalty and profitability are exceptional. A key service design feature we see in the Shouldice experience is the heavy reliance on co-production. Shouldice customers are active participants in the process, with most of the time they spend at the hospital being actively engaged in surrogate interaction (including interaction with other patients). All healthcare cannot be as focused as Shouldice, but surely other fields of healthcare could learn from their effective example of strategic process positioning.

---

[38] According to the Wikipedia entry for Shouldice Hernia Centre.

Chapter 17 – Financial Services case study

The financial services industry has had tremendous shake-ups in recent years. For example, in 2008, the four largest investment banks in the US were Merrill Lynch, Morgan Stanley, Goldman Sachs, and Lehman Brothers. In 2008, Merrill Lynch was purchased by Bank of America for about 40 percent of its September 2007 price. Subsequently, Morgan Stanley's stock price plummeted to 20 percent of its 2007 level. Goldman Sachs' stock price dropped to 40 percent of its 2007 level. In 2008, Lehman Brothers went out of business.

As you might imagine, financial services have become victims of deservitization. Financial services can be delivered in various ways, and incumbent providers often find themselves in an inefficient interactive or surrogate-interactive business model.

For example, Figure 61 shows process positioning options for an "analyze investments" step of a financial management process. The provider is a firm with investment expertise and the customer is an investor needing to make investments. With option 1, the firm performs the investment analysis independently from any client investor. With option 2, the firm analyzes a client investor's investments portfolio in a back office operation that does not require direct interaction with the client. Option 3 accomplishes the investment analysis through direct interaction. Option 4 switches over to the customer's process domain, meaning that the customer executes the analysis, using the provider's resources. Finally, option 5 represents the customer doing the analysis independently from the firm.

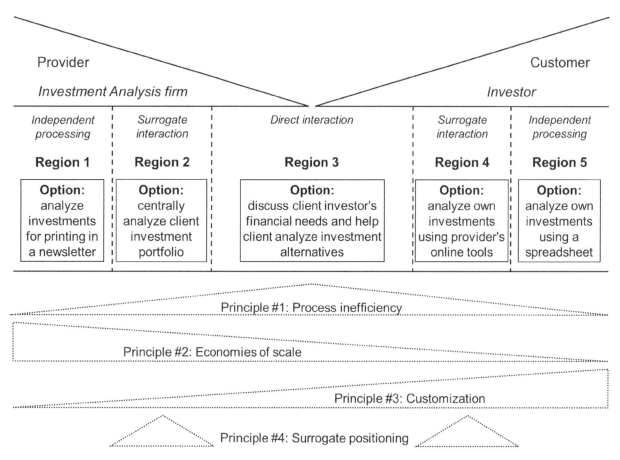

Figure 61: Investment analysis process options and principles

Figure 61 also reminds us of the four process positioning principles discussed in Chapter 5. The interactive options (especially the option in Region 3) are the least efficient, possibly requiring the customer to visit the provider's location (or vice versa) and provide information inputs for the investment analysis, with the location and interaction being important parts of the value proposition. If the customer desires extensive customization and control of the analysis process, positioning the step closer to the customer's central region (Region 5) has advantages. However, that comes with a cost of economies of scale, and it may require that the customer have the type of specialized investment analysis knowledge that one would expect an investment firm to have. The option in Region 1 can have tremendous economies of scale, allowing the provider's expertise to easily be shared with an unlimited number of investors who receive the newsletter, assuming the investors do not need customized investment advice from the firm. The surrogate options (Regions 2 and 4) provide balance between these operational factors.

Traditional investment firms tended to focus their processing on Region 3 and Region 2, gathering information about the client and centrally managing an investment portfolio that is appropriate. However, developing an investment portfolio for each individual customer ignores the inherent homogeneity within specific classes of investors. Mutual funds are managed much closer to Region 1, ignoring the unique needs of individual investors and instead creating a portfolio that meets the needs of a large group of investors.

Deservitization trends

The biggest area of growth in recent years has been in online investing that operates primarily in Region 4. One of the early examples is the firm Charles Schwab, which focused on providing advice to individual investors and helping them manage their own investment portfolios. This move to Region 4 provided Charles Schwab with operating efficiencies and allowed them to operate profitably as a so-called discount broker.

Other firms like TD Ameritrade and e-Trade further capitalized on the deservitization within the investment industry. Some firms, like Scottrade provide self-directed (PCN Region 4) investing services, but also have brick-and-mortar offices around the U.S., allowing investors to choose their mode of service delivery, and their price. As of this writing, online investing costs as low as $7 per trade[39]. The fee for using their voice-response telephone system is $17 per trade, and a broker-assisted trade is $27. This illustrates the increased efficiency with direct interaction.

It is interesting that Charles Schwab actually started as a publisher of an investment advice newsletter, and then temporarily switched to a full-service broker before hitting the pot of gold of providing self-directed investment services. Other companies have prospered on the trend toward do-it-yourself investing.

An example is The Motley Fool (http://www.fool.com), which provides free and paid-subscription investment advice and newsletters. It is not a very big company and only employs a few hundred employees. However, Motley Fool has a tremendous reach (an economy of scale) by providing investment advice primarily through Region 5—producing advice independent from individual investors.

Mortgage lenders

On a few occasions I have consulted in the banking industry. Banks, like investment firms, are subject to pressures of deservitization. Surrogate interaction mechanisms like Automatic Teller Machines (ATM) and online banking have become all the rage. In fact, one important customer (my wife) tells me how much she prefers using the ATM rather than going into the bank or even using the drive-in teller station. She is a very social person, but prefers to spend her time socializing with other than bank employees.

On one occasion I was asked to speak to an association of bank executives, including some that were from the bank where I previously had my home mortgage. It was a little uncomfortable reporting the process I went through to get a mortgage with them, in comparison to the process I went through to get a mortgage with an online mortgage broker. I have had great experiences with that bank since the early 1970's, but their mortgage process was a bit antiquated.

---

[39] From http://www.scottrade.com/documents/alt/CommissionsandFees.pdf downloaded July 27, 2012.

Figure 62 shows a typical mortgage loan process involving a brick-and-mortar lender and an aspiring homeowner seeking mortgage funding. The customer acquires loan application forms from the bank or mortgage company, gathers relevant information, and completes the loan application. Relevant information may include a property appraisal, income history, debt records, and so forth.

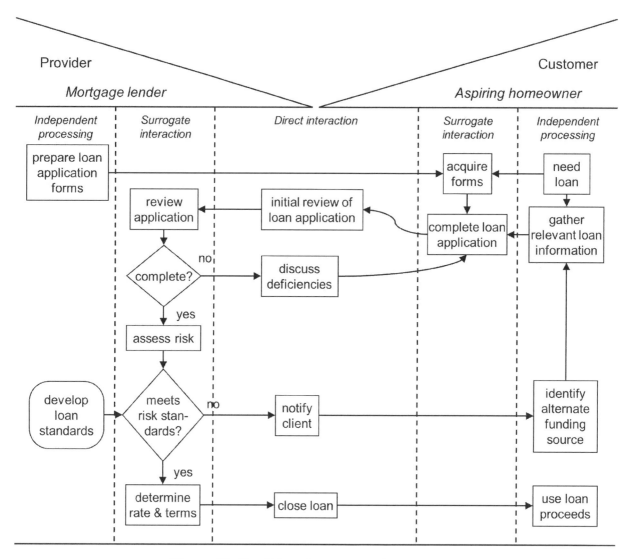

Figure 62: Traditional mortgage loan process

When I took my completed mortgage application to my bank they initially checked it for completeness. Then, I waited for them to review the application. If it is complete and my data meets the risk standards then they determine the rate and terms. Figure 62 does not show details like locking a rate, conducting a title search, and scheduling a closing data. Eventually the loan is closed, and I can use the proceeds to either pay off another loan or purchase a new home.

This process is simple, but not without its flaws. Figure 62 also does not show all of the time I spend waiting to hear back about loan approval or playing telephone tag with a loan officer who may be out of the office. Still, the process is adequate, but not exceptional.

Alternatively, I have gotten residential mortgages on a few occasions from an online mortgage broker called LoansAtWholesale.com. I do not have any idea where Loans at Wholesale is located. Actually, I do know where they are located—on the Internet and on my home phone.

The Loans at Wholesale (I will call it "L@W") process is depicted in Figure 63. One big value-adding feature provided by L@W is a providing a compilation of rates and terms available from a wide range of actual lenders. Loans at Wholesale does not actually loan money, but arranges loans for other mortgage lenders such as GMAC. This may give you the impression that L@W is less tied to customers than a bank lender would be, but even a bank lender can sell your mortgage to a third-party mortgage investment firm.

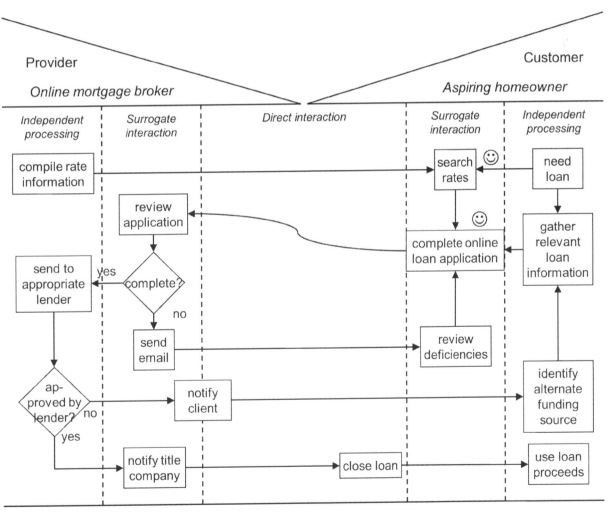

Figure 63: Online mortgage broker process

Completing the online loan application is surprisingly easy. Initially, all interaction with L@W is online, but they will call you if there are specific questions or concerns. L@W forwards completed applications to the appropriate lender for approval. Ultimately, the borrower meets with a local title company to close the loan, which is similar to the bank loan process.

The L@W website touts "Same day approval!" which may be achievable under ideal circumstances. Still, my impression is that the L@W process is much quicker and keeps the customer much more informed than the traditional bank mortgage process. L@W has minimized the need for direct interaction, which can increase efficiency as well as reduce the need for interacting with a specific loan officer. (However, even with my local bank they had to manage much of the mortgage approval process through their centralized mortgage division.)

A key to success for L@W is the way they have configured and managed their network partner lenders as well as local title companies. L@W seems to have an extremely productive relationship with lenders. This includes clear understandings of loan requirements, of what information is needed from borrowers, about what problems could occur that might be anticipated, and so forth. L@W is resistant to disintermediation because, in my experience, they have mastered the interaction with the customer in a way that other lenders could aspire to.

Figure 64 provides a simple depiction of this L@W process network. Key to this is the customer experience, which relatively simple and well informed. The primary direct interaction is when the borrower meets with the title company to close the loan. In one sense it is as though L@W has outsourced loan closing to a title company. In a broader sense, the title company is a partner with L@W to assure smooth and enjoyable customer experience.

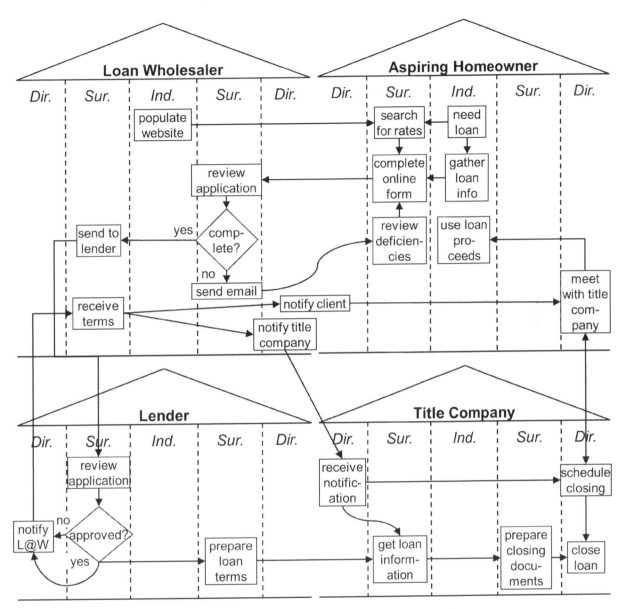

Figure 64: Loan wholesaler process network

Building a Service Value Network

How can a local brick-and-mortar bank compete with a deservitized process that is more efficient *and* provides a smoother customer experience? In some sense, residential mortgages have become a commodity, competing almost exclusively on price (including interest rate and term). A clue is given by the experience of my student, Aaron Oyler.

Aaron was in my class during the last semester of his MBA program. He already had a job, and needed to purchase a house. He began by interacting with a real estate agent who provided him with printouts of MLS listings that supposedly would meet his needs. (MLS is the

Multiple-Listing Service used by registered real estate brokers and agents to review properties listed by other brokers and agents, and is not normally accessible by individual buyers.)

Aaron's frustration was that this real estate agent seemed to be motivated primarily by his sales commission (as one might imagine), which was not necessarily acting in Aaron's best interest. Aaron reported his impression that the real estate agent was acting both as a gatekeeper to the information and an up-seller of more expensive properties. As a result, Aaron did not trust this agent.

Subsequently, Aaron was introduced to a different real estate broker through a Wells Fargo bank branch. This new broker provided Aaron with information and links to government agencies that provide assistance for first-time home buyers. The broker also provided links to qualified residential building contractors, should they decide to build instead of buy. Rather than provide a hand-picked selection of MLS items, this broker gave Aaron a login to a large database of for-sale properties, allowing Aaron to browse at his leisure.

One might argue that this new real estate broker was putting her profits at risk by enabling Aaron to meet his needs in ways that might not maximize the sales commission. However, Aaron found tremendous value in the broker's knowledge and contacts. Aaron's loyalty to this broker was not based on the broker's specialized competency, but on the Service Value Network the broker managed and engaged to meet Aaron's needs.

Figure 65 shows an example of such a Service Value Network. This broker not only understands the process of real estate sales, but understands the complexities of the customer's process of purchasing and occupying a new home.

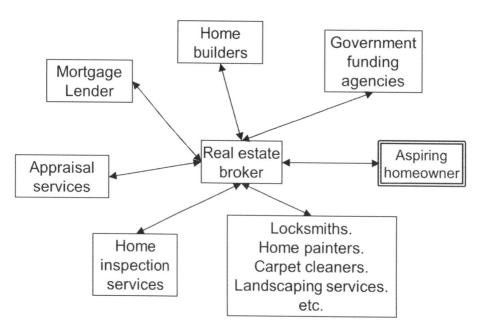

Figure 65: Real estate broker Service Value Network

Purchasing a home includes locating a property and acquiring funding, which also includes property appraisals and home inspections. Moving into a home may also involve engaging a myriad of other service providers such as locksmiths, painters, carpet cleaners, etc. The big questions include who is responsible for making all of these service contacts and coordinating their efforts, and what role should/could a real estate broker play? Some brokers sell properties. Other brokers coordinate and provide access to a Service Value Network, which can be a much greater value proposition.

Chapter 18 – Computer retail case study

Personal computers (PCs) were introduced in the early 1970's although at that time they were mostly kits that were sold to electronics hobbyists by mail-order companies. The first mass-market PC was the Commodore PET, which was introduced in 1977 and sold through an extensive dealer network. As evidence of its usefulness, in 1979 I got a part-time job programming a PET to calculate stock broker commissions. The dealer network was especially important because of the complexity of the PC.

Later in 1977, Tandy Corporation introduced the TRS-80, which they sold through their Radio Shack electronics retail stores. Also in 1977, Apple Computer introduced the Apple II, again sold through a network of retailers. I purchased my first Apple II in 1979 (and a friend of mine and I tried to become dealers so that we could sell to the school district).

PCs made the biggest leap from hobbyist use to practical use in 1981 when IBM introduced the "IBM Personal Computer." These were also sold to consumers through an extensive dealer network, and to companies through the large IBM sales force.

Full-service sales

In 1982 I went to work for Infomax Computers in Walnut Creek, California. We sold Apple IIs, Apple IIIs, and IBM PCs. In those days the general population had relatively little knowledge about computers, and customers were relatively unsophisticated. Customers who walked into the Infomax store would often ask, "So what is it about these personal computers? What are they good for?" Our response was something like the following:

- Boot up a VisiCalc spreadsheet. Type in three numbers with a @SUM() function at the bottom. Change one of the numbers and let the customer be awe-struck when the sum changed automatically!
- Show a simple database program for storing recipes. Impress the customer by asking, "so, let's say you are out of salt." We simply enter a query of ~salt (not salt) and see all of the recipes that do not require salt!
- If that was not enough to impress the customer, we could show them a really cool game of pong!

As you might imagine, in those days the PC sales process was very interactive, as depicted in Figure 66. Customers needed a significant amount of handholding in making the purchase decision, including decisions about how much RAM (memory) to purchase, whether to buy an external floppy drive, and so forth.

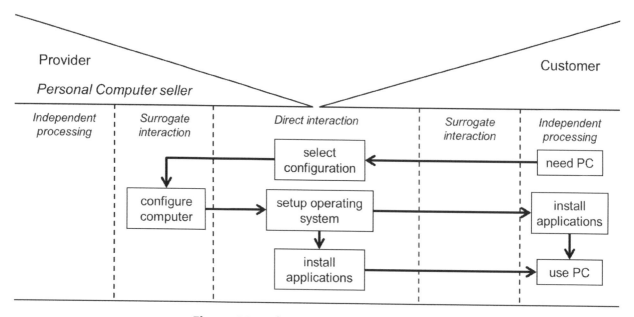

Figure 66: Infomax full-service PC sales

Once the customer made the purchase decision, we would open the box and necessary memory chips and interface cards. (I actually spent a significant part of my time soldering printer cables for customers, since they were not readily available otherwise.) The operating system would have to be told how much memory was installed and what peripherals were using which DMA ports, which we would do with or for the customer. If the customer purchased a hard drive, we would also help them install applications like WordStar or MultMate (basically copying it to the hard drive). If they only had floppy drives, there was nothing to install (they would just run the application from the floppy drive).

The interactive model for PC sales was popular, albeit not the most efficient. The sales process was largely an educational experience for the customers. The extensive handholding was worth it, knowing that we were helping people deal with the crisis of cooking without salt.

I understand that Infomax may have been acquired by the ComputerLand chain, which had the same basic model for computer sales. ComputerLand became defunct in 1999, and was purchased by a company that ceased operation in 2000.

Deservitization

The prospect for full-service PC retail were put at risk by a new influx of mail order retailers such as Dell. In 1985 Michael Dell introduced his first "Turbo PC" that he sold through national computer magazines. The Turbo PC was less expensive than a typical computer sold by a full-service retailer, plus it was configured according to customer specifications.

In its first year of operation, Dell sold more than $73 million worth of computers. Over subsequent years Dell expanded globally, and in 1996 began selling over the embryonic Internet. Dell became the world's largest PC manufacturer in 1999.

Dell's explosive growth is largely attributed to an ability to obtain great economies of scale and customization at the same time. Figure 67 depicts the Dell process. In this case, the customer base has become more knowledgeable, and needs a PC but without a lot of handholding. However, the Dell catalogs and websites were quite informative, helping prospective customers with things such as deciding why they should purchase more or less RAM based on the intended use for the PC.

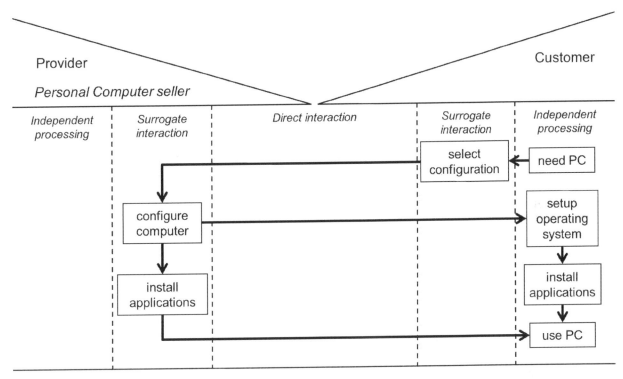

Figure 67: Dell mass-customization PC sales

Once an order was submitted by phone or via the Dell website, it was configured (likely at the facility in Round Rock, Texas). Dell committed to a two- or three-week delivery schedule from time of order to arrival. Dell used common carriers to drop-ship ordered computers on the customers' doorsteps (or offices for business purchases).

One major advantage Dell had over ComputerLand and other full-service retailers was the tremendous economies of scale that came from centralized configuration of computers. Dell operated at such large volumes that they were able to keep only a few weeks of component inventory at their Round Rock Texas assembly plant. Since customers needed to pay for the system at the time of purchase, it was rumored that Dell was able to achieve negative account payable.

Dell was also able to efficiently provide value by pre-installing selected applications like Microsoft Office on customers' computers. The customers still needed to set up the operating system on their own, including specifying login accounts, network logins and security, and so forth. Business users could get assistance by their own company's Information Technology support staff. Individual users would get assistance either by accessing the Dell knowledge base or by call a Dell support line.

These support lines were initially staffed in the U.S., but eventually shipped overseas to regions of lower-cost labor. This caused some problems for the segment of customers that needed more handholding. Dell focused on corporate customers that tended to need less handholding from Dell and were less price sensitive–at least for a time.

Commoditization

In 2006 Dell lost its PC market leadership to rival Hewlett Packard (HP). HP merged with Compaq Computer in 2001, making HP/Compaq for a short time. Dell continued to grow, but HP grew faster. Then, Dell's market share started to decline as HP's continued to climb[40]. Dell's market share was also hampered by Taiwanese manufacturer Acer, which went from 4.6% PC market share in 2005 to 12% market share in 2009. In October of 2009 Acer surpassed Dell as the second-largest PC maker (after HP).

What HP and Acer brought to the table was an even more efficient business model depicted in Figure 68. Key to this model was the fact that computers had become commodities, with customers needing less and less custom configuration. HP and Acer would produce standard configurations with a myriad of valued features and sell them for less than the price of a custom system with fewer features.

---

[40] see http://www.statisticbrain.com/computer-sales-statistics/
Also http://en.wikipedia.org/wiki/Market_share_of_leading_PC_vendors

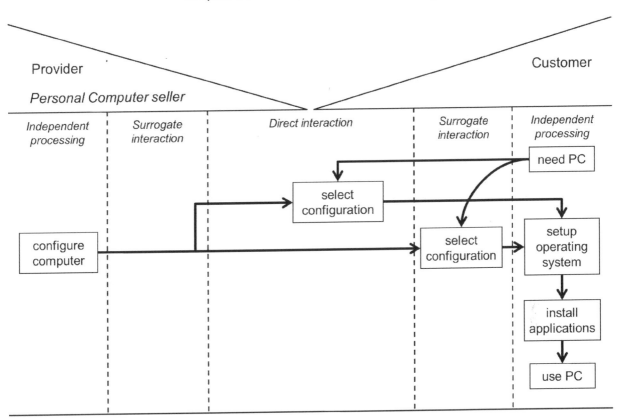

Figure 68: HP/Acer mass produced PC sales

For example, a custom Dell system could be configured with 2 gigabytes, 4 gigabytes, or 8 gigabytes of RAM. The basic HP systems would come standard with 4 gigabytes, and a high-end system would come standard with 8 gigabytes. Customers had fewer decisions to make because the basic models probably had more features than they actually would need. And they were produced in the region of independent processing with low-cost labor and mass-production efficiencies!

The HP/Acer computers were often purchased at general retailers like Walmart, with employees who were expected to know almost nothing about computers. For more information they could be purchased from various online retailers which, like Dell, often provided detailed explanations. The big difference is that HP and Acer did not typically accept configuration options, since the PCs were already configured.

Of course, under this highly-efficient PC-commodity model the customer would have to setup the operating system and install applications, although some models came with applications (or trial versions of applications) pre-installed.

As suggested in Chapter 11, this deservitization is motivated by two factors: provider learning and customer learning. Providers learned more about the typical needs of customer segments, allow standardization and commoditization of products. The customers learned more about PC selection criteria, so could make more informed decisions without as much handholding as was needed in prior decades.

At this point we might think we are on a sure path of deservitization in PC sales. However, one company has bucked the trend by opening large number of very popular brick-and-mortar PC stores. It is as though the company has managed to overcome the deservitizaiton trend, and do it quite profitably. As of 2011, that company has captured 10.7% of PC sales worldwide. Even more impressive is attaining status as the world's most valuable company by stock market valuation. You have probably guessed who we are talking about: Apple.

The amazing re-servitization

In 1997, Steve Jobs returned to Apple as interim CEO. In 1998, Apple had 5.9% of the global PC market share, which declined to 3.7% in 2000. Then, somehow, Apple's market share began a gradual increase, exceeding 10% in 2011, and, counting tablet computers as PCs, briefly surpassed HP as the market leader[41].

Some may argue that the increase in Apple's PC market share is attributed to superior products that are easy to use, but there is also evidence to the contrary. There is something else going on here that has to do with Apple's retail strategy. That something else is the Apple Stores and App Store.

In Chapter 13 we saw that Apple introduced the iPod and iTunes in 2001. Apple also opened the first Apple Stores In 2001 (the first two in Tysons Corner, Virginia and Glendale, California). The sales model of an Apple Store was highly interactive with both employees and products.

For the ever-dwindling number of people who have not purchased a product at an Apple store, I provide Figure 69 as a simplified depiction (also showing the four principles from Chapter 5). There are a number of distinctive features of this sales process. First, Apple rarely provides custom configurations of computer systems. The computers are mass produced by contract manufacturers in Asia with relatively few available configurations. This gives Apple tremendous economies of scale, and demonstrates how Apple knows more about what customers need than they do.

---

[41] Poeter, Damon, Report: HP Regains PC Market Share Crown from Apple, PC Magazine, May 4, 2012.

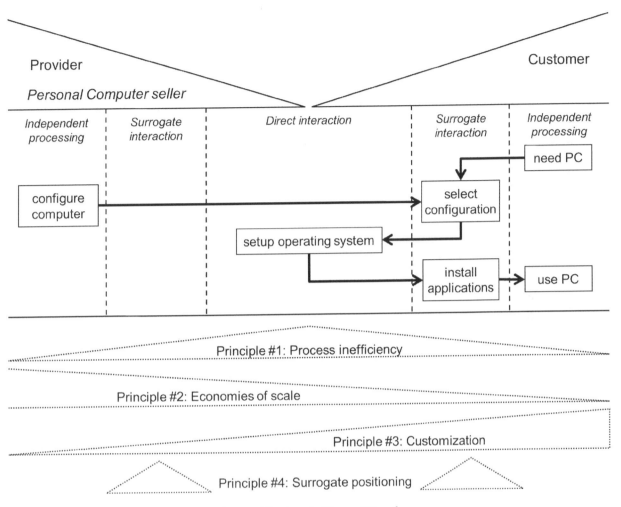

Figure 69: Apple Store PC sales

Selecting an Apple PC (iMac or MacBook) is a hands-on process. The stores are comprised largely of almost barren tables with devices attached that invite customer use. An employee will either greet you at the door or meet you at a device table to ask if you need any help. However, most of the selection process is intended to be self-serve surrogate interaction between the customer and the device.

After selecting a particular computer, an employee will retrieve the appropriate model and meet you at one the "Personal Setup" tables near the middle of the store. Although I own five Apple mac computers, I have not actually purchased one at an Apple Store. Instead, I recently observed an amazingly orchestrated "Personal Setup" at an Apple Store in Chicago.

A woman and her male companion had just purchased a MacBook Pro computer. The employee opened the box and set the computer in front of her, pointing out the small ridge where it is opened up. When she opened it, the employee quickly slid off the foam sheet protecting the keyboard, lest it detract from the beauty of the device. The employee showed her where the power switch was, which is flush with the case (so somewhat difficult to see). After a few attempts of turning it on the employee nonchalantly reached over and turned it on for her (disaster averted!). Meanwhile, her companion stood back, seemingly a bit intimidated by this fancy new device.

The employee spent the next five minutes or so showing the customer how to select a keyboard language and other setup items. When it asked for her network connection and email account he explained something about how she could obtain that information. At the end of the "Personal Setup" session the employee asked if the customer was good with things, then politely excused himself. The customer carefully put the computer back in the box and departed.

What is the value of this highly interactive setup? I am sure Apple has done research and found that for new PC users the biggest frustration is most likely in the first five minutes. If the customer has problems with the setup, it is off to a bad start. By moving the setup step to the region of direct interaction, Apple is able to accommodate the vast range of customer needs by providing customized experience with the specialized competency of employees. Based on the experience I observed this seemed to be the optimal process positioning.

There is one aspect of servitization that is part of the genius of the Apple sales system: installation of applications. In the olden-days of full-service retail, we would be happy to install applications for customers. But with the advent of auto-install scripts we were able to let customers install their applications independently. However, installing applications is no longer such an easy task, since many application software companies provide weekly updates. Further, the prevalence of viruses and malware has made installing applications somewhat of a risky endeavor.

Apple moved installing applications to surrogate interaction through their "Mac App Store." The Mac App Store is an application that, as of 2011, comes built in to the operating system. The Mac App Store allows Apple to regulate and control software that is installed on a Mac computer, supposedly providing less risk of viruses. Applications installed through the Mac App Store can also automatically update themselves when necessary.

Moving application installation to surrogate interaction provides Apple customers with additional value and provides Apple with a tremendous revenue opportunity. This is a tremendous example of Principle #4 from Chapter 5: using surrogate interaction as an effective way of balancing the benefits of interaction and independent processing.

Apple's iPod content network

One other example of successful servitization by Apple was the way they introduced the iPod in October of 2001. Oddly enough, the original iPod was neither the first portable digital music player, nor was it based on particularly impressive technology.

The first commercially successful portable digital music player was the Diamond Rio, introduced by Creative Labs in 1993. The Diamond Rio was quite similar to the original iPod, with memory, a screen, navigation buttons, and so forth. Based on raw technology, the iPod was not much of an improvement.

However, the Diamond Rio ultimately died in the marketplace, and the successor to Creative Labs filed bankruptcy in 2003. Meanwhile, the iPod exploded in popularity and attained a cult following. What is the difference?

I would argue that the difference between the original iPod and the Diamond Rio was not so much about device technology, but about Apple's ability to forward integrate into the customer's process for use.

To understand this we need to consider how a Diamond Rio operated in the customer's process domain. Users were supposedly able to download music or rip music off of CDs and load it into the device for subsequent playback. The process of downloading music in those days left something to be desired, although it was easier for hackers. The process of ripping CDs was also a non-trivial matter. All of that was topped by a precarious process for copying music files from a computer's hard drive to the Diamond Rio, especially if your files were in an incompatible format.

In my assessment, the key success factor for the iPod was the introduction of iTunes® in January of 2001, shortly before the iPod was introduced. iTunes is, in essence, an access portal to a network of musicians and record labels, and subsequently movie studios, television networks, book publishers and authors, and application developers, as depicted in Figure 70.

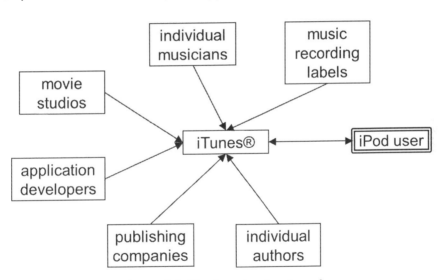

Figure 70: iPod content network

When people bought an iPod, they bought an implied process for use that provided access to all of the content they would need. The use process of an iPod included connecting the iPod to the USB port of a computer. By default, the installed iTunes software started automatically. Accessing the iPod content network was as simple as a few clicks of the computer mouse. The resulting files were automatically transferred to the iPod device for the customer's enjoyment. The process of accessing the iPod content network was seamless.

One interesting thing about the iPod content network is how little of the offering is actually within Apple's competency set. Apple is not competent at creating music or movies, writing books, or writing game applications. In fact, Apple is not even competent at manufacturing iPods, but outsources that function to contract manufacturers in Asia! What Apple is extremely competent at is forming and making it easily accessible to customers.

Chapter 19 – Video Entertainment case study

The video entertainment experience has evolved significantly over the past century. This chapter will review highlights from that evolution, or devolution, of the video entertainment industry. It is not intended to be exhaustive (for example, it does not discuss cable TV), but is illustrative of PCN Analysis of an evolving industry. We will begin with an example that significantly predates the era of video technology.

The 1599 foundation for video entertainment

In the year 1599 William Shakespeare and company built the Globe Theater in London. Theater existed well before that time, but Shakespeare was the celebrated playwright of all time, and the Globe was his public venue. Without a facility like the Globe the thespians would need to come to the audience that was likely comprised of royalty and wealthy landowners.

Figure 71 depicts a hypothetical offering at the Globe Theater. It begins with William himself writing a play, since there were likely fewer opportunities for licensing plays written by other playwrights in those days. The play is staffed and rehearsed in preparation for the performance.

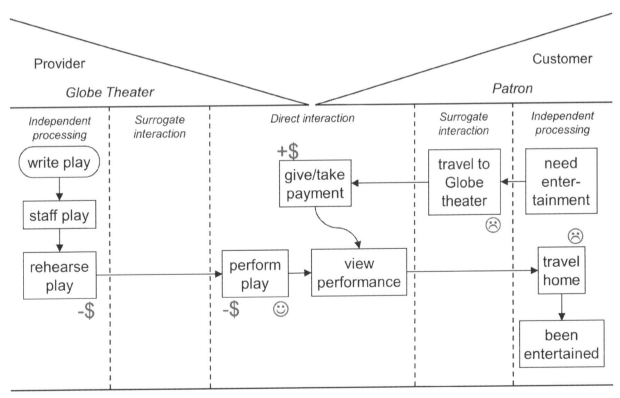

Figure 71: Watching a play at Shakespeare's Globe Theater (1599)

The patron needing entertainment travels to the Globe Theater, presumably pays their admission fee, and views the performance. After the performance is over the patron travels home and reminisces about the experience.

This is not a bad value proposition, since it leverages economies of scale by rehearsing independently from customers, allowing many patrons to view a play at reasonable cost. The need for the simultaneous physical presence of both the performers and the patrons does introduce inefficiencies, as well as limiting the reach of the offering. In other words, people in London can enjoy the play, but people from farther afield would incur great traveling costs for the experience.

Figure 71 depicts this limitation by the ☹ symbols by traveling to the globe and traveling home, which would limit the customer base who would practically patronize the theater. (These value symbols were discussed in Chapter 4.) The lack of economies of scale in performance and viewing is certainly a major factor leading to the introduction of the recorded video industry.

The 1888 introduction of the kinetograph

In 1867, William Lincoln patented the zoopraxiscope, which was a wheel with slits that provided a depiction of a moving picture.[42] However, the first practical device for motion pictures was the kinetograph, patented in 1888 by Thomas Edison. A kinetograph has a complete loop of film strung between sets of rollers in a box. The viewer would turn a crank to advance the film and watch the moving picture.

Shortly thereafter, kinetograph arcades sprung up in different cities. Figure 72 depicts the experience of a customer visiting a kinetograph arcade. As you would imagine, the arcade owners would not need to produce their own moving pictures, but procure them from manufacturers, resulting in tremendous economies of scale. A kinetograph device showing a particular movie could be mass produced and simultaneously shown in many dispersed cities around the country.

---

[42] See http://inventors.about.com/library/inventors/blmotionpictures.htm

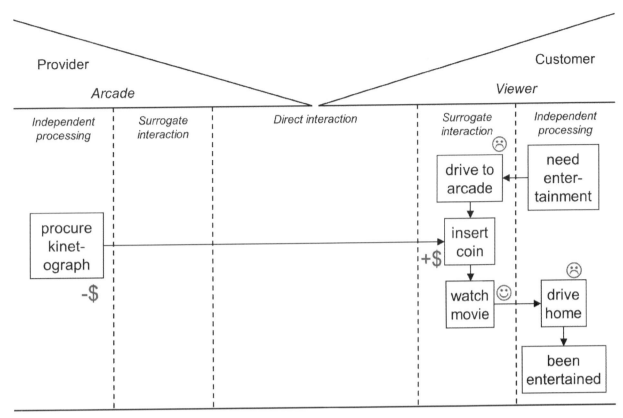

Figure 72: Visiting a kinetograph arcade (1878)

The customer experience included driving to the arcade, inserting a coin in the kinetograph, and cranking the handle to watch the movie. Operating a kinetograph was a personal experience, and only one person could use it at a time. However, movie projectors were about to come on the scene, allowing many people to view the movie simultaneously.

The 1896 premiere of the movie theater

Reportedly, the first movie theater for public use was Vitascope Hall, which opened in New Orleans in 1896. The movie theater concept built on the kinetograph offering by not only allowing many people to view the movie at the same time, but also to allow for longer movies.

Figure 73 depicts the experience going to a movie theater. The patron buys a ticket and watches the movie. The kinetograph allowed customers to watch movies at any time they choose, but the movie theater requires regularly scheduled movie times, thus requiring the customer to conform to the show schedule.

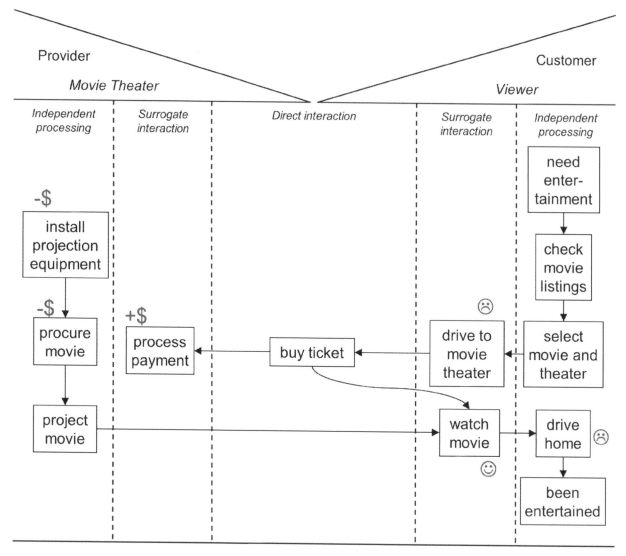

Figure 73: Going to a movie theater (1896)

Again, a disadvantage of going to the movie theater is the transportation cost of going to and from the theater. Movie theaters have been and continue to be popular. Movie theaters began to be threatened by the invention of home movie technology, specifically the video cassette player.

The 1976 disintermediation at Walmart

What if patrons did not need to go to theaters to see new movies? Of course, broadcast television was an option, but television at that time was strictly pushing of content on viewers. Movie fans still needed more options of selecting what they watch. The introduction of the video cassette player (and recorder) gave them that and more—it allowed them to decide where and when they watch as well.

Figure 74 shows the use of a home video player for entertainment. In this case, the provider is a retailer like Walmart, that sells VHS videotapes along with thousands of other items. This model has the customer procuring prerecorded videotapes at Walmart and watching them in the comfort of their homes.

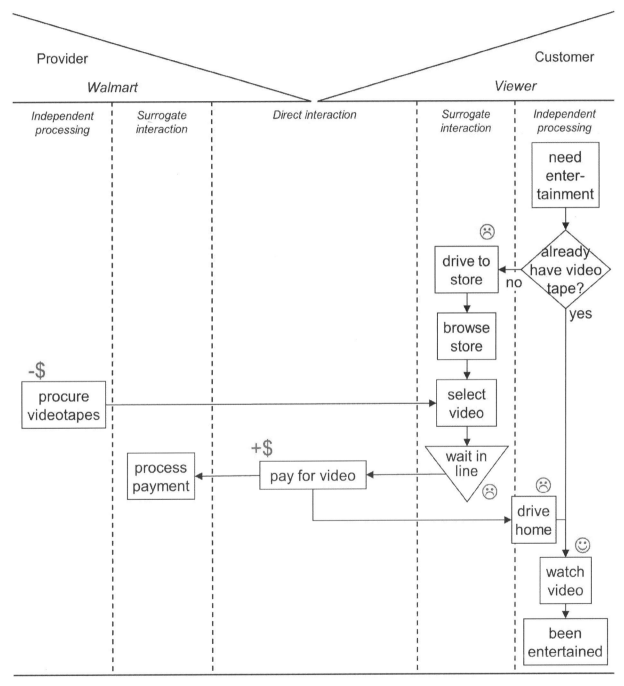

Figure 74: Watching a videotape from Walmart (1976)

Essentials of Service Design

The customers' advantage of the buy-videos-at-Walmart model is in disintermediation of movie theaters. Again, this relieves customers from being constrained to the movie times and locations of theaters. However, it also brought reduced economies of scale. With movie theaters, the theater would procure the movie and the customer only has to pay for one-time access. With the Figure 74 model, customers need to procure the video, decreasing the economy of scale of viewing. This problem was solved by video rental stores.

The 1985 re-intermediation at Blockbuster

Video rental stores became ubiquitous in the 1980's, the largest of which was the Blockbuster chain (founded in 1985). The shift to purchasing videotapes for home viewing was a process disintermediation because the "watch video" step was moved from the interactive region to the customer's independent processing region. The introduction and expansion of video rental stores was somewhat of a reintermediation, since the video store retained ownership of the videos, thus moving the "watch video" step into the customers region of surrogate interaction, as depicted in Figure 75.

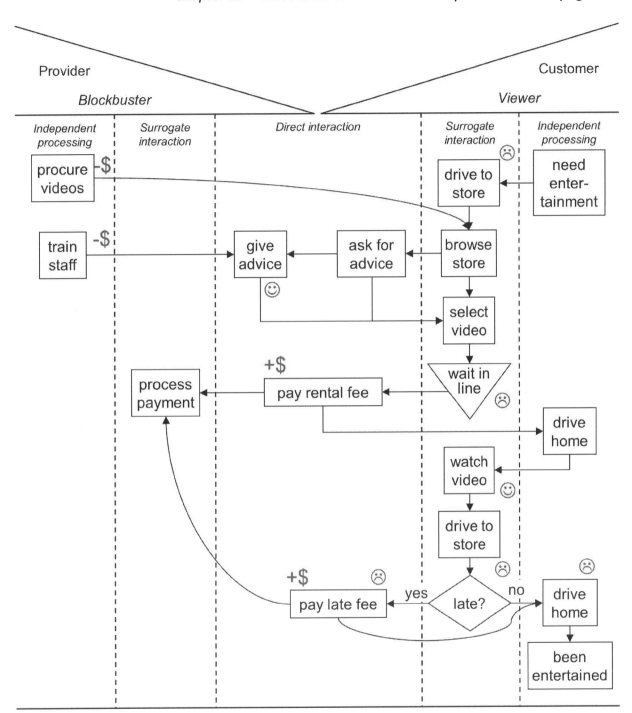

Figure 75: Renting a video from Blockbuster (1985)

Besides moving the video process into the region of surrogate interaction, the brick-and-mortar Blockbuster-type of stores also allowed for direct interaction. For example, a customer looking for possible movies that fit his or her interest could ask employees for advice, and depending on the knowledge and training of employees, receive some valued advice.

The shift to video rental did reinstate the need for traveling to and from the store. Although the video purchase model of Figure 71 required driving to the store, the customer who purchases videotapes can purchase many of them at a time and watch them repeatedly at his or her leisure. The video rental model of Figure 75 required the customer to travel to and from the video store each time video entertainment is needed.

This led to the serious problem/opportunity of late fees. Late fees were a problem for customers who forget or delay the drive back to the video rental store. They were an opportunity for rental store to make more money (although Blockbuster lost a major lawsuit having to do with exorbitant late fees).

Unfortunately, Blockbuster filed for bankruptcy in 2010, and many of the other major video rental chains closed their stores. Process innovation marched on, and other companies with process configurations that provided better value propositions took over the market.

The 1997 re-deservitization by Netflix

In 1997, Netflix was founded to address the two major shortcomings of the Blockbuster value proposition: traveling to the store and incurring late fees. The Netflix model delivered digital video disks through regular mail, as depicted in Figure 76. A key feature of the Netflix process is the customer visiting the Netflix website and selecting videos of interest that are placed in a queue. This tells Netflix what video(s) to mail to the customer next. This is important because it assures that the customer will always have a video, except for a few days the videos are in transit between exchanges.

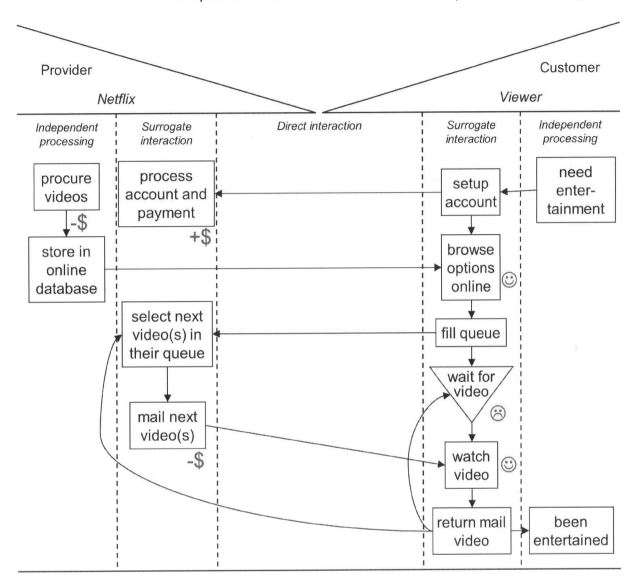

Provider   **Customer**

Netflix   *Viewer*

Independent processing	*Surrogate interaction*	*Direct interaction*	*Surrogate interaction*	*Independent processing*

Figure 76: Using Netflix mail delivery (1997)

Also key to the Netflix process is a fixed subscription fee instead of the pay-per-video pricing model used by Blockbuster and other video rental chains. Customers are thus motivated to return videos in a timely manner in order to see as many as possible. However, Netflix also eliminated late fees, since a subscription allows customers to keep a particular video for an unlimited amount of time (as long as Netflix continues to get their subscription fee, which is a monthly charge to the customer's credit card).

In one sense, the Netflix model was a digression—somewhat of a re-deservitization. By requiring customers to select a queue of videos in advance, the immediate selection of the next video is done in Netflix's surrogate interaction region. This decreases the spontaneity potential that was present in the Blockbuster model. Although customers could browse and change their queue entries at the moment they are sending a viewed video back, the changes selection still required waiting for the postal delivery schedule. The customer could not choose a movie for viewing the same day.

The 2002 revival of spontaneity at Redbox

Redbox overcame the Netflix mail limitation by putting automated kiosks at numerous locations, including at the already ubiquitous McDonald's restaurants. (McDonald's provided some of the initial funding for Redbox.) The Redbox website reports that more than 68 percent of the U.S. population lives within five minutes of a Redbox kiosk.

The Redbox process configuration (shown Figure 77) is actually more like the Blockbuster process (Figure 75) than the Netflix process (Figure 76). Redbox provides Blockbuster's potential for spontaneity but with increased convenience.

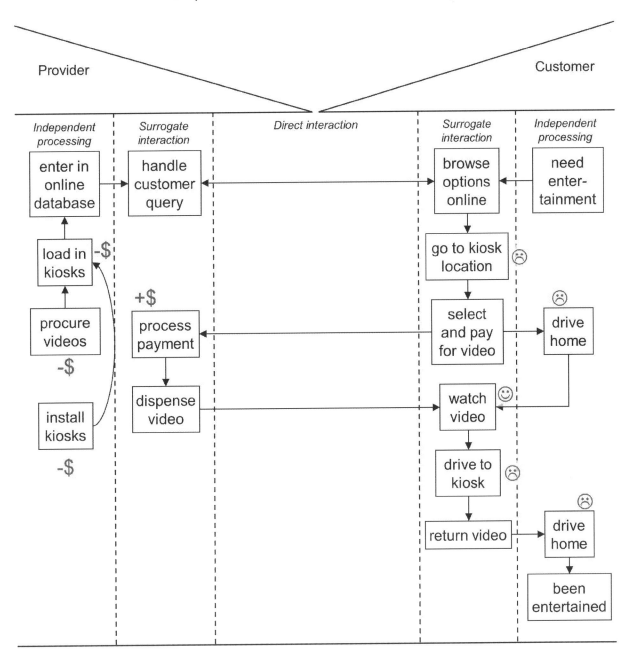

Figure 77: Renting a video from a Redbox Kiosk (2003)

Part of that convenience comes from the widespread prevalence of the kiosks. At this writing, Redbox has 31,500 kiosks in the U.S.. (There are apparently 50 Redbox kiosks within my suburban Utah zip code, including some locations that have multiple kiosks.)

However, even more convenience comes from the automated process that operates exclusively in regions of surrogate interaction. Let us just consider the process segment that begins with arriving at the location and ends with departing the location.

That process segment for Blockbuster is depicted in Figure 78. The customer enters the store and looks for the desired video. (For simplicity, we are omitting the browsing steps.) If the video cannot be found (they were quite large stores, organized by genre, theme, new releases, etc.), the customer might ask an employee for help. A trained employee might tell them where to find it, or perhaps even go with them. If the video is not there, it may be rented out, so the employee can check availability, including the date it is expected back. Ultimately the customer finds a video and proceeds to checkout. My experience was that there were usually non-trivial lines at Blockbuster (I tended to go at busy times, and was upset that they did not open more checkout stations). The customer presents and swipes his or her Blockbuster membership card and presents the video(s) to rent. The employee scans the videos and somehow demagnetizes them, so as not to set off the store alarm at the door. The system automatically reports late fees to the employee, which are told to the customer. The customer swipes the credit card and enters a PIN or signs as necessary. The employee presents the receipt, allowing the customer to return to his or her car. Whew!

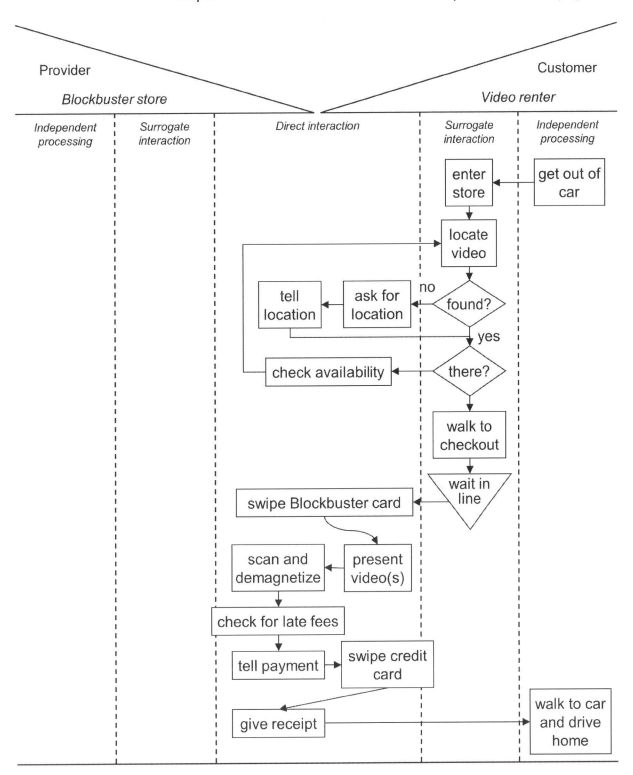

Figure 78: Car-to-car process for Blockbuster store

Conversely, consider the car-to-car process for Redbox, as depicted in Figure 79. The customer still has to walk to the kiosk, although my experience has been that I can usually park right in front of the kiosk. There is a risk of another customer being at the kiosk, but I do not seem to recall ever seeing more than one customer waiting. For one thing, there seems to be some cultural pressure for the person at the kiosk to "step it up" when another customer is waiting, which may include cutting short any arbitrary browsing. When my family uses Redbox we usually check video availability online before going to the kiosk, and we can reserve the video online if we are really set on that one movie, which further reduces the need for at-the-kiosk browsing. The desired video is easily selected on the kiosk screen, the credit card is swiped, and the video magically appears through the kiosk video slot. (There is an option of entering an email address for a receipt, but that can be done at the initial time you setup a Redbox account online.) I think most customers just grab the video and hop in their car, which may still have the engine running (at least in Utah). Total time: about a minute.

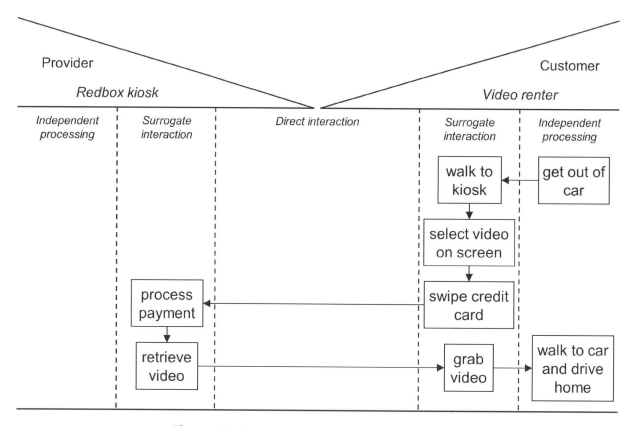

Figure 79: Car-to-car process for Redbox kiosk

It is interesting to report that NCR, an electronic equipment manufacturer, licensed the name and set up more than 10,000 "Blockbuster Express" kiosks, which NCR sold to Redbox in February of 2012. We might think Redbox is on the way to having kiosks around every corner of the country. Or, we might think that Redbox is doomed due to an outdated service process.

Indeed, a more efficient value proposition has already begun the march to take over the video entertainment world: streaming.

The 2005 video entertainment revolution

In July of 2012, Redbox began testing a video entertainment delivery service called "Redbox Instant" that is sure to cannibalize rentals at their kiosks. In 2007, Netflix took similar action by allowing customers to stream videos over the Internet. The potential for streaming video could render the physical infrastructure of Redbox and Netflix obsolete. These cannibalistic actions were surely in response to hyper-innovator, Apple, entering the online video business in 2005.

Apple's 2001 introduction of iTunes (linking to the online Apple Store) was mentioned in Chapter 13 as being key to the success of iPods, and Chapter 18 as being key to the process strategy for Apple PCs. In 2005, iTunes introduced video support, making Apple a leading innovator in online video rental and sales. Figure 80 depicts the video streaming process used by iTunes, with a similar process used by Netflix. (At this writing the Redbox Instant service is not available to the public.)

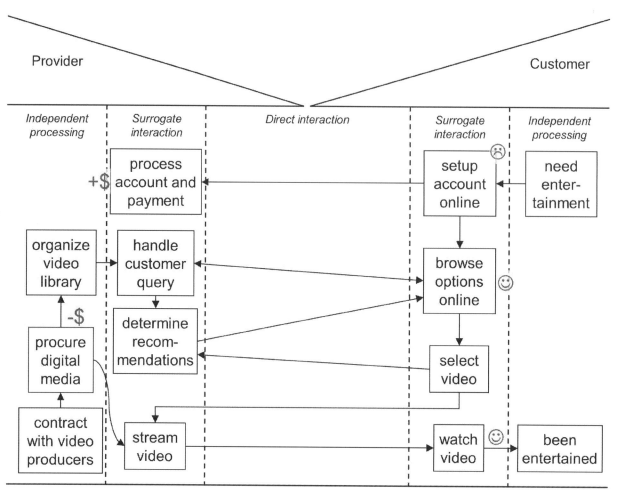

Figure 80: Streaming a video from iTunes (2005) or Netflix (2007)

The video streaming process combines the location-convenience of the Netflix mail service (although the customer does not even need to walk to the mailbox) with the spontaneity benefit of Blockbuster and Redbox. One other advantage of the video streaming method is that it automates the expert recommendation components that used to be somewhat available at Blockbuster and other video stores.

Netflix has turned the art of giving video recommendations into a science, which is to say that they have converted a divergent process step (the art) into a highly complex process (the science). This is demonstrated by the contest they held in 2006 that offered $1 million to the first individual or team who could beat Netflix's automated system for predicting what videos customers would like based on their ratings of what they have seen previously. Finally in 2009, three team of researchers combined their efforts and were able to win the prize. Given the great difficulty, and process benefit, of substituting divergence with complexity, the $1 million was a relatively small price to pay.

The ubiquity of video streaming services is assured by the rapidly approaching ubiquity of handheld Internet devices formerly known as phones, plus tablets, plus desktop computers, plus video game consoles, plus video streaming boxes (as though anyone would want a device that *only* streams videos).

Attempts at re-servitization

Lest Netflix and Apple get too comfortable with their process configuration superiority, we recognize that other providers are attempting to improve their value proposition through innovation. Movie theaters have introduced technologies involving improved sound and image detail. New technologies for 3D movies are becoming more prevalent and increasingly less nauseating to viewers. Some theaters are starting to provide so-called "4D" effects of vibration and movement—providing an even more realistic effect of nausea to keep customers coming back.

To really see where video entertainment processes might be going, I defer to my Uncle Jim from Ogden, Utah. In the late 70's and early 80's we shared a penchant for new technology. One day he told me "if you want to see where technology is going, watch the video game industry." Indeed, video games have continually pushed the limits of computer hardware and software, and also driven innovation in video entertainment.

Perhaps the most ominous example of how video games may redefine the process of delivering video entertainment is MMORPG—even the acronym is somewhat frightening. MMORPG stands for massively multiplayer online role-playing game. A MMORPG is basically a movie in which the viewer has an active part in the plot. A typical MMORPG has a script and plot involving various performers. The viewer is one of the performers and other online viewers are other performers, each assuming specific roles. The participants are given objectives and often computer-generated enemies to conquer.

MMORPG are delivered via an interactive service, as depicted in Figure 81. The customers subscribe to the game and play the game online. Some MMORPGs allow customers to purchase items for use in the game, such as farm equipment or weapons. Some MMORPGs even allow participants to create virtual items that they can then sell to other players.

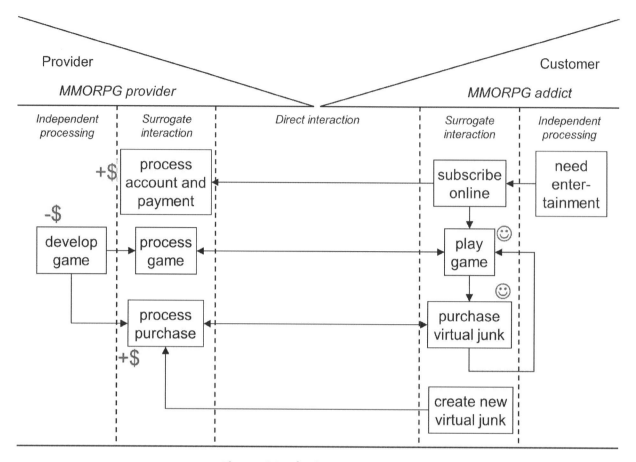

Figure 81: Playing a MMORPG

There has been a lot of debate about the value of MMORPGs to society, and some have suggested that they can be highly addictive and a major waste of time and detrimental to productivity. What is not subject to debate is their extreme popularity. For example, a Star Wars MMORPG introduced in 2011 gained one million subscribers the first three days of its release.[43]

The key distinction of the MMORPG form of video entertainment is the increased level of customization. The prior process evolution described in this chapter largely focused on improving *when* and *where* video entertainment was delivered, with the actual development of the video story being performed independently by movie studios. However, the MMORPG process leaves the final development of the video story being to consumers. This increase in customization seems to provide a more compelling customer experience.

The Motion Picture Association of America reports that the global movie industry brought in box office revenues of $31.7 billion in 2010.[44] Reuters reported that the global videogame industry brought in $62.7 billion in 2010, which is almost double the movie industry

---

[43] Michael Rundel, Star Wars: The Old Republic Is 'Fastest-Growing MMO Ever' With 1m Users, *Huffington Post UK*, 12/27/2011.

[44] Theatrical Market Statistics, 2011, Motion Picture Association of America, Inc.

revenue! MMORPGs are only part of the video game industry, but a real threat to other traditional and contemporary forms of video entertainment.

Chapter 20 – Visualizing Concepts from Service Models

I stand on the shoulders of giants. PCN Analysis was developed by integrating important concepts that have been set forth by great researchers and theorists over many decades. This chapter demonstrates how PCN Analysis relates to some of the major published models of service management from prior literature.

Indeed, one valuable application of PCN Diagrams is in helping us visualize (from a process perspective) constructs and principles from old and new theories of service provision. By such, the framework can bring together some important perspectives of services, drawing on various managerial insights, and showing how the perspectives relate to one another. This section will consider six popular service theories, first three from service operations perspective and then three from service marketing researchers. Space limitations prevent other than a cursory reference to each theory and the reader can see the cited references for more details.

Visualizing Chase's Customer Contact model

Fundamental concepts of PCN Diagrams were discussed by Chase (1978; 1981; 1983), but using different words that were more relevant in that earlier context. As mentioned, Chase suggested that the primary distinguishing characteristic of service processes was customer contact, which is an older approximation of the concept of customer interaction. Chase defined customer contact as "the physical presence of the customer in the system" which was adequate in an environment that lacked the interaction technologies that are common today. A modern system may be a website, with "physical presence" perhaps meaning the customer being at the web address.

Chase split the process domain of entities into four regions – pure service, mixed service, quasimanufacturing, and manufacturing – which are approximated in Figure 82. He spoke of differences between front-office and back-office operations, and referred to Thompson's "technical core" that should be decoupled from outside influences (e.g. customers) in order to maintain stable processing and quality (Thompson 1967).

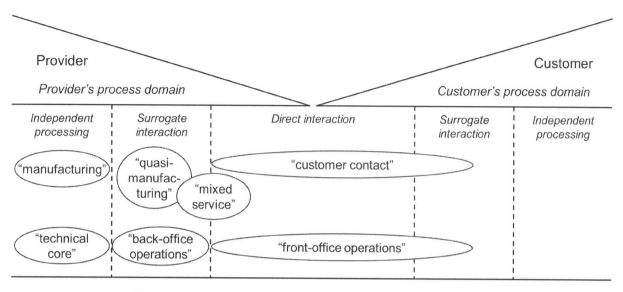

Figure 82: Concepts from Chase's Customer Contact model

Chase emphasized the process control issue by stating, "Obviously, the greater the percentage of contact time between the service system and the customer, the greater the degree of interaction between the two during the production process. From this conceptualization, it follows that service systems with high customer contact are more difficult to control and more difficult to rationalize than those with low customer contact" (1978, p. 138). He subsequently operationalized that concept by modeling potential operating efficiency as the inverse of customer contact (1981; 1983).

Another of Chase's valuable contributions is identifying some of the many ways processes in "high-contact systems" (i.e., direct interaction) differ from those in "low-contact systems" (i.e., independent processing). Related examples were shown in Table 1 (page 6), and others are listed by Chase (1978, p. 139). Chase's work reminds us that there are major managerial differences between the regions of a process domain.

Visualizing Schmenner's Service-Process Matrix

Schmenner's original Service-Process Matrix is useful for analyzing the positioning of a service operation relative to that of competing firms. The original two-dimensional matrix depicted a horizontal axis of "degree of customer interaction and customization" and a horizontal axis of "degree of labor intensity." The central idea was that firms with more customer interaction and customization typically have greater labor intensity, as represented by the "diagonal" of the matrix. Some firms would find their operations positioned off of the diagonal, yet Schmenner discusses a trend for firms to move toward the diagonal and up the diagonal towards regions of low-interaction (1986, p. 28). He attributed that trend to "pressures for control and lower costs" (1986, p. 31), and subsequently to improved productivity (2004).

Schmenner acknowledged that "customer interaction and customization" are actually "two similar but distinct concepts," which can be observed through a PCN Diagram. As shown in Figure 83, customer interaction occurs in the process region between process entities, with surrogate interaction being a lesser degree of interaction than direct interaction. Customer interaction tracks with customization, but only within the firm's process domain. In fact, willing and able customers can attain a higher degree of customization by taking control of the process themselves. Customers acting independently almost always have more customization than any interactive alternative, as long as the customer has sufficient ability and motivation to take on the process. The principle is that the maximum customization is within the customer's process domain, and customization is not unique to "service."

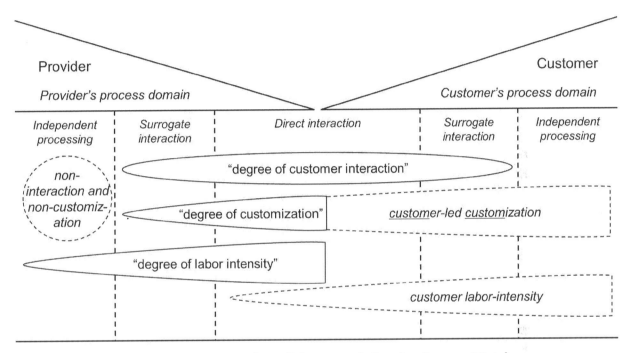

Figure 83: Concepts from Schmenner's Service-Process Matrix

More recently, Schmenner updated the Service-Process Matrix concept by generalizing the horizontal axis to represent "degree of variation," of which "customization for and interaction with customers" is a leading source (2004). "Degree of labor intensity" was replaced with "relative throughput time," more fully encapsulating the productivity concept. Correspondingly, we may assume lower relative throughput time for independent processing than direct interaction.

Visualizing Sampson's Unified Service Theory

As suggested in Chapter 2, PCN Analysis has root in the Unified Service Theory (UST), which defines service as process segments that involve "customer inputs" comprised of customers, their belongings, and/or their information (Sampson 2000; Sampson 2001; Sampson 2010a; Sampson 2010b). The UST considers customer action (i.e. customer labor) as a process input in co-productive activities (Sampson and Froehle 2006, p. 332).

Figure 84 shows a general representation of the interactive regions of UST service. Of particular note are the independent processing regions that are outside of the range of service. The UST points out how "do-it-yourself" customers are or can be competitors of most services (discussed in Chapter 9 and Chapter 11): restaurant patrons can cook their own food, students can learn on their own, brokerage customers can manage their own investments, patients can contrive their own healthcare, etc. (Sampson 2001, p. 202).

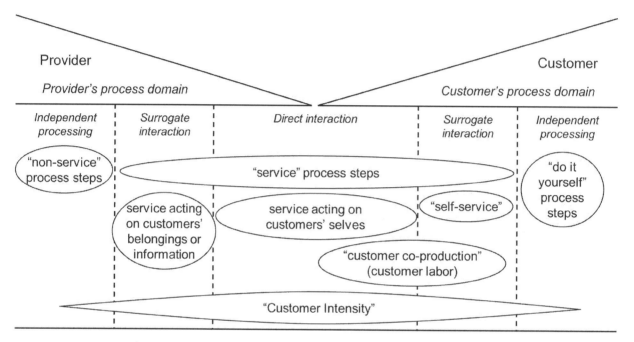

Figure 84: Concepts from Sampson's Unified Service Theory

The UST also differentiates between customer contribution and customer co-production (Sampson and Froehle 2006, p. 335). All service process steps involve some customer resources, but not always an active co-production resource. Co-production is a sufficient but not a necessary condition for a process segment to be a service (Sampson 2010a, p. 116).

A contemporary concept related to the UST is customer intensity (discussed in Chapter 6), which represents the degree of impact or influence individual customers have on a firm's operations (Sampson 2010a, p. 116; Sampson 2010b, p. 38). Not surprisingly, direct interaction is the region of highest customer intensity, and, by definition, independent processing has low to no customer intensity. In parallel with the thoughts of Chase, Schmenner, and others, increasing the potential operating efficiency and productivity of a process usually requires decreasing customer intensity, which implies moving towards regions of independent processing. Surrogate interaction provides a useful intermediate level of customer intensity.

Visualizing Shostack's Service Blueprinting

An interactive process flowcharting method that is well-known to service researchers is Service Blueprinting, which was introduced by Shostack (1984; 1987). At a fundamental level,

Service Blueprints differentiate between service process steps that customers can see—"above the line of visibility"—and those they cannot see. As depicted in Figure 85, a service blueprint categorizes process steps according to customer actions, visible employee actions, invisible employee actions, support processes, and managerial functions (Fließ and Kleinaltenkamp 2004). Service Blueprinting has been expanded over the years to consider issues such as organizational structure, physical evidence, and depiction of customer roles in service delivery (Bitner et al. 2008). The Service Blueprinting methodology does a tremendous job of documenting process actions and interactions at and around the customer-firm interface.

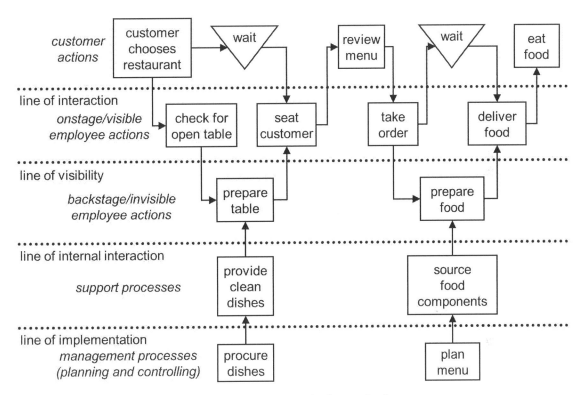

Figure 85: Service Blueprint example for a sit-down restaurant

PCN Diagrams and PCN Analysis improve on traditional Service Blueprinting in three fundamental ways. First, the PCN Analysis considers *the nature of interaction*, rather than process visibility, to be the primary basis for differentiating process steps. Actions are categorized according to the involvement of one or more parties in an interaction, regardless of whether the actions are visible to others. Second, PCN Diagrams depict all entities—providers and customers—as having distinct regions of interactive and independent processing. Eichentopf, Kleinaltenkamp, and Van Stiphout (2011) recognize that in traditional Service Blueprinting, customer actions are often treated as "a black box," and propose "mirroring [the service blueprint] structure on the customer's side" to give customers their own line of visibility, line of interaction, and so forth (p. 660). PCN Diagrams achieve a similar effect, but in a way that is less cumbersome and that easily accommodates processes that span more than just a single provider and single customer.

Third, PCN Diagrams thus improve on traditional Service Blueprinting by easily accommodating a network representation of service processes—or what Normann and Ramirez (1993) call "value constellations"—including multiple entities that can each operate independently or interactively with other entities. Patricio, et al. (2011) address this blueprinting deficiency by identifying the value constellation network at one phase of analysis then subsequently and separately designing specific dyadic service encounters with enhanced Service Blueprints. PCN Diagrams take an integrated approach by simultaneously depicting the network and the interactions.

As with the other models discussed in this chapter, PCN Analysis owes a debt of gratitude to the concepts Shostack documented in Service Blueprinting. Figure 86 shows how important concepts from Service Blueprinting are depicted in a dyadic PCN Diagram, including the independent "customer action" region that is not delineated in typical Service Blueprints.

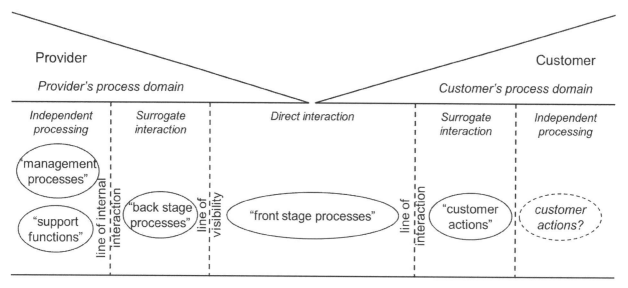

Figure 86: Concepts from Shostack's Service Blueprinting

Visualizing Judd/Lovelock/Gummesson's Rental/Access Paradigm

In 2004, Lovelock and Gummesson posed the probing question, "Is the academic field of services marketing in danger of losing its broad and in many respects coherent perspective?" (2004, p. 20) The basis for their alarm is the questionable validity of the long-standing foundation of service marketing on intangibility, heterogeneity, inseparability, and perishability – the so-called IHIP characteristics of services. Their criticism of IHIP has been echoed by other service marketers (Grove, Fisk, and John 2003; Vargo and Lusch 2004b).

As an alternative, Lovelock and Gummesson proposed revisiting a "nonownership" perspective on service that was previously espoused by Judd (cited above) – which defines services as a market transaction "where the object of the market transaction is other than the transfer of ownership of a tangible commodity" (Judd 1964, p. 59). Figure 87 depicts two process alternatives. One is firms making something tangible and then transferring ownership to the customer. The other is customers receiving access to provider resources (either through direct or surrogate interaction as we suppose) without taking ownership – a "service."

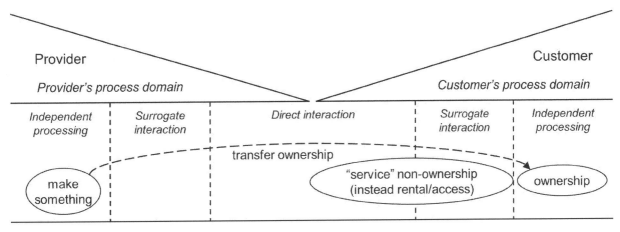

Figure 87: Concepts from the Rental/Access Paradigm

Lovelock and Gummesson refer to this as a rental/access paradigm, since customers can rent or access resources owned by service providers (2004, p. 35). The paradigm makes sense for many "service businesses" but not for others: Restaurants transfer ownership of tangible food, retailers transfer ownership of tangible goods, custom home builders transfer ownership of homes, and so forth. Lovelock and Gummesson state, "we do not claim that [the paradigm] offers a panacea with necessarily general properties. Rather, we propose it as a lens to present aspects not clearly visible in current theory."(Lovelock and Gummesson 2004, p. 34)

Visualizing Vargo & Lusch's Service-Dominant Logic

In a perspective they call Service-Dominant Logic (SDL), Vargo and Lusch define service "as the application of specialized competences (knowledge and skills) through deeds, processes, and performances for the benefit of another entity or the entity itself" (Vargo and Lusch 2004a, p. 2; Vargo and Lusch 2006, p. 43). This represents beneficial process skills that span all regions of process domains, as shown in Figure 88. They subsequently left off "...or the entity itself," which seems to narrow the scope of service to not include customers applying skills independently for their own benefit (Vargo and Lusch 2008a, p. 3; Vargo and Lusch 2010, p. 141).

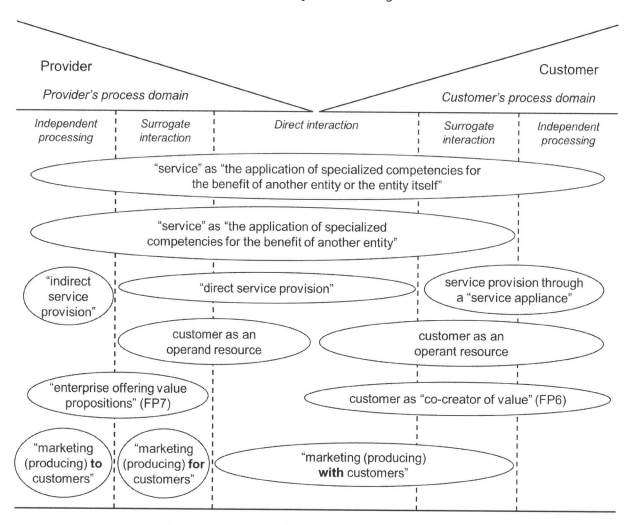

Figure 88: Concepts from Service-Dominant Logic

SDL provides many valuable perspectives on how firms operate. Vargo and Lusch make a distinction between what they call "indirect service provision" which is creating goods ("service appliances") that can later be used by customers to create value (2004a, p. 9). In Chapter 3 we discussed the important delineation of *operant* and *operand* resources, which is credited to their insightful writings. SDL includes ten "Foundational Premises," including FP6 "The customer is always a co-creator of value" and FP7 "The enterprise cannot deliver value, but only make value propositions" (Vargo and Lusch 2008b, p. 7), which are depicted in Figure 88. SDL suggests that co-production is an optional occurrence that involves the provider and the customer working together in what we may consider to be the region of direct interaction. However, SDL favors the concept of value co-creation, which can occur anywhere within the customer's process domain.

One of the tremendous ideas of SDL, discussed in Chapter 6, is contrasting the views of marketing *to* customers, marketing *for* customers, and marketing *with* customers, with the former being a goods-dominant view and the latter being a service-dominant view. The bottom of Figure 88 shows the parallel concept in our PCN framework – where providers' independent processing means processing to future customer needs, providers' surrogate interaction being processing for current customer specifications and resources, and other interactive steps being processing with customers. The PCN perspective is that all three types can occur within a given process chain.

One major modification of SDL depicted in PCN Diagrams is focusing on the process step as the unit of analysis instead of the overall process or business unit. Sure, process steps must be linked to other process steps in order to provide the desired benefit to the customer. However, individual process steps within a process chain can have very different managerial characteristics depending on whose process domain they occur in and on what region of the process domain.

Another major PCN Analysis distinction from traditional SDL is a suggestion that defining all processes as service processes is counterproductive, since it denies the distinguishing relevance of interaction (Sampson, Menor, and Bone 2010). SDL asserts that "all businesses are service businesses" (Vargo and Lusch 2008b, p. 4), which perhaps could be taken to say that all process chains eventually have customer-interactive process steps that are essential for value realization. The fact that all roads lead to Rome does not imply that all roads are Roman. The PCN framework suggests that process chains involve service process steps of direct and surrogate interaction, but they also contain non-service process steps of independent processing. One or the other may be dominant in any given process chain, and neither is universally superior or desirable.

Chapter 21 – Physical Summary

This final chapter summarizes important concepts coming from PCN Analysis, providing illustrative analogies from the physical sciences.

1. The diversity of business operations are built upon three fundamental process regions.

Some have suggested that the diversity of service businesses may require "developing separate paradigms for different categories of services" (Lovelock and Gummesson 2004, p. 37). For example, Edvardsson, et al. reviewed 57 research articles on defining service and surveyed 11 top service researchers, and concluded that "on lower abstraction levels a general service definition does not exist. It has to be determined at a specific time, in a specific company, for a specific service, from a specific perspective" (2005, p. 119).

Scientists seem to be faced with a similar problem in that many diverse materials exist on earth and in the cosmos: organic and inorganic, radioactive and inert, solid, liquid, and gaseous. There could be an unlimited number of models for matter. However, chemists maintain that common materials are made of three fundamental particles: protons, neutrons, and electrons. The periodic table of elements suggests that commonality exists between elements according to the composition of the three fundamental particles.

Correspondingly, the PCN framework suggests that processes possessing similar patterns of independent, surrogate interactive, and direct interactive steps will have similar operating characteristics, even if they are in seemingly disparate businesses. For example, auto repair involves independent processing to prepare skills and technology, direct interaction to review symptoms, surrogate interaction to diagnose, direct interaction to confirm a repair plan, surrogate interaction to perform the actual repair, and direct interaction to handle payment. That process chain is surprisingly similar to process chains found in management consulting, kitchen remodeling, healthcare, and estate planning. Indeed, the basic structural elements of PCN Diagrams can reveal commonality among seemingly disparate lines of business.

2. Every business has a mix of interactive processes and independent processing.

As mentioned, some researchers have suggested that all businesses are service businesses. That may imply that all process chains ultimately involve value-laden interactions with customers, which may be true, but it provides little in the way of strategic direction (Sampson et al. 2010). All businesses also involve essential aspects of independent processing, which does not imply that all businesses are make-to-stock manufacturing (the quintessential non-service process). The PCN framework shows how process chains contain both independent and interactive process elements—and we will not likely find any businesses that involve only interactive service processes or only independent processing.

For many years light was considered a wave similar to sound and other waves that permeate space. Einstein demonstrated the photoelectric effect which asserted that light was a particle. However, light was not aware of that and continued to exhibit wave characteristics such as diffraction patterns. The conclusion is that under current limits of knowledge, light of any color is considered a "particle-wave" containing both elements. Likewise, process chains contain both independent and interactive process elements – and we will not likely find any businesses that are *only* involved in interactive processing or *only* involved in independent processing.

3. The nature of the process mix makes a difference in how the process should be managed.

Some processes are conducive to interaction, and others are not. Table 1 listed some examples of significant managerial distinctions between independent processing and direct interaction, and others are described by Sampson (2001) and Sampson and Froehle (2006). Service interaction requires some degree of integration of processes across multiple entities, and can, therefore, be more difficult to design and execute than independent processes.

In a chemistry analogy we see that some particle entities interact and integrate while others do not. For example, hydrogen bonds quite well with oxygen to form water, but water molecules do not bond with the organic molecules of oils and other lipids. Further, there is a big difference between the properties of compounds (bonding molecules) and mixtures (aggregations of molecules that do not bond). Both have value, but it usually takes a lot more energy to make a compound than a mixture. Correspondingly, interactive processes can be more difficult to design and execute than independent processes, due to the need for integration across entities.

4. The foundation of organizations and interactions is value, comprised of value potential leading to value realization.

Ultimately, the central purpose of all organizations and interactions is to promote the happiness and well-being of various stakeholders – to promote value. Providers can usually only provide value potential, meaning providing processes and resources that subsequently can be used to realize value. Value potential and value realization go hand-in-hand.

This can be understood by another physical analogy. Physicists describe two general categories of energy: potential energy and kinetic energy. Potential energy is seen in the positioning of a ball on a hill, the arrangement of electrons in a battery, and so forth. It is energy, but just not put to work. When potential energy leads to motion – the ball starts rolling down the hill or the electrons start moving down wires – the result is kinetic energy. Kinetic energy actually gets work done, but kinetic energy does not appear out of nowhere. It comes out of potential energy.

Similarly, value realization is the end goal, but it is accomplished through appropriate configuration of value potential. The purpose and aim of specialized providers is to deliver value potential that can subsequently become value realization.

5. It is normal for interactive business processes to commoditize just like products, which can be slowed through divergent processing and overcome through innovation.

Think of a value proposition as a well-structured physical system that accomplishes an important purpose. The physics concept of entropy means that the organized structure of a system has decayed (such as through heat transfer), and that the system has less work potential and becomes less useful. The Second Law of Thermodynamics states that in isolated systems entropy always increases, implying that the potential to get work done decreases over time.

The analogy is that an interactive process may have value at one point in time, but over time the value of the interaction is likely to decrease, at least in isolation. Processes that are interactive at one time are likely to become less interactive at later points in time, and may eventually become non-interactive. However, the "in isolation" conditions can be analogous to being independent of innovation. Innovation is actually an external force imposed on the system, allowing the order of the system to increase and possibly reinstating the value of interaction of various types. In other words, if you want to overcome entropy, or deservitization, you should focus on innovation.

6. The fundamental skill of service managers is Process-Chain-Network configuration.

Service managers want to get more value out of limited resources. Value in interactive processes is determined by the process configuration. PCN Analysis helps managers analyze their process configuration and identify opportunities for improvement.

PCN Analysis is a power tool, but in the physics analogy it can be thought of as a supercollider. Supercolliders are used by physics researchers to explore what happens if atomic particles of one type interact with atomic particles of another type. The researcher has valuable theories and principles about the nature of particles, and sets up experiments to identify interactions that will reveal new and exciting phenomena.

The analogy is that PCN Analysis is a powerful tool to allow service managers to study (in a controlled environment on a PCN Diagram) interactions that might lead to new and exciting value propositions. The PCN Diagram is a laboratory for studying networks of entities that interact for valuable purposes that span process chains.

Ideally, service managers should be service system integrators, or what Normann referred to as "Prime Movers" (2001, pp. 26-36). This means they need to have a broad understanding of the firm's interactive and independent processes, and also the related processes along the process chains with which the firm is involved. This requires understanding the firm's operations, understanding customer interfaces, understanding the breadth of interrelated customer needs, and understanding network of entities that extend outside of the firm that can help satisfy those needs. This non-trivial task is enabled by a sound understanding and application of PCN Analysis.

Referenced Sources

Bitner, M. J., 1992. Servicescapes: The impact of physical surroundings on customers and employees. *Journal of Marketing* 56 (2), Apr, pp. 57.

Bitner, M. J., Faranda, W. T., Hubbert, A. R., and Zeithaml, V. A., 1997. Customer contributions and roles in service delivery. *International Journal of Service Industry Management* 8 (3), pp. 193-205.

Bitner, M. J., Ostrom, A. L., and Morgan, F. N., 2008. Service blueprinting: A practical technique for service innovation. *California Management Review* 50 (3), Spring, pp. 66-94.

Campbell, C., Maglio, P., and Davis, M., 2011. From self-service to super-service: a resource mapping framework for co-creating value by shifting the boundary between provider and customer. *Information Systems and E-Business Management* 9 (2), pp. 173-191.

Chase, R. B., 1978. Where Does the Customer Fit in a Service Operation? *Harvard Business Review* 56 (6), November-December, pp. 137-142.

Chase, R. B., 1981. The Customer Contact Approach to Services: Theoretical Bases and Practical Extensions. *Operations Research* 29 (4), pp. 698-706.

Chase, R. B., and Aquilano, N. J., 1995. *Production and Operations Management: Manufacturing and Services*, Seventh Edition, Irwin/McGraw-Hill, Chicago.

Chase, R. B., and Tansik, D. A., 1983. The Customer Contact Model for Organization Design. *Management Science* 29 (9), pp. 1037-1050.

Chervonnaya, O., 2003. Customer role and skill trajectories in services. *International Journal of Service Industry Management* 14 (3), pp. 347-363.

Chopra, S., and Meindl, P., 2001. *Supply Chain Management: Strategy, Planning and Operations*, Prentice Hall, Upper Saddle River, New Jersey.

Constantin, J. A., and Lusch, R. F., 1994. *Understanding Resource Management*, The Planning Forum, Oxford, Ohio.

Deming, W. E., 2000. *Out of the Crisis*, MIT Press, Cambridge, Mass.

Dubé, L., Johnson, M. D., and Renaghan, L. M., 1999. Adapting the QFD approach to extended service transactions. *Production and Operations Management* 8 (3), Fall, pp. 301-317.

Edvardsson, B., Gustafsson, A., and Roos, I., 2005. Service portraits in service research: a critical review. *International Journal of Service Industry Management* 16 (1), pp. 107-121.

Eichentopf, T., Kleinaltenkamp, M., and Van Stiphout, J., 2011. Modeling customer process activities in interactive value creation. *Journal of Service Management* 22 (5), pp. 650-663.

Fitzsimmons, J. A., and Fitzsimmons, M. J., 2004. *Service Management: Operations, Strategy, and Information Technology*, 4th Edition, Irwin / McGraw-Hill, New York.

Fitzsimmons, J. A., and Fitzsimmons, M. J., 2006. *Service Management: Operations, Strategy, and Information Technology*, 5th Edition, Irwin / McGraw-Hill, New York.

Fließ, S., and Kleinaltenkamp, M., 2004. Blueprinting the service company: Managing service processes efficiently *Journal of Business Research* 57 (4), April, pp. 392-404.

Frei, F. X., 2006. Breaking the trade-off between efficiency and service. *Harvard Business Review* 84 (11), November, pp. 93-101.

Froehle, C. M., and Roth, A. V., 2004. New measurement scales for evaluating perceptions of the technology-mediated customer service experience. *Journal of Operations Management* 22 (1), pp. 1-21.

Graham, B. B., 2004. *Detail Process Charting: Speaking the language of process*, John Wiley & Sons, Hoboken, New Jersey.

Greenfield, H. I., 2002. A note on the goods/services dichotomy. *The Service Industries Journal* 22 (4), Oct, pp. 19.

Grönroos, C., 2008. Service logic revisited: who creates value? And who co-creates? *European Business Review* 20 (4), pp. 298-314.

Grove, S. J., Fisk, R. P., and John, J., 2003. The future of services marketing: Forecasts from ten services experts. *The Journal of Services Marketing* 17 (2/3), pp. 107.

Hill, T. P., 1977. On Goods and Services. *Review of Income & Wealth* 23 (4), 12, pp. 315-338.

Judd, R. C., 1964. The case for redefining services. *Journal of Marketing* 28 (1), Jan, pp. 58.

Kelley, S. W., Donnelly, J. H., Jr., and Skinner, S. J., 1990. Customer Participation in Service Production and Delivery. *Journal of Retailing* 66 (4), Fall, pp. 315-335.

Lengnick-Hall, C. A., 1996. Customer Contributions to Quality: A Different View of the Customer-Oriented Firm. *Academy of Management Review* 21 (3), July, pp. 791-824.

Lengnick-Hall, C. A., Claycomb, V. C., and Inks, L. W., 2000. From recipient to contributor: examining customer roles and experience outcomes. *European Journal of Marketing* 34 (3/4), pp. 359-383.

Lovelock, C., 1983. Classifying Services to Gain Strategic Marketing Insights. *Journal of Marketing* 47 (3), Summer, pp. 9-20.

Lovelock, C., and Gummesson, E., 2004. Whither Services Marketing? In Search of a New Paradigm and Fresh Perspectives. *Journal of Service Research* 7 (1), August, pp. 20-41.

Lundkvist, A., and Yakhlef, A., 2004. Customer involvement in new service development: A conversational approach. *Managing Service Quality* 14 (2/3), pp. 249.

Lusch, R. F., Brown, S. W., and Brunswick, G. J., 1992. A General Framework for Explaining Internal vs. External Exchange. *Journal of the Academy of Marketing Science* 20 (2), Spring, pp. 119-135.

Maister, D. H., 1985. The psychology of waiting lines. *The Service Encounter*, J. A. Czepiel, M. R. Solomon, and C. F. Suprenant, eds., Lexington Books, Lexington, MA, pp. 113-124.

Matthing, J., Sanden, B., and Edvardsson, B., 2004. New service development: learning from and with customers. *International Journal of Service Industry Management* 15 (5), pp. 479-498.

Menor, L. J., Tatikonda, M. V., and Sampson, S. E., 2002. New service development: Areas for exploitation and exploration. *Journal of Operations Management* 20 (2), April, pp. 135.

Merriam-Webster, 2011. Online dictionary.

Mills, P. K., and Morris, J. H., 1986. Clients as "Partial" Employees of Service Organizations: Role Development in Client Participation. *Academy of Management Review* 11 (4), October, pp. 726-735.

Morey, R., 1976. Operations management in selected nonmanufacturing organizations. *Academy of Management Journal* 19 (1), March, pp. 120.

Morris, B., and Johnston, R., 1987. Dealing with Inherent Variability: The Differences Between Manufacturing and Service? *International Journal of Operations & Production Management* 7 (4), pp. 13.

Namasivayam, K., and Hinkin, T. R., 2003. The Customer's Role in the Service Encounter: The Effects of Control and Fairness. *Cornell Hotel and Restaurant Administration Quarterly* 44 (3), June, pp. 26-36.

Neely, A., 2008. Exploring the Financial Consequences of the Servitization of Manufacturing. *Operations Management Research* 1 (2), December, pp. 103-118.

Nie, W., and Kellogg, D. L., 1999. How Professors of Operations Management View Service Operations? *Production and Operations Management* 8 (3), Fall, pp. 339-355.

Normann, R., 2001. *Reframing Business: When the Map Changes the Landscape*, John Wiley & Sons, Hoboken, New Jersey.

Normann, R., and Ramírez, R., 1993. From value chain to value constellation: Designing interactive strategy. *Harvard Business Review* 71 (4), July/August, pp. 65-77.

Oliveira, P., and Von Hippel, E., 2011. Users as service innovators: The case of banking services. *Research Policy* 40 (6), July, pp. 806-818.

Parasuraman, A., Zeithaml, V. A., and Berry, L. L., 1985. A conceptual model of service quality and its implications for future research. *Journal of Marketing* 49 (4), September, pp. 41-50.

Patricio, L., Fisk, R. P., e Cunha, J. F., and Constantine, L., 2011. Multilevel Service Design: From Customer Value Constellation to Service Experience Blueprinting. *Journal of Service Research* 14 (2), May, pp. 180-200.

Porter, M., 1980. *Competitive Strategy: Techniques for Analyzing Industries and Competitors*, Free Press.

Reichheld, F. F., 2003. The one number you need to grow. *Harvard Business Review* 81, December, pp. 46-54.

Reichheld, F. F., and Sasser, W. E., Jr., 1990. Zero Defections: Quality Comes to Services. *Harvard Business Review* 68 (5), pp. 105-111.

Sampson, S. E., 1999. An Empirically Defined Framework for Designing Customer Feedback Systems. *Quality Management Journal* 6 (3), pp. 64-80.

Sampson, S. E., 2000. Customer-supplier duality and bidirectional supply chains in service organizations. *International Journal of Service Industry Management* 11 (4), pp. 348-364.

Sampson, S. E., 2001. *Understanding Service Businesses: Applying principles of the Unified Services Theory*, 2nd Edition, John Wiley & Sons, New York.

Sampson, S. E., 2010a. The Unified Service Theory: A paradigm for Service Science. *Handbook of Service Science*, P. P. Maglio, C. Kieliszewski, and J. C. Spohrer, eds., Springer, New York, pp. 107-131.

Sampson, S. E., 2010b. A Unified Services Theory. *Introduction to Service Engineering*, G. Salvendy and W. Karwowski, eds., John Wiley & Sons, Hoboken, New Jersey, pp. 34-56.

Sampson, S. E., 2012. Visualizing Service Operations. *Journal of Service Research* 15 (2), May, pp. 182-198.

Sampson, S. E., and Froehle, C. M., 2006. Foundations and Implications of a Proposed Unified Services Theory. *Production and Operations Management* 15 (2), Summer, pp. 329-343.

Sampson, S. E., Menor, L. J., and Bone, S. A., 2010. Why We Need a Service Logic: A Comparative Review. *Journal of Applied Management and Entrepreneurship* 15 (3), July, pp. 17-32.

Sampson, S. E., and Spring, M., 2012. Customer Roles in Service Supply Chains and Opportunities for Innovation. *Journal of Supply Chain Management* 48 (4).

Schmenner, R., 2004. Service Businesses and Productivity. *Decision Sciences* 35 (3), pp. 333-347.

Schmenner, R. W., 1986. How Can Service Businesses Survive and Prosper? *Sloan Management Review* 27 (3), Spring, pp. 21-32.

Schmenner, R. W., 1995. *Service Operations Management*, Prentice Hall, Englewood Cliffs, NJ.

Schneider, B., and Bowen, D., 1995. *Winning the Service Game*, Harvard Business School Press, Boston.

Shostack, G. L., 1984. Designing services that deliver. *Harvard Business Review* 62 (1), January-February, pp. 133-139.

Shostack, G. L., 1987. Service Positioning through Structural Change. *Journal of Marketing* 51 (1), January 1987, pp. 34-43.

TARP, 1979. Consumer Complaint Handling in America: Final Report. U.S. Office of Consumer Affairs, Technical Assistance Research Programs, Washington, D.C.

TARP, 1986. Consumer Complaint Handling in America: An Updated Study. The Office of the Special Advisor to the President for Consumer Affairs, Technical Assistance Research Programs, Washington, D.C.

Thompson, G. M., 1998. Labor scheduling, part 1. *Cornell Hotel and Restaurant Administration Quarterly* 39 (5), October, pp. 22.

Thompson, J. D., 1967. *Organizations in Action*, McGraw-Hill, New York.

van der Aalst, W. M. P., 1999. Formalization and Verification of Event-driven Process Chains. *Information & Software Technology* 41 (10), pp. 639-650.

Vargo, S. L., and Lusch, R. F., 2004a. Evolving to a New Dominant Logic for Marketing. *Journal of Marketing* 68 (1), Jan, pp. 1.

Vargo, S. L., and Lusch, R. F., 2004b. The Four Service Marketing Myths: Remnants of a Goods-Based, Manufacturing Model. *Journal of Service Research* 6 (4), May, pp. 324-435.

Vargo, S. L., and Lusch, R. F., 2006. Service-dominant logic: What it is, what it is not, what it might be. *The service-dominant logic of marketing: Dialog, debate, and directions*, S. L. Vargo and R. F. Lusch, eds., ME Sharpe, Armonk, NY, pp. 43-56.

Vargo, S. L., and Lusch, R. F., 2008a. From goods to service(s): Divergences and convergences of logics. *Industrial Marketing Management* 37 (3), May, pp. 254-259.

Vargo, S. L., and Lusch, R. F., 2008b. Service-dominant logic: continuing the evolution. *Journal of the Academy of Marketing Science* 36 (1), pp. 1-10.

Vargo, S. L., and Lusch, R. F., 2010. Advancing Service Science with Service-Dominant Logic. *Handbook of Service Science*, P. P. Maglio, C. Kieliszewski, and J. C. Spohrer, eds., Springer, New York, pp. 133-156.

Webb, D., 2000. Understanding Customer Role and its Importance in the Formation of Service Quality Expectations. *The Service Industries Journal* 20 (1), January, pp. 1-21.

Wemmerlöv, U., 1990. A taxonomy for service processes and its implications for system design. *International Journal of Service Industry Management* 1 (3), pp. 13-27.

White, S. A., Miers, D., and Fischer, L., 2008. *BPMN Modeling and Reference Guide*, Future Strategies Inc., Lighthouse Pt, FL.

Xue, M., and Harker, P. T., 2002. Customer Efficiency: Concept and Its Impact on E-Business Management. *Journal of Service Research* 4 (4), May, pp. 253-267.

Zeithaml, V. A., 1981. How Consumer Evaluation Processes Differ Between Goods and Services. *Marketing in Services*, J. H. Donnelly and W. R. George, eds., American Marketing Association, Chicago, pp. 186-190.

List of Figures

Index

18248478R00133

Made in the USA
Charleston, SC
24 March 2013